To: Keith Pearson

The story of my father, part one (2nd ed)

Vincent Hancock

11th Aug 2019

BY THE TALE
OF THE
Dragonfly

Vincent Hancock

authorHOUSE®

AuthorHouse™ UK
1663 Liberty Drive
Bloomington, IN 47403 USA
www.authorhouse.co.uk
Phone: 0800 047 8203 (Domestic TFN)
        +44 1908 723714 (International)

Published by AuthorHouse 07/12/2019

ISBN: 978-1-7283-9058-1 (sc)
ISBN: 978-1-7283-9059-8 (hc)
ISBN: 978-1-7283-9064-2 (e)

I am an old man now, and I have nothing to leave to my children except the story of my life—but it is a remarkable one. Thus, I will write my book so that all may know me well. I must be true to myself, and so I write only when I am inspired and never only because someone expects me to. People have said, "No one will remember me." I have sung, and I was both the singer and the song. I've walked the hills and mountains, spent much time in rainforest jungles, hunted and been hunted! I've travelled far on land, sand, and sea. But most of all, I have loved and been loved! If you are reading this private journal now, then I am no longer in this life but in that of the next, with my ancestors, on my greatest adventures.

Rex
30-05-1924 to 10-05-1989
RIP

Foreword

Having spent much of my school years between 1966 and 1973 living in Malaysia, I find this book strikes a chord. My father was a senior officer at RAAF base Butterworth, involved in Australian operations during the Vietnam War. My mother was a child of Dutch colonials in Indonesia during the Japanese occupation and could therefore speak Malay quite well. We did feel at home there.

One of my father's best friends there was a Scotsman who had been serving with the British Army in Malaya before independence (when Malaya became Malaysia). He had served during the Malayan Emergency prior to transferring to the RAAF as an officer, and he returned while his memories were still fresh. He would chat about it with my parents, and I would often listen in. Even as a kid, I was aware of the recent history and ongoing communist insurgency. I remember having time off school because the security risk to buses full of Australian kids was too great. However, the memories of that time and place are generally fond ones of a relaxed and vibrant multicultural society, with a multitude of religions and religious holidays to celebrate. We always felt welcomed by the local people.

Reading this book, I can hear the strains of Indian and Chinese music competing for attention, the constant heat and humidity of the tropics, and the exquisite, exotic, and confronting smells—the mouth-watering aroma of *rendang* at midday, and the ambivalent perfume of *durian* in the relative cool of the night market. The book is redolent with memories of a bygone age. On the other hand, *The Tale of the Dragonfly* reminds us of the courage and vigilance required from the few to secure peace and freedom for the many. It was a weird, yet fitting, twist of fate that the author and I both ended up serving in the Royal Engineers in Northern Ireland during the "troubles".

Stephen Plowright
Forensic Examiner, IBM
Author of *Learning Logic: Critical Thinking with Intuitive Notation*

Contents

I was educated by French Canadian catholic missionaries and grew up during the last days of British colonial rule in her Far East colonies. I gave up my dual nationality and relocated back to the United Kingdom when I turned sixteen years old. I shortly afterwards enlisted with the Corp of Royal Engineers as a boy soldier serving six years as a professional soldier with the British army on tours in Northern Ireland, Central America and Europe. I now spend my semi-retirement writing with a view to improve my work further and catch up with more research into my favourite subject areas which are ancient civilisations, magic and mythology.

And I dedicate this book to my mother Roffina.

Introduction

The author grew up during the ebbing days of British colonial rule in her Far East colonies. Educated by French Canadian Catholic missionaries, he grew up with the romance of empire. As a young man, the author relocated to Great Britain with his parents. He enlisted with the Corp of Royal Engineers as a boy soldier with the British Army, serving six years as a professional soldier in Central America and Europe. He experienced active service in Ulster during the troubles there in the seventies. Educated at the degree level, he now lives with his wife in the West Midlands and works in information technology. They have a son who is currently a serving military officer for the Royal Air Force.

This book is a true-to-life account based on five existing journals of my late father. He was born to a poor mining family in a small village called Ebbw Vale, South Wales, during the Great Depression of the early twentieth century. His family moved to Staffordshire in search of better employment opportunities when the Second World War broke out. His father was a police special constable during the blitz, but he enlisted with the Corp of Royal Engineers and was sent to Normandy, France, on June 4th, 1944, landing at Gold Beach, Arromanches. The battle for the port of Antwerp was his last European battlefront from Normandy.

Rex was then posted across to India to fight the war against the Japanese. After the Japanese surrender, our protagonist decided to opt for a life of high adventure by applying his scuba diving skills as a mercenary of the high seas in the South Pacific. Missing information to connect the dots comes from my teenage memories of fond conversations with Rex, my father, and remaining scraps of notes he loosely jotted down, breaking up some of the timelines. *By the Tale of the Dragonfly* is the summation of the first two of five journals, based around the period of 1947 to 1952.

Chapter 1

The End of Colonialism in Malaya

The year is 1947, and it seems a relatively short time, like yesterday, since the cessation of hostilities from World War Two Japanese Imperialists in the Pacific. But many war survivors still remember and have recurring nightmares, the brutal legacy of their former Nippon occupying conquerors! Post-traumatic stress disorder was not well known back in the late 1940s; the upper-level, nonchalant civilian personnel hiding in their safe Home Offices within the corridors of power might have called it shellshock or even cowardice.

I often ponder how many white feathers were given out undeservedly during the First and Second World Wars to these broken young men. They had witnessed first-hand the brutality, large-scale execution of prisoners of war and civilians alike, and the indiscriminate targeted rapes of white nurses and local females—things that no young man or woman should ever have to experience. The Imperial Japanese military forces during World War II made a mockery of *bushido*—the code of honour developed by Japanese samurai—savagely killing indiscriminately throughout their war campaign in China, South East Asia, and the Pacific.

The Japanese military forces of that period refused to recognize the Geneva Convention and treated all prisoners of war with much contempt for surrendering instead of fighting to the death or committing suicide. The occupation forces also brutalized and killed with fervour a great number of innocent civilians through orchestrated mass murders carried out on behalf of their High Command. General Tomoyuki Yamashita, referred to as the Tiger of Malaya, authorized his men to cooperate with the Japanese Military Police or *Kempeitei*.

Under the brutal command of Colonel Tsuji Masanobu, a purge of Chinese anti-Japanese elements who were likely to undermine the Japanese occupation was carried out. The British island colony of Singapore capitulated on 15 February 1942, with the surrender of some 120,000 British Commonwealth and Allied troops under

1

Lieutenant General Arthur Ernest Percival to only 30,000 Japanese soldiers following the Battle of Singapore. Then the Sook Ching massacre began. These mass summary executions, in two phases, were carried out under Japanese General Yamashita's directive, from 18 February to March 4, 1942, at various isolated killing fields throughout the island of Singapore. All Chinese men above the age of 18 were ordered to respond to a Japanese mass registration on the island. Failure to do so would be at their own peril, warned the Japanese order. Some quarter of a million Chinese men and women attended the mass registration, but several thousand were randomly routed after failing a very brief and bogus anti-Japanese filtering interview. They were considered a threat to the Japanese occupation, Chinese young men in particular.

These men and some women, along with their children, were sent on trucks to remote sites such as Changi, Punggol, Blakang Mati, and Bedok for immediate execution by drowning at sea or machine-gunning. The whole killing operation was overseen by the Kempeitei. High-secrecy protocols placed by the Japanese occupation forces limited accurate records surrounding these summary executions of innocent civilians. During later exhumations of the many mass execution sites, estimates suggested between 70,000 and 100,000 Chinese souls lost their lives.

General Tomoyuki Yamashita was branded as a war criminal. He took the blame for Pacific region Second World War atrocities, although he was not the only Japanese officer executed. Yamashita, through his legal team, attempted to deny the charges against him, but he was unanimously found guilty by the Allies in Manila, the Philippines Islands, and executed by hanging on 23 February 1946.

Colonel Tsuji Masanobu, in charge of the Kempeitei and leader of Sook Ching, fared better; he managed to escape justice. After Japan surrendered, Tsuji escaped to Japan via Indochina and China, disguised as a Buddhist priest. Arriving in Japan in 1949, after the Far East Tribunal had completed the trials of the major war criminals, he escaped attention from Allied occupation authorities. The Chinese term for the massacre, *Sook Ching*, is defined as "a purge through cleansing". The Japanese called it *Daikensho*, suggesting the "great inspection". It became known as the *Shingapōru Kakyōgyakusatsujiken*, or the Singapore Chinese massacres. Sook Ching was the systematic indiscriminate extermination of perceived hostile elements, mainly Chinese, and the makeshift British local militia called Dalforce, who disappeared after putting up a fierce battle at Bukit Timah (Timah Hill).

The survivors of this Dalforce most likely went underground, along with the communist guerrilla fighters, later called the Malayan People's Anti-Japanese Army. They continued the war with hit-and-run tactics against Japanese forces. The communist guerrillas learned from Malayan aboriginal tribes how to disappear deep in the jungles of Malaya. They even hid out in leper colonies, where they knew the Japanese pursuers would not follow them. The Chinese-led communist resistance had planned well ahead, with weapon caches hidden all over the country for guerrilla war.

When the British in Malaya and Singapore finally surrendered to the Imperial Japanese forces, all that was left to oppose them was the Malayan People's Anti-Japanese Army, who were mainly Chinese communist guerrilla fighters with some Malay sympathizers. These "freedom fighters," who modelled themselves on the example set by Josef Stalin, set aside their differences during the war against the British colonialists to focus on their common enemy, the Japanese. The old leaders of the resistance fighters were routed out by the Kempeitei.

A young Chinese Marxist revolutionary called Ong Boon Hua, better known to the British as Chin Peng, took over command of the Japanese resistance army, with the help of Special Operations Executive Far East. SOEFE was a highly classified Second World War British commando unit known as Force 136. They re-armed these Malayan communist fighters on provision that after the war against the Japanese ended, the British-supported resistance army would disband and relinquish all such weapons back to Britain. When the war ended, the Malayan Communist Party, along with their military arm, the Malayan Peoples' Anti-Japanese Army (MPAJA), refused to disband after failing to win influence politically.

Instead, they started an insurgency to gain power in Malaya as Chinese communists within the Malayan Communist party, believing they had a right to rule the colony because of their sole guerrilla-war efforts against the Japanese occupiers during the Second World War. The Malayan Communist Party embraced the Malayan Nationalist Liberation Army (MNLA) in bloody armed conflict towards their former British colonial masters. Choosing to continue the struggle to rid Malaya of British rule via the gun instead of the ballot box, they killed and mutilated innocent civilians. The MNLA, formerly MPAJA, was essentially a communist-inspired uprising that began with many brutal murders of colonial expatriate rubber plantation owners and their families.

The communists also targeted the families of British colonists in Malaya, including their children. They set fire to their properties, buses with innocent children still inside them, and rubber plantation estates, as well as murdering local policemen and policewomen. Bloody violence flared up in the streets and then escalated, becoming a problem for British rule in Malaya post-Second World War and kicking off a large-scale communist terrorist insurgency—better known today, for insurance purposes, as the Malayan Emergency (1948–1960). A new kind of soldier was needed, as the cream of British veterans had disbanded after the war.

The National Service men of post-war Britain were no match for the experience-hardened veteran jungle fighters of the new communist insurgents. These—under a renewed second insurgency in 1968, long after the British had left the conflict in Malaya—renamed themselves the Malayan National Liberation Army. To deal with the new threat, the decommissioned Second World War Special Air Service of David Sterling's North Africa group was reborn, under the command of ex-Chindit veteran jungle fighter Brigadier "Mad Mike" Calvert.

General Sir John Harding, commander-in-chief for the Far East, decided he needed independent advice and brought in an expert on jungle warfare to fight these hard-core battle-seasoned Chinese terrorists. They were later called communist terrorists or CTs. Mad Mike Calvert was a veteran leader of the controversial Chindit long-range penetration groups. Major-General Orde Charles Wingate masterminded long-range operations in Burma during the Second World War. But after Wingate's death in an untimely air crash, Michael Calvert, who also had considerable experience of hard jungle-terrain fighting behind enemy lines, carried on leading the Chindits. Mad Mike Calvert was notorious for getting the job done. He knew how to fight the Japanese and defeat them.

Charles Wingate (centre) with Michael Calvert (third from left) and Chindits, Burma, 1944

The term *chindit* is an English corruption of the Burmese word *chinthe*, describing a mythical lion. The name was adopted by a legendary band of irregular British-Allied troops during the war in Burma. Calvert was also one of the prime movers in ensuring the Special Air Service (SAS) ethic didn't die out at the end of the war. Calvert set up his own special force, a jungle fighting unit he called the Malayan Scouts SAS. This was intended to operate only for the duration of the emergency, under Far East Command. The Malayan scouts wore shoulder titles on their olive-green jungle uniforms, and under the titles were the green patch and yellow kris fighting knife. The basic training of British National Service men or regular soldiers was not enough to counter a brutal guerrilla war. An elite counterterrorist jungle warfare group was required to meet with the new growing communist threat in the Malayan colonies.

This eventually led to the jungle-warfare school being set up at Kota Tinggi, Johore, in Malaya. The original British jungle-fighting school was set up by the Malayan Scouts Special Air Service and operated from 1948 until 1971. There are those even today who sympathize; they were once a part of treason against their own nation or bought into the idea of a great people's revolution against the British Empire of the Far East. In my opinion, our colonies fared a great deal better than many others who came before us. They should have remained under British control. Dissenters who sought to get rid of British rule in her colonies did so through a policy of large-scale murder of innocent civilians.

All those loyal to the British also became targets of the communist terrorists. It started with the random killing of plantation owners and rubber tappers, along with kidnapping and gang-raping their daughters. The brutality extended to killing innocent schoolchildren by setting fire to their buses. Our not-so-noble enemies in the colonies got what they had coming to them. These murderous thugs needed to be eliminated; they were not "freedom fighters" but brutal killers who adopted a policy of intimidation, protection rackets, and sheer terror to raise funds, along with beheadings and disembowelling of their enemies.

Those who remained loyal to the British they contemptuously called "running dogs". For the most part, the Malayan Emergency was one of many forgotten wars that the British and her colonial forces fought after the end of the Second World War in our Far East colony. I watched Bache, a loyal Malay friend and fellow security forces police officer, bleed out and die horribly on me. I tried to rush him to hospital on rough jungle roads after he was shot in the stomach; he had taken the bullet meant for me in an ambush by communist terrorists.

Members of my jungle Q squad, 1952

We also changed tactics, using the officially denied "Q" squads to great effect, and achieved what could not be done otherwise. Q Squads were British officer-led guerrilla warfare infiltration operations, wherein highly motivated locally trained and recruited jungle fighters dressed up as the enemy to engage them on their own terms. These were a kind of officially denied search-and-destroy kill teams akin to American Special Forces A teams, whose principal operating methods fell outside the rules of engagement. British Q squads often came across regular British Army or local security forces jungle patrols but pulled back into the bush when they did. But of course this never happened, at least not officially.

Historians have argued that the fall of Singapore was the greatest British military defeat during the Second World War, citing that a smaller force of just 30,000 Imperial Japanese forces had defeated the 120,000-strong British and Allied forces in Malaya and Singapore. Winston Churchill had failed to reinforce her weaker Navy, Air

Force, and ground forces in Malaya with any credible effective military deterrent, scavenging all that he could from Malaya to bolster the war in Europe. The sinking by enemy aircraft of two British capital battleships of Force Z, namely *HMS Prince of Wales* and *HMS Repulse*, which reportedly sank off the isthmus of Kra, sealed the fate of Malaya.

HMS Indomitable, a 35,500-ton aircraft carrier intended to give air cover to Force Z, ran aground off Jamaica. Force Z was a British naval squadron hurriedly put together during the Second World War to halt Japanese aggression on the British colony of Malaya and the naval base of Singapore. It consisted of the battleship *HMS Prince of Wales*, the battlecruiser *HMS Repulse*, plus four accompanying destroyers. Yamashita, the Japanese commander for the attack on Malaya, was not short of men. To maintain his logistics, Japanese forces of around 30,000 troops amassed in the jungles of Johore for the final attack on Singapore, which by then was running low on drinking water.

The fact that the 30,000 Japanese forces were undersupplied and low on ammunition at that time would not have changed the outcome of the attack on "Fortress Singapore," as huge battalion-strength reinforcements were not far behind. What is missed out by later day historians was that the Japanese forces also had several thousands of battle-hardened Manchurian campaign troops held in reserve, including tanks, planes, and armour that could be brought into play. Allied forces in Malaya and Singapore on December 1, 1941 were as follows: 19,000 British, 15,000 Australian, 37,000 Indian Army (including the eleventh division), plus 17,000 local Malay troops.

Approximately 7,500 Allied soldiers were killed; 10,000 were wounded, escaped, or were listed missing in the Battle of Malaya. On January 29, 1942, approximately 20,000 green troops of the eighteenth division arrived in Singapore, bringing the actual rather than reported total Allied forces strength up to around 85,000 men—not 120,000 as previously claimed. After Singapore fell, a tally of Allied losses revealed 5,000 killed and wounded or missing. In retrospect, on the Japanese side, more than 10,000 were killed in Malaya and Singapore, with some further 25,000 wounded or missing in action. Historians and military strategists regard the fall of Singapore as the greatest British military disaster—or clusterfuck—of the Second World War.

After the battle of Singapore, many thousands of British prisoners of war were taken as slave labour for the Japanese Burma railway. They subsequently perished there, from brutal beatings by their Japanese guards, malnutrition, exhaustion, or tropical diseases. British and colonial Far East troops in Malaya were inexperienced at jungle warfare, generally being considered untested or "green". Soldiers lacked the discipline of battle against a well-trained, determined enemy. The British officers in command led them poorly, with no real effective coordination of ground or air movements. Inaction against the initial Japanese landings in Siam, as well as poor intelligence regarding Japanese movements, was a factor. Without any real air support or naval aircraft carriers, the colony of Singapore was known to be doomed by her commanders.

Despite the propaganda that led the colonial British to believe themselves invincible early on during the Malaya campaign, I suggest there were greater losses at stake and that their Far East colonies of Malaya and Singapore were sacrificed by the British to focus on fighting and winning the war in Europe. A 1939 COS Subcommittee Report known as CAB 53/50 stated that to effectively defend Malaya, Britain would have had to deploy at least eight capital ships.

That should have been the minimum British Naval Task force mustered to counter the threat of nine Japanese battleships and battlecruisers. The fact that we needed battleships and heavy cruisers with at least two modern aircraft carriers to defend our Naval Task Force is incidental, as none materialized nor existed back then in the region. The British Empire relied heavily instead on the bullshit propaganda that Britain "ruled the waves". Using her untested and poorly led large colonial army—more suited to keeping public order than fighting an all-out war—was a serious mistake. She had at the time neither the resources nor strategic military naval assets to fight a major world war on two fronts.

The defeat of the British in the East Indies, culminating with the fall of Singapore, had more far-reaching consequences post-war. A humiliating military defeat by a nation considered to be an inferior military power at that time was politically catastrophic. The belief that Britain was technologically and militarily superior to their Japanese counterparts was misguided. What did not help was an acute lack of any immediate military action by the British commanders, such as bolstering Malaya's northern border defences or taking the war to Siam, where the Japanese landed on neutral territory. Britain's defence strategy was based on outdated WWI modules.

Incorrect deployment of limited and obsolete aircraft and the ground forces clusterfuck by British commanders contributed to the huge military defeat that was the invasion of Malaya on 8 December 1941. The Japanese navy, army, and air force, especially with their Mitsubishi Zeros, were far superior militarily, very well coordinated, and a formidable fighting force compared to any British forces in the region at that time. The loss of their strategic island colony, "Fortress Singapore," and her newly upgraded British naval base had also damaged prestige for Britain as a protector of her colonies; it also aided the Japanese.

This eventually triggered the quest for independence from British rule that signalled the beginning of the end for the British Empire. For the first time ever, the inhabitants of British colonies in the Far East realized that Britannia was no longer invincible, and that British imperialism could be beaten. Losing the war in the Far East British colonies changed the way the local people viewed their former imperial masters. In the days of British imperialism, if a white British man or woman was walking along a street, local Chinese or Malay peoples would automatically cross over to the other side so as not to run head-on into white British people. All this ended when local-population politicians decided to press for independence from British rule. They no longer crossed over the street to give way to the British colonials.

The Japanese lost some 10,000 men in Malaya and Singapore, and more than 25,000 Japanese soldiers were wounded or missing. So, contrary to all that has been said, the Japanese military did not walk into Malaya without cost.

There must at this stage be no thought of saving the troops or sparing the population. The battle must be fought to the bitter end at all costs. The eighteenth division has a chance to make its name in history. Commanders and senior officers should die with their troops. The honour of the British Empire and of the British Army is at stake.

—Winston Churchill, to the eighteenth Division, 1942

Chapter 2

Living the Dream
Wednesday, 1 January 1947 (New Year's Day)

Most people simply daydream without end; others wishfully think *What if?* But as Thomas Edward Lawrence once said,

> "All men dream, but not equally. Those who dream by night in the dusty recesses of their minds wake in the day to find that it was vanity: but the dreamers of the day are dangerous men, for they may act their dreams with open eyes, to make them possible."

Do you moralize the ideal, or do you remember these atrocities committed against humanity in the name of idealism? I am not very good at subterfuge. When I was young, I looked at people and saw that I had a decision to make. I could run with the pack or go it alone. I decided that I would be in advance of the others and throw myself into the winds of fortune. There are some things in life of value, and these you may strive hard to achieve or acquire. But whatever you choose to do with your life, do so honestly and with integrity. This I did with varying degrees of success and failure during my time as an itinerant soldier of fortune.

My journey began on a small vessel somewhere out in the Savu Sea, sometimes called Sawu Sea, located within the Indonesian archipelago and named after the island of Savu. The post-war era was a time for new opportunities, with great adventures for daring entrepreneurs willing to take risks in the game of life. But it was also a time of many fractured post-war families and broken military men looking to start afresh. Not all wounds are visible, and nightmares persist. I decided to make a better life for myself, out in the colonies, redefining who and what I was on the other side of the world.

Language is a public affair which no one really controls. The Saxon word *worm*, for instance, can also mean dragon. The word for *dragon* in Germanic mythology is worm in Old English: *wyrm*. In Old High German it's *wurm* and in Old Norse *ormr*, suggesting a snake or serpent. A word is just another sound and the written word merely a series of marks. We live in terms of language, which is, when properly considered, a history of words and rules that determines their use. I have always kept a journal, odd disjointed jottings and anecdotes of my thoughts at the time. I note these quickly on pieces of paper but write them up fully later when I have a few spare moments. In this sense, my journals are a record of my disjointed thoughts at the time of their writing.

Roy is a *wally* and Cecil a *gallah* (an Australian bird). Wally is Aussie slang for an idiot. They both took off in a hurry, leaving me high and dry in the boatyard at Fakfak, a significant port town in West Papua, New Guinea. Apparently they were heading for Foochow on the South China coast in their pearl lugger. It is New Year's Day! We are three days out of Fakfak, in New Guinea, heading for Ndao in the Java Sea. Ndao is one of the southernmost islands along the Indonesian archipelago. It is a picturesque, pacific, oceanic blue sky today, with my crewmen, Abu and Idris, who are sat on the planks of the deck, weaving tiny, delicately coloured *momi* and *kaheleani* shells into a necklace.

We are running a month late, but have you perhaps never chased a rainbow or gone off in pursuit of a dream? Divers are notably notorious for not wanting others to know about their underwater finds, and if we are honest, we can't blame them. Some very spectacular finds have been made, several of which have been worth a great deal of money. Perhaps their attitude is not unreasonable, for after all, many of them have spent quite some time searching for that something special in life, their dream of discovering lost gold or buried treasure.

We have just concluded a five-month trip through the South Pacific and spent Christmas in Fakfak, Dutch New Guinea. Our cargo is rather a mixture now, most of which we will trade off at various ports of call on our way home to Singapore. We have *kappa*, the bark cloth made by the women of the South Pacific from mulberry bark. After being pounded, the scrapings are left fermenting in seawater before being sun-bleached. After that, the fine gauze-like cloth is printed with designs using vegetable dyes. As well we have pearl shell, which the Chinese use to inlay and ornament their furniture, and mother-of-pearl, which could fetch a good price in Singapore.

We also have one or two white and blueish-grey pearls of the size and type approximately five points between ruby and diamond. But although the pearl-oyster seabeds were good to us, we did not find those precious tear-tooth black pearls we came in search of, the mythical lost treasure of King Kamehameha. Cecil called us on the radio this morning, but for the time being we are maintaining radio silence. This is not because there is any animosity between us. We are currently en route to a shipwreck in Dutch Rotinese waters. Pulau Rote (Rote Island) lies 500 km (311 miles) northwest of the Australian coast and 170 km (106 miles) north of the Ashmore and Cartier Islands, southwest of the larger island of Timor.

I don't relish the possibility of a Dutch gunboat turning up out of the blue to catch us in the act of making profit. After all, there is quite an insurrection going on in the Dutch East Indies around Java, and of course the Dutch authorities keep an eye open, especially for gunrunners.

I think it was Anton Chekhov who said, "The task of a writer is not to solve the problem but to state the problem correctly." I have yet to write up my 1946 journals from the notes I made during that busy time. This 1947 journal will overlap briefly and commence in Hawaii, moving quickly to Fakfak. China must have been quite a place, all things considered.

The Kuomintang under General Chiang Kai-Shek were fighting bolshevism in the south, and the *tuchuns*—self-styled warlords little better than bandits operating on a large scale—were making war on one another, plundering the impoverished and war-weary peasants. Now, the poor of China had a rather nasty habit of leaving unwanted baby girls on a mountaintop, where they would die of cold or be taken in by one of the monasteries. My Chinese emissary female was one such case. Luck must have been with her back in 1920, because the Taoist monk who found her as a baby later became the clan master of the Green Dragon Mountain Society.

We will leave her story for the moment, while I get my 1947 journal into its correct sequence. My business partner, Roy, and I left Singapore for Hawaii in search of some fabulous treasure he had learnt of during his enforced stay in a Japanese prisoner of war camp at Changi, Singapore, during the Second World War. Myth or not, this story helped keep Roy alive during that very trying part of his life, so that seeking to recover it became a compulsion for him. This was the lost treasure of King Kamehameha.

When Kekuiapoiwa II, a Hawaiian chieftess and the mother of King Kamehameha, was pregnant back in 1758—a notable year during which Halley's Comet was visible over Hawaii—she had a strange craving for the eyeball of a chief.

It is said that instead she was given the eye of a man-eater, the tiger shark. The *kahuna* (Hawaiian for a priest, sorcerer, magician, wizard, minister, or expert in any profession) immediately prophesized that her unborn child would be a rebel and killer of chiefs. As a remedy against this prophesy, Alapainui, the old king and then ruler of Hawaii, made plans to have the child killed secretly. According to legend, the baby, Kamehameha, was carried to safety by a local chief named Naeole, at a place called Awini, on the north coast of the island. The child was carried hidden in a basket covered with *olona* fibres, which are used for making fishing nets.

Kamehameha grew up and later became a very powerful war chief and then king, during a long and bloody campaign of conquest across all of the Hawaiian Islands. Some say that his treasure of black pearls was lost during a battle at Morotai, in the Halmahera, Indonesia. Others say that he himself tossed those black pearls into the fire of Kilauea, as his tribute to the Hawaiian goddess Pele. Yet another story suggest that the pearls were lost during a battle in Tahiti. But his last battle was at Pitu.

Oyster-bed girls in Hawaii

Wailana—"Peaceful Water"—is chanted in Hawaiian on the slopes of Waia to evoke the uplands. *"Olelo no ke ola, I ka olelo no ka make."* She (the goddess Pele) speaks the language of life and death, here amidst the falling white ash of Kilauea, one of the world's most active volcanos. The *kahuna* say that this is the home of their goddess Pele.

"Hokule'a." Follow the stars to Tahiti. *"Aloha."*

We took the garlands of *ti* leaves and delicate *ohai ali'i* and *ilima* blossoms and went our way, following the path of Kamehameha to Tahiti. Of course, the location of the oyster bed was to all intents and purpose taboo. We were never permitted near them. To break the taboo would have invited the full vengeance of Kukailimoku, the appointed guardian and war god to whom the local chiefs sacrificed animals, criminals, and conquered warriors. Both Roy and I had no intention of becoming meat for the god's bird-feather visage set with dog teeth. Perhaps the legend of the black pearls was just a ruse—the fox pretending to be dead as a ruse to confuse the hunters.

People were making offerings of fresh fruit wrapped in ti leaves to Laka, the goddess of the hula dances and of the forest. They were also making offerings to *amakua*, their family gods, and telling stories of how these spirits in the shapes of lizards, owls, sharks, or other creatures intervened in their lives. The full moon had peaked above Mauna Ka and began to turn red. The red deepened as the moon moved closer into the earth's shadow. Both Roy and I felt it was time for us to leave the place. Perhaps the strict taboo was the cause of the uneasiness we felt sitting under the blood moon. We left the people to their belief in their ancient gods and set a new south-easterly course for Tahiti.

I rounded up my boat's crew and waited for the high tide before setting my new heading. I left my ex-Royal Malayan Navy coxswain, Zainal, to take my boat to our new destination whilst I did some catch-up with a long-deserved sleep. Thoughts of England, my mother, and my wife, Pam, flooded back during my dream time, that special landscape, lost outside of time and space, where we live our hopes and ambitions without the burden of consequence for our actions.

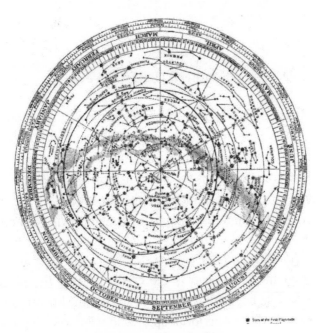

Northern Hemisphere

This map shows all the principal stars visible in the Northern Hemisphere throughout the year, and it thus includes many stars also found in the Southern Hemisphere of the sky. If you hold it nearly over your head, so that its centre is in the direction of the Pole Star, and then rotate it until the day of the month is at the bottom, it will show the positions of the stars at midnight.

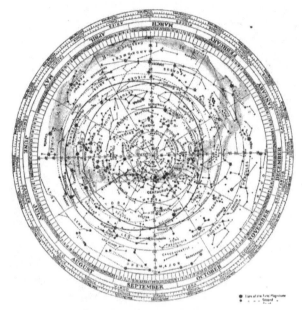

Southern Hemisphere

This map shows the stars for people living in the Southern Hemisphere. Here the first thing is to face the South Pole, so that you set up your map with the date at the bottom, as before, and turn so that the Southern Cross corresponds with the position of Crux on the map. To observe at a time earlier than midnight, proceed as in the Northern Hemisphere, only rotate the map in an anticlockwise direction.

Thursday, 2 January 1947

They say that the ocean is the cradle of life, the place where everything had its beginning. We must admire the bravery of the man Kamehameha and his warrior people, who went foraging the Pacific in their flimsy outriggers.

The Tahitian women are quite beautiful among the local island women of the Pacific. They have light-olive skin, which contrasts with their black hair and crowns of woven gardenias, the scarlet blossoms they wear behind their ears.

The dark-grey beach, which shows black here, is where the dead coral has been broken up and pounded into fine sand by the ocean waves. Branches of pink coral are strewn everywhere, and the sword-back ledges project in ragged crests of rock, standing out in small towers and combs and teeth, set one upon another.

Here on the slope that stretches down to the lagoon, palms lean over the sea mirror of unruffled waters. Presently the women depart, their light cotton sarongs falling about their legs as they walk. With the sunset comes the cooling of the heated air, and the lights twinkle through the red walls of the translucent palm-thatched huts. Lights can be seen gliding to and fro, flickering through the darkness as the canoes ride the still lagoon. Darkness swiftly descends in this part of the world and fades just as quickly. When at length the singing and dancing cease, the women bring out the sleeping mats and unwind their necklaces of flowers. Talk is not necessary, and the murmur of the tide fades.

This is "aloha!" Here sleep comes easily, without anxiety. We are full of little gold fish baked and served in a coconut sauce, bread fruit baked and served hot, banana pudding, and pancakes. Roy thinks he could stay forever! I am told that King Kamehameha's last battle was at Morotai Island, or Pulau Morotai, one the northernmost islands in the Halmahera group of Eastern Indonesia's Maluku Islands. This is where he lost his treasure and where we are searching for our dream.

The Polynesian Triangle has its corners over 4,000 miles apart at Hawaii, Easter Island, Tahiti, and New Zealand. Of course there are also several Polynesian Islands within the adjoining Melanesian and Micronesian groups, involving tiny populations on almost every inhabitable island—obviously, the result of countless long-distance voyages over a period of perhaps thousands of years. The origins of the Polynesians is subject to debate and speculation. On the other hand, we have the theory put forward by writer and explorer Thor Heyerdahl, who is attempting to prove the accidental one-way voyages with his Kon-Tiki expedition, a drifting voyage from Peru to the Tuamotu islands later this year.

Are the Polynesians the lost Inca of Peru? I have an open mind, though my own theory remains that the Polynesians are a hybrid people of Mongoloid, Caucasian, and Negroid racial origins, a mix that has probably been isolated since around 2000 BCE. My first clue came from the similarity of many Polynesian words, which can be traced back to ancient Malay; no other linguistic elements are quite so apparent despite dialect changes across the area. The Hawaiians believed Captain James Cook to be a god because of his appearance and at first worshipped him. Their disillusionment later led to his death when he broke their taboo by his desecration of Polynesian *mana*.

The concept of mana among Melanesian and Polynesian peoples is of a supernatural force or power that may be ascribed to persons, spirits, or inanimate objects. Mana may be either good or evil, beneficial or dangerous. The taboo exists in all Polynesian societies without exception. The belief in a white god is found amongst the Bugis of South Sulawesi. *Arung*, a word taken from *anum*, or *ratu anum*, denotes "handsome prince". This Bugis prince is considered to come from the highest lineage of white blood, the descendant of a heavenly being sent down to earth to bring order to a chaotic world.

Friday, 3 January 1947

These people of the Celebes are Bugis (the word is more accurately pronounced as *boo-gis*), a Malay-speaking collective of smugglers and pirates whose territorial waters are the Indian Ocean and the South China seas. The Bugis are a South East Asian people, numbering over a few million, whose homeland is the south-western peninsula of Celebes island, called Sulawesi in modern Indonesia. They belong to the great family of the Austronesian peoples. Of course the question is rather obvious: Did the Polynesians acquire this belief from the Bugis? Or was it vice versa! The war paint is for the benefit of the Tahitian women. Idris is the only Bugis member of the crew; both Sulaiman and Zainal are Malays.

Now, the French of Tahiti are nothing like the people living in

France. They lack the intellect and liveliness of the French, especially that of the Parisian. These French expatriates are the old nobility who survived and refurbished their clothes, creating an effect of smartness even though the material of their frocks appears to be somewhat old and shiny. Here in their tropical colonies, they live for each other and find a great deal of amusement in so doing, reliving their past noble colonial heritage. We British laugh at a man if he runs after a woman. Both Roy and I are considered beachcombers by most them, although we are more inclined to see ourselves as daring, bold, or even audacious itinerant soldiers of fortune and opportunity.

The pearl banks are held under French monopoly, and while the French are quite prepared to make full use of our diving skills, they have never trusted us nor believed in our honesty or integrity. After all, we had gone "native" and away from the white man's reservations. We lived off the grid, but more importantly, as free men we were outside of society rules and regulations. Our only loyalty was to each other and our fellow crew fraternity.

As far as the French Polynesians are concerned, life is lived in a rather serious, tyrannical fashion, and we have no place in their dreams of the old nobility.

We left Tahiti and set course for Pitu, Moratai.

From left to right, Idris, me, Sulaiman, and Zainal at Tahiti

21

Saturday, 4 January 1947

When we arrived on the Indonesian island of Pitu in Moratai, at least the children were glad to see us. But then, perhaps it was curiosity which brought them down to the beach to greet us by shouting hearty and friendly hellos. It was refreshing to see such young children playing and cheering strangers from the sea in this most magical of all places in the world. I initially felt like the explorer Captain Cook, just off the British *HM Bark Endeavour* at Botany Bay in Australia. We all have our dreams, after all. But the difference has always been with the dreamers who realize their ambitions through hard work, a little luck, and sheer perseverance.

Two Pitu women, 1947

Pitu women were dark-brown skinned and garlanded with dog-tooth and shark-tooth necklaces for decoration; they each wore also a bone through their nostrils. I suppose their appearance was rather ludicrous by Western standards. But then who are we, with our standards of Western morality—which brought destruction upon the world in two major world wars—to dare consider that our technological mass-scale killing machines make us more civilized than they? Race distinction and the idea of racial superiority has always been separable by culture, although racial heredity is usually invoked to rally a group of people together.

Nineteenth-century Germanic nationalist romanticism and the search for identity led to the idea of the Aryan or Indo-Europeans being of superior race, based on the colour of their white skin. The concept of *Übermensch,* or superman, belongs to Friedrich Nietzsche; this also became synonymous with Nazi political ideologies against the so called *Untermensch,* referred to as subhuman or inferior Slavic races. This Germanic "master-race" doctrine led to the horrors of the holocaust. The brutal Nazi extermination of perceived non-Aryan "inferior" races during the Second World War decimated many Northern European cultures on a level never previously experienced in Europe.

The writer, poet, and Freemason Rudyard Kipling, who penned the poem "The White Man's Burden" (1899), proposes that there is a moral obligation to rule the non-white peoples of the Earth, whilst encouraging their economic, cultural, and social progress, until they can independently manage their own affairs. But perhaps primitive man never looked out across the world and saw mankind as a collective group or felt his common cause with his species. From the beginning he was a provincial who raised the barriers high. Whether it was a question of choosing a wife or the taking of someone's head, the first important distinction was between his own human group and those beyond the pale.

His own group and all its ways of behaving was always unique. So modern man differentiated into subgroups of "chosen people" and those that became considered dangerous alien groups within his own civilization. And yet we are humans who remain genetically and culturally related to one another. This is the fundamental fact that bigots and separatists, who cannot see the woods for the trees, choose to blatantly ignore. For all men are brothers after all, despite the external variances of skin pigmentation. But with the next breath, we are always both the tribes and the outsiders, with a strange thirst to default into the organized chaos of subcultures.

From left to right, Roy, me, Cecil, and Edward

I suppose this is the way of our world, ready to wage war and mayhem against each other based on these differences. Those who choose to live outside the provisions of the moral compass or code which holds within the limits of their own people usually end up summarily denied a place anywhere in the human scheme and become outcasts. But is not one item of man's tribal social organization, language, or local religion carried in his germ cell?

Sunday, 5 January 1947

Edward and Cecil are two Australian divers from the Darwin area; we came across them whilst exploring the reef off Pitu. They run a pearl lugger; that's a small ship with four-cornered sails set fore and aft, bent on yard slung at a third and or a quarter of its length from one end. Edward found a market for mother-of-pearl at Amoy and Foochow on the South China coast.

We worked the reef together for the next few days, which of course gave us all a little more advantage in hunting on the seabed for the shell we required. We took it in turns to work for an hour only at a time, to make the best of our underwater work and avoid nitrogen narcosis, or the "rapture of the deep" as it is sometimes called. Many divers compare nitrogen narcosis to a feeling of pleasant drunkenness, but in our line of work we can ill afford any mishaps to any of our diving crew, as there is no real immediate help here in the open seas. There is no decompression chamber and certainly no well-equipped and trained medical staff on hand should anything go south.

Depending of course on depth, my golden rule remains as far as diving with compressed air is concerned—one hour down with two hours of mandatory rest on the surface. No exceptions! I am fully aware of Boyle–Mariotte law, or Mariotte's law, and its implication when diving using compressed air, which can have tragic results for the unwary diver. Of course, another danger is the build-up of carbon dioxide in the blood of the diver who, being under high pressure, cannot properly expel this respiratory gas with each exhalation. Then there is the danger of the "bends," due to the use of compressed air under pressure. This occurs when we start to ascend and pass into a zone of lighter pressure after being more than two hours underwater, for example, at a depth of 132 feet (forty metres) below the surface.

Atmospheric pressure on the human body is approximately 73.5 (5 bars) per square inch. A lot of people mistakenly believe that the gas divers breathe while scuba diving is pure oxygen. Although the human body needs oxygen to survive, deep underwater pressures causes pure oxygen to become poisonous to a scuba diver, and the onset of oxygen toxicity syndrome can kill the diver. Thus the gas scuba divers use is compressed ordinary air, which changes its nature in a diver's bloodstreams at depth.

Monday, 6 January 1947

Before the Dutch established control of the region at the beginning of the twentieth century, South Sulawesi consisted of a large number of petty kingdoms, each ruled by a prince of the highest white blood. Each local ruler, or *arung*, was considered as a direct descendant of a heavenly being sent to earth to bring order to a chaotic world. The Dutch recognized the authority of more powerful rulers and gave them additional power under a system of indirect rule. The result was that life in the Dutch East Indies has been little affected fundamentally by the march of time under this extremely efficient Dutch administration, and the people continue to live along traditional lines.

We arrived at Pulau Karimata (Karimata Island) at 0545 hours PST (Pacific Standard Time) and immediately commenced unloading into the small native *sagur*, which is a kind of dug-out canoe they call *perahu-sagur*. For ease of handling, the consignment is always kept in the form of small packages, which in the case of medical supplies is waterproof. It also makes for quick loading and unloading, which would be very necessary should one of the frequent coastal Dutch gunboats decide to pay us a visit and force us to make a quick getaway out to sea. In that case, my specially modified Motor Torpedo Boat can outrun those Dutch gunboats for about an hour at top speed.

I always maintain emergency high-octane aviation gasoline before setting off on any venture, and this fuel remains our last resort should all else fail. The reserve fuel tanks contain marine diesel. My crew are all trained to shoot well in any firefight, but my boat's .303 light machine guns, rifles, and pistols are no match for the four Dutch gunboats' deadly accurate heavier 4.7" guns or their complement of four 40 mm machine canons, including several .50-calibre heavy machine guns well placed on her gun decks.

It would be suicide to take on the full and deadly accurate firepower of a Dutch naval gunboat. As I have no torpedoes to defend my vessel against Dutch gunboats, my only viable option is to outrun the Dutch navy, never to engage them. In the case of this island, Pulau Karimata, my exit strategy would be to make my getaway at maximum speed towards Sambas, on the very tip of Dutch Borneo and, once there, another hour's run at normal speed, switching over to the diesel engine.

This is a necessity, because most of the emergency aviation fuel that powers the two-high performance marine engines would have been spent by then. My heading, at normal speed, would then be into the waters of the Malaysian state of Sarawak and onwards to safety. Once in Kuching, I would refuel and lay up in hiding for a few days until the pursuing Dutch gunboats have given up the chase. After that I would make a new heading and return at a steady speed to the more familiar home waters on the island of British Singapore, for a well-deserved rest.

On the reef off Morotai

Tuesday, 7 January 1947

We are not loading anything at Pulau Karimata on this trip, and at 0800 hours local time I get my boat underway again, this time heading for Pulau Tambelan (Tambelan Island) off the coast of Singawang. This is on the tip of Dutch Borneo, where I am going to pick up that family of Dutch Eurasians from the island of Bunguran in the Great Natuna group. The weather is fine, with a little wind, and we are making good time. Pulau Tambelan is a rather quiet little island where we don't anticipate any problems with the local people, who are not into local Indonesian politics. My boat is a former Royal Navy Motor Torpedo Boat, designated as MTB.

The US Navy sent several of their Pacific Fleet Patrol Torpedo (better known as PT boats) to support the Royal Navy during the war. We have stripped and modified these for our contraband trade. We are currently running on a Grey diesel marine engine taken out of a British landing craft. Centrally sited in my engine room, it gives me a steady fifteen knots in fair weather at sea. I am running empty, since being laden with cargo would slow us down. My marine plywood-constructed vessel still retains two of the craft's original Packard marine V-12 engines, whose maximum revolutions are 3,000 per minute and use the more expensive 100-octane aviation gasoline.

These engines develop approximately 1850 horsepower at 2,500 rpm, increasing our speed to around twenty knots at a moment's notice, for a quick getaway should any gunboat show up on my radar. Those engines are only used in an emergency, as they are not as economical to run as the diesel engine. I will need to refuel with diesel once we arrive at Pulau Tambelan and top up all my fuel tanks, although we currently have sufficient fuel to make the run around Cape Datu to Kuching on marine diesel alone.

It will also be a good time to get fresh-food provisions for the crew and fresh drinking water. Its 1500 hours PST, and we are well off Pontianak, on the coast of Dutch Borneo. Pontianak is the capital of the Indonesian province of West Kalimantan and remains the largest trading-port city on the island of Borneo. Pontianak was one of our problems on this run, due to a Dutch trader vessel that puts to sea around high tide, heading for Batavia in Java. If the old tramp came near us, the crew would radio our position to one of their gunboats, and the chase would be on for our very survival. High tide is around 1700 hours PST today, so we are on schedule, with an hour left to spare and Pontianak out of the way.

According to local Indonesian and Malaysian mythology, a *pontianak* is a female vampire ghost, much feared, especially by men in that region. The Malayan/Indonesian pontianaks are usually depicted as pale-skinned women with long black hair and red eyes, dressed in bloodied white dresses. But they are said to be able to shapeshift into beautiful females, since they prey on men. The Malays are a rather superstitious people. Pregnant Malay women, it seems, feel rather vulnerable if this vampire ghost of legend has been sighted. According to local folklore, a pontianak will rise from her grave during a full moon, with high-pitched baby's cries.

It is an impressive sight to watch dolphins playing, and this is made more so by the way the dolphins frolic together. One moment they will be swimming in a line; then one will leap into the air, and a second later, all will bunch together, rolling and twisting about, splashing each other. One moment they will roll on their backs and the next leap vertically out of the water and land back in a kind of belly flop. Then they will all be at it, leaping in and out in a perfect line-abreast formation. These are the common dolphins, easily recognizable because of their distinctive creamy-yellow hourglass pattern along the sides, with a dark-grey back, tail, and flippers and a cream-coloured belly.

A common dolphin's beak is relatively long and slender, and it is believed that its lifespan varies between twenty and thirty years. I would further add that dolphins are very intelligent creatures.

Pearls are produced by bivalve creatures, such as mussels and oysters, on the insides of their shells, somewhat like blisters between the shell and the creature. But the violence associated with removing the pearls from their natural abode has given the pearl a reputation as being unlucky for some, bringing bad fortune to their owners, though this is superstition.

All along the north coast of the Australian continent, pearlers were busy from Exmouth Gulf to the Torres Strait. Broome, Darwin, and Thursday Island were the principal bases for the pearl luggers. The crews on these three-sailed vessels, akin to small wooden fishing sail boats, practically lived on board these purpose-built craft. Basic day-to-day amenities were non-existent, but these men worked long hours, from sunup to sundown, in seas with some of the biggest tides in the world. All sorts of weather conditions hampered their progress, with major cyclones, rip tides and unforgiving currents that could sink their tiny lugger into the vast, destructive sudden whirlpools which often cropped up out of nowhere.

The crew members were mainly indentured workers who had to toil hard for minimal rewards. Being a highly competitive diving-for-fortune industry, the pay-out in return for work rendered was often poor. Bonuses were based on the size of the catch. The head diver was the guy who usually doubled as the skipper or captain. He directed the work from the seabed, using a recognized code of tugs on his lifeline. His life and the success of the dive depended upon the alertness and skills of his tender. On board the pearl luggers, the crew had to work hard together, with great trust and understanding, to ensure that divers were able to collect as much shell as possible.

The oyster beds we seek remain in small groups amongst the razor-sharp coral, and the trick is to locate quickly the spot where the largest group of seabed oysters have congregated and to lift the large ones, by means of a basket, up to the boat waiting above. The smaller shells we leave to grow and mature; we only take the larger shells. This is important if we are to preserve this natural resource for the future. The underwater world is a strangely quiet world of coral, rocks, and seaweed, but the fish who swim these waters take very little notice of us—unless of course we scare them by making sudden quick movements.

There have been many interesting discoveries made here on the reef. Some of the marvellously coloured formations of coral can give a diver a terrible rash if touched without the protection of gloves. *Millepora* coral is highly venomous, with a burning effect if you touch it with your bare skin. There are also a great number of stingrays in these waters, which carry a poisonous sting in their tails. But it is the grouper fish, with its bristles and spines, that concern us the most. Now, most of our diving gear is war surplus but very reliable, although in these tropical waters we prefer to dive and work minus the Navy-issue wetsuits and weighted belts.

I have never seen a giant squid, that ten-legged cephalopod mollusc of the genus *Loligo*. It is allegedly a type of "kraken" found in these deep waters. In my view, giant squids are the most dangerous of all the creatures we are likely to come across in these parts. At least, so I have been told by more knowledgeable "sea gypsies", a name given to the pearl hunters who have operated in this region over many years. However, this is an octopus, a rather timid creature that is doing its utmost to avoid my interest. Storytellers would have us believe that the octopus is a terrifying, menacing monster of the deep. Cecil has a way of turning them inside out.

I let this one go and then regulated the quantities of compressed air from the two tanks on my back so that the pressure within my body was equal to that of the sea surrounding me. Then I went deeper down the reef.

Some of these oysters weigh as much as four pounds, but it is the gold-lipped pearl oyster that is the most luxurious and valuable of these seashells. The fine pearls (not so often found in the flesh of the enclosed shellfish, or rather molluscs, which is the correct scientific name for shellfish) are a by-product. The mother-of-pearl on the inside of the shell is what we are after.

***Trochus* shell**

We also took Trochus, a top-shaped, striped shell approximately three inches high, for its pearl shell. Pearl shells sometimes lie flat on the seabed, covered by coral, seaweed, or sea fern. They may be partly buried in mud or sand by the eddies of the tide passing around the shell. If you are lucky and you know what you are doing, sometimes you can spot them as they open and close during feeding.

We went back on board towards the end of our extended dives, when the light started failing. The evening quickly crept up on us; time to get some rest and to organize all of our day's work as well as the next day's dive rota. Supper this evening was *sambal ikan bellis* (dried anchovies in a hot sauce) with rice, which is a Malaysian delicacy.

I experienced one of those nights when I had a series of lucid dreams, kind of broken up and seemingly unconnected dreamscape scenes in my mind, which took me back home to my first wartime romance with my English wife, Pamela, and my former life in the South of England. Guess I am in some ways homesick for the motherland, as all ex-pats seem to be.

I took the first dive next morning with Zainal. We always dived in pairs for safety. I adjusted my air regulator as I went down deeper into the clear, blue waters.

The Malay generic name for sharks, dogfish, and rays resembling sharks is Yu. The hammerhead shark or wing-head shark is known as *Yu Bekong* in Malay. Of the nine known species of hammerhead sharks, only three of them are particularly dangerous to humans, namely the scalloped, great, and smooth hammerheads. The wing-head shark (*Eusphyra blochii*) is a species of hammerhead shark indigenous to the Pacific region; it is part of the family *Sphyrnidae*. Reaching a total length of 1.9 metres, or approximately 6 foot 3 inches, this small brown or grey shark has a slender body, with a tall, sickle-shaped first dorsal fin.

Shark rays (*Rhina ancylostoma*), on the other hand, are not true sharks, although at first sight they may appear so. The front section is broad, like a ray, with prehistoric ridges along the head, while the back section resembles a shark with dual dorsal fins. *Yu gila* or the slender bamboo shark (*Chiloscyllium indicum*) is a bottom feeder. *Yu laras*, or the star-spotted smooth-hound (*Mustelus manazo*) is a hound shark of the family *Triakidae*. *Yu rimau* is the Tiger shark (*Galeocerdo cuvier*), a species of requiem shark and the only extant member of the genus *Galeocerdo*.

Commonly known as sea tigers, *Yu sambaran* are the ground sharks, order *Carcharhiniformes*. They remain the largest order of sharks, having 270 known species. We know from experience that sharks are most dangerous in shallow waters, and of course they are likely to swoop suddenly on a diver. After all, they are from my point of thinking nothing more than a rather unpleasant eating machine that cleans up the seas. It isn't personal; this is what sharks do. However, as any experienced ocean diver will tell you, in deep water sharks remain curious and will move in on your position, but they are not likely to attack.

The thing is to swim towards them very slowly; usually they will turn away. Most inexperienced scuba divers will immediately bolt straight for the surface in terror and awe on sighting these marine creatures. Bad mistake! It is by far safer to make your way to the seabed and keep still till they pass you by. Sharks are sensitive to any sudden movement, so you should never turn in uncontrollable terror and head for the surface when sighting them. Sharks will pick up on your fear and panic and will attack if you do so.

This particular shark was the oceanic whitetip shark (*Carcharhinus longimanus*), also known as Brown Milbert's sand bar shark, brown shark, or nigano shark. Oceanic whitetip sharks are a large pelagic requiem shark inhabiting tropical and warm temperate seas. The shark is approximately eight to ten feet long, and prefers a depth of fifty feet, with pilot and sucker fishes in attendance.

Oceanic Whitetip Shark

It was Felipe Poey, a Cuban naturalist, who originally described the oceanic whitetip shark as *Squalus longimanus* in 1861. It is possible that many attacks from oceanic whitetip sharks are not recorded because they occur not close to landfall but on mariners adrift far out on the open sea, particularly after shipwrecks or aircraft crashes. The most notorious example of this behaviour came after the torpedoing of the *USS Indianapolis* by a Japanese submarine in August of 1945, when whitetips were thought to be responsible for the deaths of 800 or more American sailors stranded on the Pacific Ocean.

Staying calm and collected as a diver amongst sharks takes a lot of self-discipline, and I do know this is easier said than done. For what it is worth, sharks have always scared the hell out of me. One last thing—avoid at all cost cutting yourself whilst you are diving near coral, especially in shark-infested waters. All sharks can detect blood from miles away, or so I am told by other, more experienced, divers. Sharks are probably among the best hunting and eating mechanisms on planet earth. My advice stands, though: swim slowly towards them if you find yourself in deep waters with one of these predators. Stay calm, keep cool and, I reiterate, never, ever bolt for the surface on sighting a shark.

Many inexperienced sports scuba divers make this serious mistake, but it is their undoing, as sharks have an uncanny ability to sense and even smell fear or panic from their intended prey. People may laugh when I tell them that marine creatures have a sense of smell—but believe me, they do! Sharks possess an acute olfactory system which is far superior to that of human beings. Sharks' nostrils are located on the underside of their snouts and are used solely for smelling, not breathing. The nostrils are lined with specialized cells that comprise the olfactory epithelium.

As sea water flows into their nostrils, the dissolved chemicals present encounter tissue, exciting receptors in the cells. These signals are then transmitted to the brain and interpreted as smells. It is unusual to face as shark, as prey usually tries to escape the situation rather than confront it headlong. If the shark turns away, carry on at the same slow pace, and if possible head for the seabed rather than the surface, keeping a close watch in case the shark does a U-turn and comes straight back at you! But once the sea creature has cleared your diving area and you are sure it has left, start to head slowly for the surface and the boat.

Once safely aboard your dive boat, you will need a stiff drink, as I always do, plus a quick visit to the ship's head, if you have not already crapped in your pants underwater! I am not fond of sharks, but I do respect the danger they pose. Sharks are the oceans' natural scavengers, so it's never personal. But no diver, including myself, is without fear of being eaten alive by these underwater eating machines. We all take the risk every time we go down in search of wrecks or treasure. Contrary to popular myth by romanticists about these creatures, sharks do nor circle around their prey before attacking.

More likely they will come up fast from below and attack you head-on with incredible speed and awesome strength. Sharks have different types of attacks strategies. If the shark attack is territorial, or when a shark has come across you without warning and is curious, it will circle to check you out. So its circling you does not necessarily mean the shark is preparing for an imminent attack. Like their human counterparts, sharks are curious creatures who will want to know exactly what is moving about in their territorial waters. If a shark observes an object of interest, it will adjust its swimming pattern to allow it to get a better view. There is much prejudice about these creatures who clean up the seas.

Chapter 3

Dirty John Hedges
Wednesday, 8 January 1947

Mission Station at Fakfak, 1947

Having spent the better part of the week diving for pearl treasures, we packed up all our gear and headed out once again to Fakfak in Dutch New Guinea. At that time, the mission station at Fakfak New Guinea was operated by a group of Dutch Protestant missionaries, and most of the people these mission crusaders had managed to convert were young girls from one of the hill tribes. Now, if you think that the Catholic missionaries are narrow-minded, do try the Dutch Protestant and compare them.

"Bring your coconuts for sale, and we will sell them." Two for their Dutch guilder and one for you! We, however, were permissive and adventurous and given short shrift by the missionaries.

The island girls had a few good ideas of their own. Now, Edward had "cracked a fat" and had gone off with Roy in search of some well-meaning native girl to remedy the situation. Roy had gone along to keep him out of trouble. For those not in the know, cracking the fat is a very British phrase that refers to having an erection, or bone on—a troublesome thing, particularly for young men running high on hormonal urges.

It must be said that this affliction of cracking the proverbial fat is not exclusive to young men. Older men get the urge also from time to time, especially when spending too many long and lonely nights and days at sea without the comfort of accommodating females. Cecil and I were sitting on the lawn in front of the guest house, watching two-long tail macaque (*Macaca fascicularis*) crab-eating monkeys at play. These two lived on my boat and were full of annoyances and playfulness at the same time. We were having little luck looking for King Kamehameha's treasures.

Cecil suggested that we spend the next three months searching the area of Timor for the wreck of *HMS Pandora*, which sank on 28 August 1791. *HMS Pandora* was a twenty-four gun Porcupine-class sixth-rate ship, launched in 1779, which was reputed to have sunk with a large cargo of gold in her hold. The gold was never recovered. *Pandora* was a Royal Navy warship dispatched to the South Pacific in pursuit of the infamous *Bounty* mutineers. Few people know of or appreciate the archaeological significance of the wreck or the contents, still waiting to be discovered.

My main concern right then was the boat, which required barnacle removal and having her bottom checked. "Dirty John!" Cecil exclaimed suddenly; he had been introducing his pet pup to my monkey while I snapped the camera shutter. Ram the monkey promptly bit the pup, which yelped with pain, much to Cecil's annoyance. It was just a nip, and the pup was more scared than injured.

"You want to shoot that fucking monkey!" Cecil said with a scowl on his face.

"Who is this Dirty John?" I asked by way of changing the subject. "John's a crocodile hunter with a small boatyard. You will like John; he is as mad as a dingo with rabies and two gins," he replied.

I visualized some form of alcoholic with two glasses of gin at the ready, bearing a glazed zombie-like expression on his face.

"If he's pissed out of his mind all the time," I said, "how the hell can he hunt crocodile and run a boatyard?"

"Two *jinns*, not two bloody gin and tonics, you daft Pommy bastard," Cecil said with a laugh.

"Jinns?" I said, and he nodded.

"You mean as in Mohamedan mythology, an order of Arabian spirits lower than angels, with supernatural power over men?" I said.

Cecil's mouth fell open as if he were speaking but without making any sound. "Well, fuck me hurray!" he said at last. "Two black Sheilas," he said in a rather exasperated tone of voice. "I am going to teach you to speak Australian if it kills us both." He laughed again.

When Cecil and I arrived at his place, Dirty John Hedges was busy hosing down a live crocodile from the deck of his boat. The reptile had its mouth wide open and appeared to be enjoying the bath. "He's cleaning it before killing and skinning it," Cecil explained. "Play the water on its head, and the beast keeps its mouth open to breathe," he went on. "John will knock it on the head and then cut it along its spine so that he can skin it and clean it. Then he will get the belly hide off in its entirety, because it is the most valuable part of the reptile. Fancy a jar?" he offered. I nodded and followed him up to Dirty John's office, which was a rather haphazard collection of old colonial paraphernalia with a mix of eclectic furniture arrangements.

Dirty John Hedges hosing live crocodile

John shouted and left what he was doing to join us in his makeshift office. He was a rather squat middle-aged man, with a bald crown which made him a little self-conscious. Cecil told me that once during a drinking spree at the Chinese bar in Fakfak he had jokingly told him to rub salt into his bald patch, saying, "I reckon the hair under your skin will get thirsty and come up for a drink. Then you grab hold and tie a knot in it before it can go back down again!"

Cecil advised me, "He's got a punch like the kick of a large randy kangaroo, so watch his right hand!"

The corn whisky I was offered was the best I had tasted since leaving the port of Singapore.

"Sly grog, distilled from a mash made up of not less than 80 per cent corn," John proclaimed. "I make it myself, the best grog this side of Darwin," he said. John waited while I drained my glass.

"It's good"! I said, and he smiled benevolently.

"The Pom knows his grog," John said.

Cecil nodded his head in agreement. John replenished each glass and placed the bottle down on the table in front of him. "Well, Pom," he said, "what can I do for you?"

"I want to scrape a few barnacles off the hull of my boat and repaint it. I thought perhaps I could use your slipway," I said.

John smiled at me and said, "Have another drink, and let's talk some more business. Perhaps we can come to an agreement on the price I have in mind."

It was that sort of no-hurry day, which eased my confidence and level of trust in this mad Aussie with the jinns. There was an honesty to this man I have not seen often, especially in my dealings with less trustworthy people in my underworld contraband and gunrunner trade. John struck me as a no-messing, straight-talking kind of guy, and I liked that about his character. The Malay word for crocodile is *buaya*. *Buaya tembaga* refers to the colour of the reptile; *tembaga* in Malay suggests copper, bronze, brass, or gold (the word is Sanskrit). I much prefer the common village name *buaya katak*—old frog face—which is given to the common crocodile (*Crocodilus porosus*), at least in these parts.

Buaya serunai is a name given to several types of musical instruments, especially the wooden whistle with a slide for varying the pitch, which is why this name is given to the gavial *Tomistoma schlegelii*. The gavial or gharial freshwater crocodile *Gavialis gangeticus* (*Gmelin* in Linnaeus, 1789) is also called *buaya jenjulong* by the locals—or "logs in the river".

On our way along the river, we found a few shells of the *Cocos maldiva*, a coconut believed to be the fruit of the *pauh janggi*. My shipmate Idris the Bugis believed this was a good omen for the future and that we would be successful and prosper.

Malayan legends suggest strongly and the Malays who are superstitious believe that the tree *pauh janggi* is to be found at a remaining sand bank in the centre of a great ocean. This sand bank holding the tree represents all that is left of a once-great but now-submerged continent and ancient civilization called Atlantis. This is the fabled island continent in the ocean west of the Pillars of Hercules, a beautiful, prosperous great seat of empire overwhelmed by the sea because of the impiety of her inhabitants.

Thursday, 9 January 1947

John Hedges and I finally reached an amicable agreement with regards to my use of the slipway facilities at his small boatyard: 500 armour-piercing .303 cartridges plus three lengths of kappa cloth for his woman. Not a bad deal, considering—but then John was not a greedy man, and our little business meeting soon transformed into one glorious drinking bout! Jon had acquired the name Dirty John from his habit of rubbing himself down with rancid crocodile fat before embarking on one of his early morning escapades through the mangrove on foot. If you want to get close to a crocodile sunning itself on land, without the problem of having to keep downwind because of your stronger human scent, which would alert it to your presence, then you would rub yourself down with rancid crocodile fat!

"Thought you'd be off up the creek," Cecil said.

"Intertribal warfare got me beached for the moment," John said with a laugh.

"Straight up?" Cecil asked.

"Straight up, mate," John said with assurance. "I never poke my nose into something like that; these tribespeople have long, grudging memories. It is always better if we keep our affairs outside of theirs."

"What ethnic group do you have in this area?" I asked John.

He was thoughtful for a moment. "The Ekuti, Manki, and Nauti," he said. "They all speak different dialects of a more or less common language and carry the same social customs. But the problem here is the hill people, the Angu or Änga people, also called Kukukuku. These tribesmen have a rather nasty reputation about them. Half a dozen or so Kukukuku tribesman on a ridge above a village is all it takes to send the whole surrounding territory running for their lives, for these hill tribesmen are well noted for being exceptionally fierce warriors. The Kukukukus are feared by the local people as merciless raiders and killers. Their chief here is called Big Fellow," Dirty John exclaimed with a chuckle.

Jenny Kuku, Dirty John's woman

"I went up to his village once and had a good talk with him," John said. "It was a large circular house in the centre of the village, with a conical roof which came down almost to the ground and was thatched with pandanus palms. But in order to enter the chief's house, it was necessary to crawl in the low outer entrance, then pass halfway round to the door within the inner wall of the hut, affording those inside the chance to inspect the intruder prior to entry or to prevent the intruder's entry altogether.

"The Kukukuku are keen to possess metal knives and axes, which my old mate Happy Jack would take up there with him from time to time. Happy Jack almost got himself killed on one such occasion, when a battle dance got out of hand and two of the dance participants ended up shot full of arrows in a mad frenzy.

"I'd like to see the Kukukuku," I said.

"Look out of the window," John said.

Charlie Kuku was sat on his thighs, busy lighting a rather large bamboo pipe. "He's a Kukukuku?" I said, rather astounded.

John laughed. "He's my bodyguard! That is why you do not see any of the local people hanging around my place."

Charlie Kuku was short but solidly built, just under five feet tall. His hair was a thick, woolly mass held in place by a hairband. His ear lobes had been pierced and decorated with earrings made from bones and pieces of fur, and he had undergone the ritual piercing of his nasal septum as part of the Kukukuku male warrior initiation ceremony. He was also wearing pieces of ivory in his nose. He had a reddish-brown skin. "Not the chap to tangle with on a dark night at Kings Cross!" John said. I had to agree, though what any Kukukuku warrior would be doing in Kings Cross, Sydney, was beyond me for the moment!

Cecil saw the expression on my face. "It is where the prostitutes hang out," he said to put me right.

"Soliciting?" I asked, playing dumb just to get his goat.

"Of course they are soliciting," Cecil said with impatience. "They don't fucking give it away! Sitting on a gold mine, most of them painted sheilas, you daft Pommy bastard," he said.

"I am most grateful," I told him, and we all laughed.

"What's it like for sheilas here?" Cecil wanted to know.

"Difficult!" John said. "There is a Chinese whorehouse, a leftover from the war, compliments of the Yank PT boats flotilla," he continued.

"Chinese," Cecil remarked with contempt.

"They live on the smell of a bloody cheesecloth and breed like rabbits! I am better off with one of the local Sheilas!" Cecil said.

Young fellow Charlie Kuku, 1947

"You can't do that," John said, explaining that it would start a bloody war with one of the tribes. "But should you choose to take one of the missionary-school girls, you will have the Dutch padre around, breathing down your neck until you marry the girl."

"You have a woman?" I asked.

"Yes," John said, refilling our glasses from a fresh bottle of his sly grog. "It's a damn long story and could take all night to tell." But nonetheless he told his love saga that evening and well into the early hours, drinking his sly grog. After that I attended to my boat and settled down for the night.

The story of Happy Jack is an intriguing one, as he was an old trader with a nostalgia for the comforts of modern civilization. Jack kept a woman in most of the upriver villages: an Ekuti woman, a Manki woman, and of course a Nauti woman. Women are, after all, gentle creatures and have a cooling influence on us hot-blooded men. Happy Jack kept his ear close to the ground, so to speak. He got wind that the American Navy flotilla of PT boats based close by was due back in the good old USA; it would be replaced eventually by the Dutch Navy. Now, the land skipper of that US Navy flotilla had only one land-based flush lavatory in the whole territory, and he was determined to have that flush loo for himself. No bloody Dutchman was going to have the use of that flush lavatory, not if Jack could help it! Anyway, I thought the Dutch use a bottle of scented water to wipe their asses with."

"Tried that once," Cecil said, "when we ran out of toilet paper at sea."

"How did you get on with that?" John asked.

"Got a hand full of shit and a shoe full of water," Cecil said and laughed.

"Happy Jack and his Chinese boy Wong set to work here at the slipway and in no time at all had put in a proper septic tank and set up all that was necessary for the flush lavatory.

"The Yank skipper gave Jack the flush lavatory on the day his PT boat flotilla pulled out, and Jack left the final installation of the flush lavatory to his Chinese boy, Wong. Now, the trading steamer had arrived early the next morning, and Happy Jack had gone post-haste to check out the trade goods he was expecting from the mainland. The tragic part was that Happy Jack left the Chinese boy Wong unsupervised to complete the work on his newly acquired flush lavatory. I was away upriver doing a spot of crocodile hunting at the time," John said.

Now pausing for a moment to take a swig from his glass, he then wiped the back of his hand in one quick movement and continued the narrative. "The Chinese boy, Wong, had of course secured all the necessary pipework to the wall, fitted a couple of brackets at the required height above the lavatory pan, and placed the cistern in position. But he had mislaid a couple of components that were essential to fasten securely the hanging cistern to the supporting brackets. Wong threw a couple of buckets of clean water down the lavatory pan to see if the join was leaking, and having satisfied himself that he had done a good job, set off in search of the necessary bolts with which to fasten the cistern securely to the wall.

"Happy Jack had tied one on with his old mate the purser at the steamer. He was not stoned out of his mind. I don't think I have ever seen him stoned; but he had that well-oiled glaze in his eyes and walked with that South Pacific Ocean stroll which he always reserved for such an occasion. Jack was never mean when drunk, but he had a little almost ritualistic routine. Happy Jack would come home and chase Mary Ekuti around the house, screw seven balls out of her, and then take her to bed to sleep it off. Jack reckoned she was the best grind in the territory!" Cecil winked, and I burst out laughing.

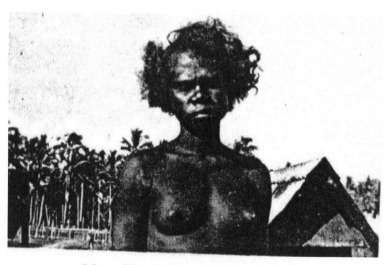

Mary Ekuti, Happy Jack's woman

"Straight up!" John said, which didn't help quell my laughter much.

"Fair dinkum," Cecil said. "Some women are like that!"

46

"I caught them at it once on the kitchen table," John said.

"It appears that Jack was going at it like one of those big Queensland traction engines, and she seemed to be giving as good as she got." John paused while opening another bottle of booze. It was fast becoming quite a drinking session. John cleared his throat and continued his story with rather quite a lot of feeling. The event had obviously emotionally upset this otherwise tough man. "Happy Jack was dead on the shitter when I found his body late that night," John said. "Jack must have given the damn flush chain a rather hard yank, because the overhanging cistern had fallen down on him and bloody well brained him!"

Both the boy who'd fitted the flush toilet and Jack's woman, Mary Ekuti, had gone bush for fear of being blamed for Jack's death by the Dutch police. It was a bloody mess, with Jack's brains all over the fucking place. The worst part is, I could not bloody well stop laughing over the whole matter. I was not too sure if this was bad luck or some strange twist of fate, collecting a debt owed. But it was so damn funny at the time!"

"What a sad way to end your days—on the shitter!" John said.

"But the Chinese boy, Wong, is back now?" Cecil asked.

"Yes," John said, grinning. John added that the Dutch police had picked him up at the Chinese whorehouse in Fakfak. The Dutch coroner concluded that it was an accidental death by misadventure. The Dutch authorities released Wong without any charges after questioning him. Some three days later Mary Ekuti came back home from the bush, glad to be back and not arrested for murder by the Dutch police.

"She's a good grind?" Cecil asked.

"You keep your fucking paws off her!" John shouted at him.

"All right, mate," Cecil said. "I was just checking."

"Well, now you bloody know!" John said.

The road down to the slipway at Fakfak

I made the necessary arrangement for my boat on the slipway first thing in the morning, after which Cecil and I went in search of Edward and Roy, who had gone off whore-chasing. The Chinese Happy Moon bar-cum-whorehouse was on the edge of town, a darkly lit, dingy place, complete with the distinct smell of lust, opium, and burning joss sticks. The air in that whorehouse was that thick you could push it along with your hand, I kid you not! "You fancy a bit of Chinese pussy, Pom?" Cecil asked

"I would not touch any of it with yours, never mind my own!" I said in no uncertain tone. We found Roy bleary-eyed from the amount of rice wine he had consumed. Edward, on the other hand, was rather more filled with enthusiasm than usual. I mentioned this to Cecil at the rest house later.

"It's a sore point," he said. "Edward was stuck on one of those bloody little islands for most of the war, checking on enemy shipping for the Navy. When Edward returned home after it was all over, his missus had taken off with another bloke. Edward was going to kill the joker, but then he heard his wife had conceived a child by her newfound lover. So he left them to it. He was a small-time criminal

48

for a while and moved around from place to place before he tied up with me. Edward lost his respect for women and picked up, sadly, the opium habit, the great panacea and cure-all.

"What most people fail to realize is that sulphate of morphia is used by physicians regularly as a remedy for so many complaints. Everything from headaches and sore eyes down to more serious ailments, such as gastritis, liver complaints, gall stones, carditis—inflammation of the heart—or aneurism, as well as for general pain relief. I don't judge, but with the widespread medical usage of opiates, is it any wonder that so many people with a monkey on their backs choose to escape the reality of their shitty lives this way?

Happy Moon bar-cum-whorehouse at Fakfak

Saturday, 11 January 1947

It was high tide at 0300 hours PST, in the bright moonlight. I required a little extra water in order to bring my boat down into position properly over the top of the slipway cradle. The alternative would have been the arduous task of lightening my MTB by offloading most of my cargo, which was not only a difficult and time-consuming operation but also would have aroused the suspicion of every port official in Fakfak. So no can do that! The very last thing I needed at that moment was some Dutch official poking his nose into my affairs.

Zainal, my Bugis crewman, had taken the wheel of my boat and reversed her engines slowly over the cradle, while Wong had taken up the slack on the slipway winch. I checked the clearance between the cradle and the boat screws and made her secure, while the rest of my crew held her steady with land lines. Cecil stood in the bow with his rifle while were in the water.

Cecil was keeping a sharp lookout for any signs of a prowling crocodile searching for food. Perhaps we were making way too much noise for them. It had taken us an hour and a half to get the boat high and dry, with the real work of scraping her hull still to do at first light in the morning. I was rather tired and ready to sleep. I settled down on the bridge of my boat for a few hours' kip rather than bothering with my bed at the guest house ashore. No sooner had I got my head down than my coxswain, Zainal, was waking me up. It was dawn.

The cup he offered me of sweet, black Malayan coffee was most welcome, for my mouth on awakening felt like the bottom of a Singapore sewer. What a taste! The black coffee did the trick, and I felt much better. It was time to get the rest of the crew organized on the hull. Scraping barnacles from the bottom of the boat is a laborious task, though she was not too badly infested, considering the journey we had so far completed. By noon we had done most of the scraping necessary. By this time the hull had dried off sufficiently in the heat of the sun for us to start painting her with red lead.

Roy then decided to appear, after a prolonged disappearance. He looked like death warmed up and swore he would never tag along with Edward again on any bloody binge. "I can't remember a bloody thing," Roy said. "It wouldn't be so bad if I was sure."

"Well, did you?" I asked.

"I just don't bloody know!" he said.

Zainal was busy repainting the stern when Dirty John showed up and viewed his work with critical eyes. "Not bad!" he said. "I'd say he was an ex-Navy man!"

"He is," I told him. Zainal was with *HMS Malaya*, originally named *HMS Pelandok*; she was one of two remaining LCT Mk III left in the Royal Navy service in 1947. *HMS Pelandok*, originally a

Landing Craft Tank belonging to the British Royal Navy, was brought to Singapore during the Second World War and was then refurbished after the war for duties in Malayan waters.

Zainal had been part of the Strait Settlement Naval Volunteer Reserve formed in Singapore (1934) and Penang (1938); it was a sort of colonial-based extension to the British Royal Navy, created for the defence of Malayan waters during the Second World War. Zainal also assisted with the rescue of survivors from the sinking of the British Battleship *HMS Prince of Wales* and the Battle Cruiser *HMS Repulse* off Malaya's east coast in 1942. Zainal was a veteran and hero by all accounts. He is also an excellent naval coxswain to have at your back under any circumstances, as well as a warrior.

John caught sight of Roy standing on the deck above us. "Dip your wick at that Chinese whorehouse last night?" he shouted. "You want to watch your cock does not drop off on you," he told him. Roy walked red-faced over to the other side of the deck and out of sight without comment.

"He can't remember," I told John.

"You won't get me to poke any sheila the Yanks have been through!" John laughed out loudly. "Pox up to their eyeballs, the lot of them whores were," he said.

"You're just prejudiced," I told him.

"Prejudiced my arse!" John roared out further. "Those fucking Yanks brought the disease over with them into these islands and put it about like the fucking flu," John said.

"Okay, mate, don't blow your top," I said.

"Here!" John said and thrust a rather tattered piece of paper at me. "It's in Chinese," he said. "It seems that Wong brought it in last night and said it was for you."

"Where is Wilhelmina Height?" I asked.

John scratched his head and pointed to the hill on the other side of town. "It's where the Dutch residents live," he said.

"Any Chinese over that way?" I enquired, attempting to be tactless about the whole affair.

"Sure," John replied. "The Chinese government joker, and there is a temple of sorts, full of little yellow bastards halfway up the hill."

"Thanks," I said.

"You can read that bloody Chinese chicken scribble?" John said seriously.

"Just about make it out," I said with a laugh.

"You want to watch those slant-eyed little bastards!" he said. "Cut your fucking throat for less than a sixpence!"

John lent me his battered old Morris, and then he piped up, "It will give me an excuse to take the whole place apart if you are not back by this evening." He laughed at that. "Anyway, what's it all about?" he queried.

"Don't know offhand. Just some joker with a proposition," I replied. I had a few words with Roy, who was not too happy about being left in charge of the boat. In any case, I'd be back in time to relaunch her on the morning tide.

Just as John had said, the temple stood on the side of the hill, half a mile beyond the last bungalow in Wilhelmina Height. I have seen larger places, but this one stood out. It was a little more than a Chinese joss house.

The temple was at the end of a long flight of steps. The Chinese seem to have an odd fixation with temples on hills. Parking at the side of the road, I leisurely climbed the steep flight of steps to the sound of steady tock-tock-tock of a fish-head gong deep within the temple.

"Friend!" the ancient Chinaman standing proud in traditional oriental robes said in perfectly fluent English as I arrived at the entrance of the temple. "Please follow me!" he called. "We are expecting you!" He led off through the rather large red doors of the temple entrance. The sudden deep boom of a larger gong drowned out my reply.

We were off through the building, with me hurriedly trailing behind. I caught a glimpse of eight or more robed women prostrate in front of the deity Kuan Yin. In Sanskrit her name is Padmapâni, or "born of the lotus". Kuan Yin alone among Buddhist gods is loved rather than feared and is the model of Chinese beauty; she is also regarded by the Chinese as the goddess of mercy. But it was the other statue that took me by surprise—it was Ucchuṣma, the all-seeing, four-handed, four-faced "killer of daemons"! This Buddhist deity is well known and believed to have powers to purify the unclean, particularly in respect to sexual diseases.

We skirted the main hall, dense with the smell of pungent joss sticks and large red wax candles, to traverse a long, dim passage into the crypt of the temple. A white-bearded Oriental even more ancient than the first sat at the round table in the centre of the room. Beside him was a young man with a heavily pox-marked face. I noted the small tiger-head tattoo on his right hand. This man was a tiger fighter and bodyguard who would take no part in the proceedings other than to defend and protect his master. On the left stood a young oriental woman in the cultivated submissive stance. I bowed respectfully and took the seat indicated at the table, sipping the green Chinese tea that had immediately been offered and served.

This was probably one of the most civilized, polite places I have ever been to, but I remained under the watchful gaze of the oriental trio and the emerald-green motif of the dragon on the wall behind them. It all suddenly clicked into place: Tz'u Hsi (1834–1908), the dowager empress who once ruled China for almost fifty years. She was from a minor Manchu family, and Yehe was her clan name. Nala (aka Nara) was her tribe name. All of this had the makings of Chinese secret societies and powerful clans lurking in the shadows. I had been taught to use caution, especially when dealing with secret societies, because they had influence almost everywhere.

Ucchuṣma, "killer of daemons"

Thus her real name was Yehenara, rather than Yehonala, as was often cited. Tz'u Hsi was concubine to the Emperor Hsien Feng, but when she seized power in China, her reactionary policies were extremely anti-European and led to the Boxer Rebellion of 1900. What came to me was a Chinese secret society, one of the most powerful at the time known to me as the Green Dragon Mountain Society. Tz'u Hsi was xenophobic to the extreme, for the dowager empress of China had a morbid fear of foreigners. No doubt this distrust stemmed the European-inspired China opium wars.

"I hear that you are an accomplished parachutist," the bearded ancient said.

"I gave it up," I replied. *Two can play the game of beat around the bush*, I thought to myself.

"Gave it up?" he repeated.

"Yes," I answered. "Falling from the sky can be very bad for your health, especially if your parachute fails to deploy correctly and decides to throw a string or two that roman candles you on your way down back to earth."

"Ah, yes." He smiled and then said, "Perhaps flying should be left to the birds?" I nodded in silent agreement.

"But you are also a skilled diver?" he went on in a quiet but serious voice.

"That I am," I answered respectfully.

"A man accomplished in falling through the air would have no fear of diving into deep oceans?" he enquired attentively.

"Perhaps not," I responded in kind.

"It appears that late in April 1945, a ship was en route to China with a cargo that was to be transferred to one of our Wang Tows at sea. But the untimely torpedoing of the ship by an enemy submarine in the Banda Sea unfortunately occurred, with far-reaching consequences for us." The bearded ancient's eyes were fixed steadfastly on mine while he spoke, as if he were trying to see though my soul whilst attempting to read me or gauge what kind of a man I was.

"The ship lies at a depth of 120 feet in the water," he went on. "This is much too deep for our own divers, who lack the proper equipment or skill to go down that far," the old elder said.

"You're talking salvage?" I asked, pointing out that I was not equipped to salvage a ship from deep waters.

"Salvage of our part of the cargo," he said.

"We will, of course, pay you five thousand Australian pounds now, in cash, if you will bring up one box," the old sage went on.

"If that box is undamaged, a further twenty-five thousand Australian pounds when you recover the other nineteen boxes. Do you agree?" he demanded.

"I will have to think about it," I said.

"No!" he spoke out firmly and aloud. "I need your answer right now."

The woman took a small box from her sleeve and placed it on the table in front of him. The box contained five thousand pounds.

"Five thousand Australian pounds plus one silver Chinese water pipe," I responded in a firm tone. Why, you might ask, did I want a silver Chinese water pipe? Well, for a start, I'd always wanted one. If you happen to be a smoker, as I am, the Chinese water pipe is much handier to smoke than the Arabian water pipe, which requires the smoker to sit cross-legged on the ground. My silver Chinese water pipe, gifted to me by the old elder, has a tobacco box and a place for the cleaning instruments of the pipe, but this type of water pipe is made of pure silver and not plated like so many other, cheaper models. Want/desire is a strange thing, but it seems as if by chance my desire to own a classic was being granted.

"You may take all three of them with you now," he said.

"All three?" I asked.

"Yes," he said. "Liu Wen-Ming will be my agent and at your complete service."

"At my complete service," I repeated, somewhat bemused by the tone of the old elder.

"She will see to your every need and represent me during the period of this business transaction," he concluded sharply. The old elder then got up and walked away to another room of the temple, followed by his tiger-tattooed bodyguard. Before disappearing, he turned to remind me, saying, "This is my act of good faith and trust in you to be honourable, as honour dictates. I wish you every success in this venture."

I got up and started to leave the temple, with Liu Wen-Ming leading the way. As we descended the steep flight of stairs together, she displayed every bit of the grace and culture of a well-trained Japanese geisha with the beautiful body of an female athlete. I switched the ignition on the battered old Morris, and we headed straight back to the boatyard.

Sunday, 12 January 1947

At the boatyard, Dirty John had a face like thunder when I

56

returned in the early hours of the morning to witness a Dutch padre breathing down his neck. It appeared that my partner Roy had done the unpardonable and been caught making a woman out of one of the Dutch mission virgins when the padre arrived on the scene. This, of course was yet another unnecessary mess that I had been left to sort out, but there was no question of rape! On the other hand, Cecil had clocked Mary Ekuti and later put to sea along with Edward and Roy. John, of course, had been drinking, and I left him to it.

The seawater level was sufficient at 0315 hours PST for me and my crew to commence refloating operations. Relaunching the boat was a piece of cake by comparison with loading her onto the slipway, and at 0330 hours my boat was set, with engines running and ready again for the open sea. I carried out a few critical test runs up and down the shallow channel waters to see whether the boat's handling was satisfactory before I risked taking her out into the open sea. Once my safety trial runs were completed to my satisfaction, I put her on a new heading for the Banda Sea.

Scraping her hull had given me two or more inches of free board, which would come in handy in a heavy sea. *Freeboard* refers to the distance from the waterline to the freeboard deck of a fully loaded boat or ship, measured amidships at the side of the hull. It shows to what depths a ship may be loaded, depending upon various service conditions. At 0400 hours we were off down channel, and at dawn we made for the open sea. My passenger on this occasion was the emissary for the Green Dragon Mountain Society, one of the rather influential Chinese secret societies, who had engaged my services to recover some property from the wreck lost in the Banda Sea.

The Banda Sea is among the Maluku Islands of Indonesia, connected to the Pacific Ocean but surrounded by hundreds of islands. Idris will be my back-up diver there, though he is rather superstitious where shipwrecks with loss of life are concerned. Otherwise he is quite a good diver. It is all a matter of choice, which is not always excellent or tasteful! I don't like working for any secret society, but from a more progressive and enlightened standpoint, this one exploratory dive could be a stepping-stone to several new possibilities. A little indiscretion can be progressive and popular, though never predictable.

As it happens, the emissary is a troubleshooter for the clan master, 27 years of age and a woman! Did I say predictable? A horse, dog, or cat are predictable. A woman is the most unpredictable of all things that are unpredictable! I'm not complaining; it was the adventure that drew me into this situation, and we shall see what we shall see. The Chinese name Liu Wen-Ming means enlightenment, and this young, fascinating, cultured but well-trained lady did enlighten me. No, not in the way you might suppose. I like to keep them in suspense a little, and they tend to work much better that way.

So whatever this mysterious cargo was, it was certainly not hard drugs. That was as far as she was prepared to go on that question for the moment. Our current heading was for Timor in the Banda Sea. There was no sign of Cecil at all. Wen-Ming had been with the secret society since childhood and was now the confidante of the old master at the Fakfak temple. It was a time of great change in China, during which the warlords and the forces of Mao Tse-Tung were pitched against each other. For ninety-nine women out of a hundred, the mainspring of existence is love. I doubt very much that they can subordinate this rather cumbersome characteristic, for all their genius is subordinate to their love.

One of my rules of life is that I never let a lover interfere in my work, but then I will never allow myself to get more deeply involved than is necessary. In the case of Liu Wen-Ming, all her genius was subordinate to her clan master and his career. She was brilliant, however, in seizing and expressing a special phase of actions or thoughts that was passing. "Achievement is the price demanded for the right to venture!" The old man knew what he was doing when he named her Wen-Ming—or enlightenment! Liu Wen-Ming and I talked long together during our journey, and I learnt much from her wisdom.

The Green Dragon Mountain Society had been formed back in 1888 by the Dowager Empress Yehenara Tz'u Hsi and had played a great part in the Boxer Rebellion of 1900. All else had changed in China since the last great Manchu empress, Tz'u Hsi said with her dying breath, "Never again leave such power in the hands of a woman." But now, because of the long war against the Japanese, with the continued persistence of Mao Tse-Tung in his quest for total power and domination over all of China, the warlords were fighting amongst themselves and had finally turned against the society that gave them power over China and her people.

Secret-society property and wealth were being looted by both sides of the present unrest, and the basic principles and very structure of Chinese society was under attack.

Now Taoism, the Chinese religious system based on the teachings of Lao-Tze, along with Confucianism and Buddhism, is a principal element in a rather complex religious culture. Neither Taoism nor Confucianism embody any authoritative dogmatic scheme. Taoism is in effect a mixture of polytheism and poly-demonism, or the worship of nature and of many gods, often connected with natural phenomena. Magic and exorcism have always been principal functions of its priests. Yet, as with both Hinduism and Buddhism, behind the popular cult lies an ancient and sophisticated doctrine that some people consider worth dying for.

Of its reputed founder, Lao-Tze, little is known. His personal name is given as Li-poh-yang and his birth assigned to 604 BCE. Taoism as a philosophy dates from the time of Chuan-tze, during the fourth and third century BC. His aim was to persuade his countrymen to abandon Confucianism for the teachings of Lao-tze, who expounded a method of "quietism". It was thought that if a man could possess the *te*, (an inner power and confidence) by contemplation, he might also possess it more easily by occult means, hence the resort to magic.

Taoism has been much influenced by Buddhism, but it has drawn to itself upon ancient animism and nature worship, the latter in the shape of polytheism with all its accompanying mythology. Lao-tze himself, of whom many wonders are related, has been to all intents deified as the highest incarnation of the Tao (a reality immaterial, omnipresent, and eternal), and his image is commonly seen in Taoist temples with the genii (or spirits of heaven and earth); both good and evil are beyond number. Taoist priests have frequently been celibate, but others have married and found secular employment.

Confucianism remains a practical ethic based on the treatises of Confucius. It does not employ any authoritative dogmatic scheme. Confucius may be said to have brought a fresh moral impulse to the ancient Chinese outlook on life without in any way presenting himself as a moral reformer. To the contrary, Confucius was essentially a conservative who equated novelty with impiety. Confucius the sage, or K'ung Fu-tsze, was born in 479 BC in the province of Shan-tung. He was orphaned at an early age and grew up in poverty. At 22 years of age he became a teacher, and thereafter he began to develop his characteristic doctrine.

He served in the government of his native state of Lu but left the country when its prince continued to neglect his advice. As an old man, he returned to Lu and spent his last five years of life there in literary work, dying in 551 BC.

The philosopher Mencius is known as the second inspired one, for he imbued the Confucian ethics with a more speculative interest. His stress on the natural goodness of human nature is greater even than that of Confucius. He accepted the prevailing worship of spirits and ancestors, but otherwise religious practice was without interest for him. But enough about Confucius and Mencius for the moment.

German philosopher and economist Karl Marx was alleged to have said, "Religion is the opium of the people" (translated from the German original, "Die Religion ist das Opium des Volkes"), which is often rendered as "Religion is the opiate of the masses." There is strong evidence that the leaders of Taoism have unfairly exploited the Chinese population for profit. There was also exploitation of the poor by Chinese warlords, who forced them into slave labour. Nature is not completely without blemish in an ancient society where man is treasured and women considered nothing more than slaves. It was always the girl children who would be left on a mountain to die or sold to enable the male children to be fed.

The peasant people of China are no longer complacent, for poverty is not the presupposed lot of the masses.

I quickly drifted into a deep slumber, only to dream of things long since past. They say that you should never leave a wounded man behind during wartime. It is uncanny and strange how the dead come back to haunt the living, with flashbacks of things that happened long ago. I guess this is the legacy of the combatants who survived a violent and brutal world war in a very different kind of no-man's land. May they all rest in peace. I know there must be a better life in the beyond than the one I experienced first-hand during the war in Europe and Burma.

I found myself back again in Normandy, France, in the year 1944, cut off with a group of two others from our main landing body. We were running along a ridge, keeping our heads low to avoid being spotted or making an open target of ourselves. There was a lot of artillery, and mortar shells were exploding all around us. It seemed amazing that none of us were hit by the shrapnel. We came up upon a clearing with a dirt-track road, where a German on a BMW motorbike with an outrider had stopped to look at the scene unfolding on the beaches. His machine gunner was missing, and I presumed the Jerry standing there was either a lone rider or his machine gunner had disappeared somewhere to take a leak.

With all the mayhem and noise from the mortar bombs, gunfire, and shells exploding all around in the distance, I quickly moved in from his blind side to dispatch the motorcyclist with my Fairburn Sykes killing knife. I snapped his neck hard back and plunged the dagger into his kidneys through his feldgrau (field grey) tunic. The war remains from my point of view one for my survival and that of those who were fighting alongside me. I had no issues with stone killing an enemy, none whatsoever, nor regrets over the matter. When I pulled the knife out, warm blood rushed onto my hand as the enemy German fell, and that broke the repeating dream.

Chapter 4

The Lady Enlightenment
Monday, 13 January 1947

We arrived during the early hours of the morning at Pulau Pantar, which happens to be the second-largest island in the Indonesian Alor Archipelago. At Pulau Pantar I discovered that a small schooner carrying a white crew and two Chinese men had put into the port of Lomblen, at S 8° 30ʼ0», E 124° 9ʼ0" early the day before. The description fit those three friends who had left Fakfak rather hurriedly. In haste, I had just declared that I was about to join them and punch a few heads, when Liu Wen-Ming suggested otherwise.

"We are near the ship!" she informed me.

"Where is it?" I asked.

"Between the islands of Savu and Ndao," she replied.

"That is at the exit from the Savu Sea," I said.

She nodded, telling me, "You can see the ship in the clear water."

"But it will take time locating the wreck's final resting place," I said.

She shook her head. "Our people have located the ship long ago but have kept quiet over the matter, maintaining, however, a constant watch over it," she said.

"But I will need my friends if I am going to dive," I told her.

"We don't trust them," she said. "One is an opium addict, and the other two are rather irresponsible."

"Who is watching the wreck?" I asked.

She was thoughtful for a few moments, as if debating the question carefully in her own mind to find a suitable response to my question.

"There are four family wang-tows," she said. "They keep away any intruder!" The wang tow is a Chinese trawling junk, a typical seagoing trawler approximately 100 feet in length with a beam of some thirty feet. The hull is divided into fish holds, with the crew's quarters and galley near the stern. The long rudder slopes forward, works in a slot in the stern, and acts also as a centreboard.

We refuelled at Pulau Pantar and put to sea shortly afterwards, making our way through Sotor Arch into the Sava Sea, on a heading for Pulau Ndao (Ndao Island). Ndao is one of the southernmost islands of the Indonesian archipelago. It remains part of Lesser Sunda Islands, located west of Rote Island, some 500 kilometres from the coast of Australia and 170 kilometres from the Ashmore and Cartier Islands.

This is Rotinese Indonesia, which has two monsoon seasons and the odd Dutch gunboat to worry about. Most of the islands here are rocky and have been heavily eroded by flash floods. You see, when the rain comes at the end of a long dry season, the soil, which has been baked hard by the sun, is unyielding. The first rains simply cannot penetrate the earth and flow deep into underground streams. Instead, all this mass of water remains on the surface, causing flash floods heading towards the sea. Thus the vegetation on these islands is limited to hardier, drought-resistant species of plant life.

Liu Wen-Ming had kept well out of the way during my dealings with the Rotinese on the question of fresh water and fuel, only appearing on deck again once we were well out to sea. I considered the huge risk I was taking now. Apart from doing this without my three other Australian divers, whom these people did not trust, I knew that the four Wang-Tows were quite possibly heavily armed and likely outgunned my boat. There was a lot at stake here, with so little margin for error and many lives hanging in the balance should anything go wrong. This was my primary concern should the deal go south for whatever reasons.

In my mind I weighed up all the odds for and against this deal. I knew from my past encounters with pirates on the high seas that I could outrun any Wang-Tow but probably not outgun. After due consideration, I thought, *Fuck it! In for a penny, in for a pound!* I had been paid for the first part of the job and the hard cash was in a very safe place. My Malay and Bugis crew did not like the Chinese, but then my men were extremely loyal and would follow my orders without question. This was because I had always looked after them, no matter what turned up for us.

I was not only their skipper; we were also shipmates and much more. We had the kind of do-or-die mentality which could only be experienced in combat. We were an unspoken band of veteran brothers, as I had had at Gold Beach, Arromanches, in Normandy on June 6, 1944, when I had just turned 20 years old. My men and I would die for each other, and that is all I am going to say on the matter. The bard Shakespeare, in his *Henry V* St Crispin's Day speech, penned it quite eloquently: "We few, we happy few, we band of brothers; For he today that sheds his blood with me, shall be my brother" (Henry V, Act IV Scene iii, 18–67).

I instructed Zainal to set up and arm the twin .303 machine gun amidships and sheet them ready for action. I took over the wheel and checked the instruments. We were on course and making good time through a calm sea, with the occasional cross-current running, some of which can be rather strong. This was the place of sudden high winds and raging seas, torrential rain followed by long periods of good weather. We are on the fringe of those fabled mystical seas full of strange creatures and fish-like monsters of the deep. My immediate concern was the large number of pirates that frequented these waters. There was nothing mystifying about them!

"Nan Hsi?" Wen-Ming asked.

"South-west," I said, and she smiled.

"Which part of China are you from?" I asked.

"Huang-ho," she replied.

That was south of the Yellow River. No wonder she had a good knowledge of boats! These people we were to rendezvous with were quite possibly Chinese pirates from the South China Sea area. The Yellow River, or Huang He, is notably the second-longest river in China, next to the Yangtze, spanning some 5,464 kilometres; it is sometimes referred to as the "mother river of China". The Yellow River basin dates into prehistory, to around 4000 BCE. It was the centre of early Chinese politics, her economy as well as her culture. It remains the sixth-longest river in the world, flowing through what was one of the most ancient of civilizations.

"Hainan-quay?" I asked hopefully.

She nodded and smiled her acknowledgement.

"Who oversees these people in their four Hainanese Wang-Tows?" I enquired.

"I have been put in charge of them all", she replied, "on behalf of the master—but please don't worry. They are all good people!"

We arrived at first light, with the South Pacific blazing sun slowly creeping up the early dawn horizon. Wen-Ming flashed her recognition signal to the waiting Wang-Tows while I slowly circled them, just out of range of any possible small-arms fire. Once contact had been established, I manoeuvred my boat closer to the largest of the four junks so that she could speak to the head man from the bridge of my craft. There was no question of allowing Wen-Ming to board any of the four anchored junks. For the present time, she remains both my guest and my hostage for the security of my crew and the boat. But I did not bind her, for that would show bad faith and increase both fear and hostility between our South China Seas pirate wreck-watchers and my crew. Besides, the situation for now remained a little volatile; making my female guest a prisoner on board would without doubt not be conducive to good health.

Tuesday, 14 January 1947

Hainanese wang tows in the Sawu Sea over the wreck

My former Malayan Royal Navy coxswain, Zainal, was instructed to restrain Wen-Ming should she decide to jump overboard during

65

my solo dives. I knew that it was not good practice to be minus a dive buddy at any depth, but the situation was what it was. As I looked down into the clear blue-green waters, the wreck appeared to be on its side. After carrying out all the necessary safety checks on my diving gear, our tanks, and our equipment, I immediately prepared to take my first exploratory descent into the deep. The goods my representative of the Chinese Secret Society required were supposed to have been stored in the very centre of the hold and marked with the Chinese characters for *Tien Shan*, or Shan Mountains.

Under the wreck

Three of the four junks stood well out of the way, only one being allowed in the salvage area through mutual agreement. This was under the immediate supervision of my helmsman Zainal, who also incidentally was very good with using the boat's twin-mounted .303 machine guns, hidden out of sight under sheets but fully locked and loaded. Idris stood by as my rescue and supporting diver should the need arise.

I anticipated that due to the length of time the wreck had been down, since late in April 1945, it was unlikely that any corpses from the wreck would come bolting up to the surface. The absence of sharks also told me that there were no longer any eatable bodily remains by the wreck. But you can never tell for certain until you are down there with them. I readied myself and went off the boat feet first from the port side.

Taking a depth marker line with me, I steadily made my way down to find that the wreck, which lay on her port side, had a rather strong underwater current sweeping around her stern. I noted two large holes, torpedo strikes, one amidships and one in her bow. The wreck's hull and deck were festooned in soft coral. Though the outline of the required hatch was still clearly visible, the depth of coral varied from an inch to three inches in places. She was the standard type of shelter deck for a general-cargo merchant ship of approximately 7,000 tons, distinguished by a large superstructure and a long forecastle. Had the ship sat upright on the bottom, I could have dived down her mast with comparative ease.

At around 15 metres from the wreck, looking from above her, I noticed that she had taken two torpedo hits in her engine room and one in her bow. Yet, strangely, the second hatch remained sealed, its tarpaulin hatch covers intact beneath the layer of coral. On closer inspection, I found that the wreck of the ship was a shambles where the torpedo had hit and explosions had followed. The ship had taken three *tin fish*, a naval term for torpedoes. Probably Type 93 long-lance Japanese torpedoes had struck her in a pattern attack.

My naval submariner's knowledge told me that any attacking submarine usually fired her torpedoes in timed, calculated sequences of twos. One torpedo would go straight after the other in a pattern shot, optimizing the possibility of a strike with one or more of the tin fish should the ship targeted at range alter course sharply. With three torpedoes strikes on this vessel, the possibility existed that a rogue Type 93 Japanese torpedo might well be lying somewhere close by and hence be a threat to us, even after all this time. This threat I could not rule out entirely, having experienced it close at hand, back in Britain early during the blitz, when I was a police officer tasked with all the shitty jobs.

I remembered pulling dead, dismembered men, women, and children out of bombed-out buildings. The danger posed from

Luftwaffe raids was the widespread deposits of UXBs—unexploded bombs—throughout most of our towns and cities. After that I decided I wanted some payback and went to war against the Nazis instead, volunteering and joining Combined Operations. This took me to the beaches of Normandy but afterwards on to India and Burma to fight against the Japanese.

With three direct torpedo strikes, the ship must have floundered almost immediately, keeled over in the terrible primary and then secondary explosions which followed, and gone down fast into the deep, with seawater overwhelming the engine room and the buoyancy of the vessel. It would have been over rather quickly, making the chances of survival improbable. All the souls in this vessel must have perished on that fateful day. If one was superstitious, it was akin to walking over the graves of the many lost souls who had perished horribly at sea. So many phantoms the sea does hold in her cradle.

It became obvious at this point that I would require the help of my second diver. Idris's role was to gain access to the wreck's hold by removing the hatch boards. It was time for me to surface and plan our next move. Where the lone diver is concerned, it is rather difficult to imagine a more hostile environment in which to work than with a wreck. The problem lies in keeping actual track of time, which is vital to a diver's well-being and, indeed, health. If he is not disciplined in dive timekeeping, the lone diver is most likely to become overzealous with the task at hand, even to the point of obsession. Many a scuba diver unwittingly overstays his maximum time deep underwater and at that point is well on the way to nitrogen narcosis.

I had completed my primary inspection of the wreck in less than seventy minutes, nearly ten minutes over the specified safety time I'd allowed myself. I have without exception been a stickler where safety is concerned, especially at that depth. As an itinerant soldier of fortune, I also know that you won't get paid if you get yourself dead! Rapture in bed with a good woman is preferable to rapture of the deep, in my eyes. I planned my safety decompression through the depth stages, using my marker line to the wreck

It is strange how you always seem to notice things around you, especially when you are on a slow, seeming endless decompression safety crawl back up to the surface after a deep dive! Perhaps this is the anticlimax to your adrenalin run? There seems to be a kind of osmosis between light, water, and colour. Just as water absorbs light, so colour is likewise absorbed. At 100 feet below the sea, it is all shades of deep blue and black. Then, as you ascend to around fifty feet, the colour yellow starts to appear; at twenty-five feet shades of orange emerge, and just at fifteen feet, red. On the surface it's blue-green.

Once I got safely topside, I communicated what I had seen directly to my partner in crime, Liu Wen-Ming. She bubbled with optimistic enthusiasm.

I told her that the second hold of the wreck appeared to be intact, but truth be told, at the moment I had not the faintest idea exactly what the interior of that second hold would be like. Wen-Ming was still very secretive concerning the actual contents of the boxes I was to recover from the wreck. In the meantime, Idris went through with me in detail the procedure we would both meticulously follow during the next dive. We also went through all of our diving gear together, checking our tanks, regulators, and hoses with great care. After another cup of coffee and a light meal, we completed the necessary preparations by the time my two hours at sea level was up.

Taking my end of the dive rope, I dropped gently into the water and made my way down once again to the wreck, followed closely by Idris. At twenty-five feet, a green turtle gave me a close look as I equalized the pressure building up in my ears and nose. I noticed that the turtle was somewhat curious and followed my dive rope back up to the surface. Turtles at sea are rather inquisitive, it seemed. Idris and I secured our end of the rope to the wreck, and I watched the rope lift till they made fast on the boat topside. We had completed our first objective, which was to stop the drift of our craft on the surface.

We decided to clear an area six by four feet in number two hold, immediately in front of the wreck's bridge. But a thick suspension of particles soon clouded the water around us when we got to work on the soft coral. This in turn attracted several fishes looking for a quick feed. Though the current took several moments to clear the floating particles, it seemed an eternity, more so because every moment was precious time lost. The particles drifted slowly away with the fish, some of which were still feeding whilst others followed out of sheer curiosity. Idris and I then cut through the large tarpaulin cover and down to the hatch boards beneath, pulling them away in one piece. Together we removed three hatch boards and allowed them to fall into the depths below us.

Now it was time to wait again, and I carefully inspected the hatch combings for any telltale signs of chemical discolouration. Foolhardy I may be, but I was not going into that hold without checking for any chemical toxicity that might be trapped with the remaining atmosphere, if any, behind that hatch. Opening even a small part of that hatch underwater, in an enclosed batten-down hatch, was rather like opening Pandora's box and unleashing all the evils that plague mankind. However, in this case there appeared to be no toxic suspension of floating particles present. Idris attached one end of my safety line to himself, and I went in.

Most of the cargo had shifted when the ship had keeled over and settled down on the bottom. There was tinned food in what once had been cardboard cartons. In the 'tween decks, behind the steel hatch ladder, I found the security area, a wire-mesh affair for bonded goods to be carried in the hold. The wire mesh was nothing that a good pair of bolt cutters couldn't deal with. Working my way along the front of the security cage within the beam shining from my sub-aqua lamp, I found a substantial number of firearms storage boxes of the type used for carbines.

With these firearms were several smaller ammunition boxes, tucked neatly away in an adjacent stack. Some of these were marked "Tien Shan!" Perhaps Liu Wen-Ming had got it wrong? Yet she had been correct about the wreck and the cargo being in the 'tween decks. I decided to recover one of each to maximize my dive time, thus saving myself having to repeat the dangers of the deep to come back for the rest later. We could sort the differences once we got our newfound salvage find of weapons and ammunition boxes topside.

Cutting a hole in the wire mesh immediately in front of each box required, I attached the end of my safety line to the rope handle of the box. I managed to work it free and out of the security cage. Idris and I placed both boxes in the steel recovery net and watched while the winch in our craft above lifted them slowly towards the surface. Idris and I then headed for the surface and the comparative safety of the boat.

Liu Wen-Ming was rather puzzled. The weapons box was correct in every detail—except it was missing the clan mark. On the other hand, the smaller ammunition box, although wrong in detail, had the necessary clan mark.

This was not in keeping with what I had been told. It required further investigation, as my contract was very specific. I never back down from what is agreed, as this is bad for my business. I always deliver as agreed.

"The clan master is never wrong," she said.

"Perhaps he is not wrong," I told her. "The ammunition box is rather heavy."

"You will now transfer both boxes to the junk," she insisted.

I flatly refused her in this instance, pointing out that while I was under contract to recover and deliver up the box marked "Tien Shan", the unmarked box was subsequently mine under the salvage law of the sea.

But I wanted to be fair to both parties. "I will open up my box for your inspection," I told her. Her eyes flashed momentarily, and I suddenly remembered the credulous belief that Orientals have in losing face.

"Not here," she said. "Take cabin."

We opened the weapon box together in the seclusion of my cabin, to discover ten American M1 carbines, still wrapped in grease paper and protected from the sea water.

"It is part of a consignment destined for nationalist resistance troops in Wuchi Shan during the war. It was en route to Hainan, in the Gulf of Tonkin," she said.

The ammunition box was not quite so easy to open, but we eventually forced it. It contained a single layer of cartridges and a layer of thick material. Underneath this and embedded in yet more packing were three bullion bars, each with a Chinese hallmark.

"Chinese gold," she said in a quiet, reserved voice.

"You knew about this all the time?" I asked.

"Yes!" she answered. "The gods are always setting tests for us mortals to complete."

"I think we had better discuss the situation fully, so that this matter can be settled between us honourably," I told her.

Liu Wen-Ming smiled and was silent, her brow furrowed with thought lines

"You will honour the clan agreement in full?" she said.

"Yes!" I said. "But only as the clan agreement, the boxes marked 'Tien Shan'."

"You may have the guns," she said. "They are of no consequence to the clan. You've heard the story concerning the rape of Nanking by the Japanese?" she asked.

"What's that got to do with it?" I asked.

"Everything and perhaps nothing!" she said.

"The clan had been betrayed by one of the *tuchuns*, self-styled warlords. Temples were ransacked by Japanese soldiers in search of clan gold, and many people were killed in the process. But the clan gold was never kept in just one temple; it was distributed among several so that the greater part of the clan wealth would always be safe. But this one tuchun had been a Taoist monk, and he knew there was gold in the clan temples. The Japanese soldiers were quick to act, and they found some of the clan gold, but most of the gold was spirited away to those clan temples outside China. When later the Japanese army moved into the islands of the Dutch East Indies, the gold was again moved, to clan members in both Australia and New Zealand for safekeeping." She said.

"The winds of change were strong in China following the dropping of the atomic bombs on Japan and the end of what had been for us Chinese a very long and protracted war indeed. But long before the war ended, the clan masters had forecast future events based on their knowledge and good judgement. The Soong daughters and H.H. Kung had set a good example of patriotism that called forth an enthusiastic response against the Japanese occupation during that long and bloody war. Prominent women like the half mythical rebel Mulan or Yang Kwei Fei, a famous Chinese legend based on a ninth century heroic Chinese female heroine character.

"But there was also the peasant girl with blue headbands, carrying ammunition and rifles and fighting alongside the men. They are the new revolution sweeping through China, but they also, like the Japanese, ransacked the clan temples. The Nationalist Chinese are unable to withstand the onslaught of this new revolution due to the corruption within their own internal government departments. It becomes only a matter of time now before it will be replaced by the new revolution. The clan master decided in January 1945 that they would set up a force of their own in Wuchow. They arranged for part of the clan gold to be returned to China so that it could be used to obtain the necessary government support for the project. The ship *Wuchow Bay* had been used on this run several times with success. Indeed, the Japanese were more concerned with the war around New Guinea at the time than the odd ship at sea.

"The grass bends and stands upright once again when the wind has passed!" Wen-Ming said. "The clan will survive where our organizations are well established in the overseas Chinese communities."

"You mean the Chinese in the colonies are Tong members?" I asked.

"Of course!" Wen-Ming said with conviction. "But influence requires capital, in terms of hard currency, if we are to generate the power required for our return to China."

In a way I supposed it was inevitable. You can't kick around the islands in this part of the world without running into the Chinese, and where they are the Tong is only one step away. The word *triad* is an adaptation of the word *trihedral*, referring to the trihedral angle, which has three faces. 1540s, "group or set of three", from Late Latin *trias* (genitive *triadis*); from Greek *trias* (genitive *triados*); a triad, the number three.

Perhaps the gold I delivered to Wen-Ming on behalf of her master belonged to the Nationalist Chinese and not the triad. Liu Wen-Ming had made a good case and more than convinced me that her story was the truth. I always trust my gut on these matters—it has never failed me yet! Organized crime throughout the world continues to follow traditional patterns. But in-group crime usually erupts and dies away. As with all criminal organizations, whatever their ultimate goals or aims are, extortion and theft remain tempting and often very rewarding sidelines.

Sometimes it pays to be a little philosophical where the Chinese are concerned—the sound of one hand clapping and all that jazz! I had the gold almost in my pocket; possession, after all, is nine tenths of the law, is it not? Oh yes, it would have been a bloody battle, and I was sure there was more than just one watchful Chinaman under the deck canvas of the large junk.

"What happened to that *tuchun*, that warlord?" I asked.
"It was not a nice death for him," Wen-Ming answered.
"You have a heavy gun under the canvas of that large Wang-Tow," I told her.
"They are pirates, and pirates have guns," she said.
"*Hainan-quay?*" I asked.
"*Ang-mo-quay?*" she answered and laughed.
"What are you laughing at?" I asked.
"You don't have a red arse!" she said.

Ang mo (simplified Chinese: 红毛; *pinyin: hóng máo*; POJ: âng-mo•) or sometimes *Ang mo quay* phonetic sound *kow* (red-haired monkeys), also spelled *ang moh*, is a racial epithet that originates from Hokkien (Min Nan). It is used to refer to white people in Malaysia and Singapore. Literally meaning red-haired, the term carries a strong stigma at present amongst a large proportion of the Caucasian minority. The term implies that the person referred to is a devil, a concept explicitly used in the Cantonese term *gweilo* (foreign devil).

Later, Jamil, our galley slave, cooked a satay, a welcome change from the fish which had been our usual fare. But then, when you live on the sea, you eat what comes out of it most of the time. Darkness had closed in on us unnoticed while we were at dinner, and I checked the deck watch before returning to my cabin.

"I suppose the Chinese revolutionaries will take over Hong Kong?" I said to Wen-Ming.

"Perhaps!" she replied. "You will dive again at first light?"

I checked the glass; it was high. "Weather permitting," I said.

"You are rather contrary to what I was told to expect," Wen-Ming said in a quiet voice. "You are much more patient than I first anticipated you would be."

She poured Chinese rice wine into the two small bowls on the cabin table and, lifting one first to her lips with both hands, then presented the bowl to me.

"*Korero ke oti!*" she said—Speak and it shall be done!

It sounded rather strange to hear a Chinese woman speaking in the language of the islands.

"A man alone, or even a lone woman, for that matter, is but half of wholeness," she said.

"The one without the other and wholeness is impossible for either of us," she went on.

"Wholeness is not simply identification and fusion but rather polarity and union. Each is involved in the development and completion of the other," the lady of enlightenment exclaimed.

"The sound of one hand clapping," I said with a laugh.

Her right hand sped quickly, striking the air beside my left ear and making an ominous sound.

"The sound of one hand clapping," she said, laughing.

I'd never heard it put quite that way before. She disrobed at her leisure, folding each of her garments carefully in a neat pile on the other bed. She was the most breath-taking woman I had seen for a long time.

"You have bobbed hair," I said, "and you look good!"

"I am not permitted to wear my hair long," she informed me. "I am the Lady Enlightenment, consort to the clan master. Did he not say I was at your service?" she pointed out.

Strange though it may seem, sleep came easy that night. Wen-Ming, the mysterious female, spirit of the valley that never sleeps, was dimly visible in the early light of dawn as if she was always there. Yet one would never drain her. What was it she'd whispered? All future possibilities are fused together in wholeness again. Life is full of happenings, each with its own rather special difference. We all live in two worlds—one which is routine, and the other, our heroic world, which is the one that matters. In this one we are ageless and on course, running along the corridors of time in those seasons far beyond the neverness of human dubiety.

Wen-Ming, the girl child left on a hill in China at birth to die, was Lady Enlightenment, the consort! It's a particularly strange feeling, this sensation of double consciousness. Certainly the clan master was very astute and assured of his own ability to decide correctly. A woman is much stronger than wine, and one of ability is of worth too great to be calculated. I learned a great deal from Liu Wen-Ming, not only concerning the clan but about China's special sets of internal cut-throat politics. She was one rather special Chinese lady. I guess you could say I was smitten by her rather unique set of charms complemented with the wisdom of such an old soul residing within her.

Wen-Ming possessed a beautiful oriental female body. Such a woman is not only rare to find but, more importantly, priceless! Wen-Ming's loyalty to her master and her clan remains beyond question. If reincarnation happens to exist, this old soul in female form has certainly fallen back to earth many times from the spiritual genepool of life! A man, according to Taoist mythology is "earth, air, metal, and fire." He is minus one substance. On the other hand, a woman is "earth, air, stone, and water" Together they complete the circuit, like the sun and the moon in perpetual orbit around the earth.

Liu Wen-Ming and I had one common attribute which had decided our compatibility; we had been both born in a leap year. She was under the sign of a dragon and I under the tiger. Had the old Chinese master worked it all out beforehand? Nothing was ever by chance with these people, or at least that is what I thought at the time. In this mix of pairings, I was the barbarian, a soldier of fortune with integrity and scruples, plus a man who could always see a deal through to its conclusion. That much could be said of me. I was a Welsh barbarian, which was considered to be a good omen, for the Welsh are believed to be the people of the winged Red Dragon, and I was a parachutist.

Liu Wen-Ming had no doubt been engaged in this contract by her master, to take my measure via getting very intimate with me both mentally and sexually, by which means that venture had been deemed a success also. Every young man should make love to an older woman, if only for the experience of gaining skill and knowledge through such a relationship. "Sexuality is not mere human-led instinct; it is an indisputably creative force that is not only the basic cause of our individual lives but a very serious factor in our psychic lives as well," Liu Wen-Ming said. The natural tendency of the barbarian is to spill the energies in the outside world.

The Chinese spiritual concept of sex is allowing the male and female fluids to blend within the female, to experience progress in self-development or the art of letting things happen. Thus, the act turns seminal essence into Jade fluid within the female crucible so that yin and yang can nourish each other. In essence, this is a blending of energy and polarities unlike any other, not just the mere act of sex and sexual fluid exchange. The sexual act in a mutual loving context without conditions is the most profound physical and spiritual bonding of the male and female souls made manifest in the physical world.

77

Principles of Dao

Wednesday, 15 January 1947

Dawn came early the next day. I could hear the compressor running, a model C700E, former British Royal Navy job, which could pump 36 cubic feet of air per minute at 200 atmospheres and was equipped with a 3,000 cubic foot five-bottle bank for filling when the compressor was not running. I guessed from my cabin that Idris was probably topping up our tanks and prepping for the morning's dive. In this part of the world, despite it being tropical, it would still be cold down there, scuba diving along the underwater currents at depths of over 120 feet first thing in the morning. Wetsuits would be required. The weather glass had dropped during the night, and to make matters worse, it was raining. It was one of those dull-looking mornings with a slight groundswell running, making large stretches of water move up and down without separate waves.

My lookout told me that there had been no shark sightings that morning on the surface, which was always a good sign, but that should never be taken as read. Those damn sharks could still be down below if the undercurrents were flowing in the right directions. We kitted up after breakfast, taking a block and tackle down with us. We set up a dragline from the hold, clearing ten weapon boxes and fourteen ammunition boxes in four one-hour dives. All in all, this was a productive day's salvage. Liu Wen-Ming had recovered for her clan master forty-five bars of Chinese gold bullion, with a final fifteen still down on the wreck, to complete her full tally of sixty missing triad gold bullion bars. I saw that she was well pleased with the progress of our salvage, as her face lit up like the morning star.

Up to that moment, we had collectively spent a total of five hours and ten minutes diving on the wreck, but I personally was one hour and ten minutes over my safety time.

The wreck stood in Dutch territorial waters and under International Maritime Law. We should have applied to the Dutch at Batavia in Java for permission to dive on the wreck. However, there was an insurrection going on in Java just then. The Dutch East Indies covered an area of around 783,000 square miles, like the scattered beads of a broken necklace, emergent mountaintops which link the Indian and Pacific oceans. There are some 13,700 islands containing 400 volcanos, with 300 ethnic groups speaking more than 250 dialects.

Nothing is? Look … and it is!
Dark Indigo vale of night
Betwixt the moment dreams take flight.
Carry her safely across the sea,
Bring my forsaken love to me.

Nothing is? Look … and it is!
Shadowy camel caravan sway,
Dusty trails to Samakhan and old Cathay.
Tinkling bells and bolts of silk,
Bangles of gold and asses' milk.

Nothing is? Listen … and it is!
Monasteries, peaked mountaintops,
Babbling streams and opium crops.
Porters bent beneath heavy loads,
Stagger the ancient bridal paths,
Where rode the Khan and his Mongol horde.

Nothing is? Listen … and it is!
The gentle roll of a steadfast boat,
Cradled on the mighty sea,
Babbling sound of the whispering wind;
Come, fly this world with me.
It's a wonderful thing to see!

Fritters, those crisp deep-fried morsels, appear in one form or another throughout the cuisine of Asia but are on most occasions eaten as a snack. Fish, fruit, and vegetables are cut into small fragments, along with finely chopped herbs and spices. They are stirred into a batter all at once before being dropped by the spoonful into hot oil. Our maritime cook is rather ingenious and creative with his makeshift cuisine, but alas, once he has gone through his long list of possible curries, it's fritters. Little wonder I become rather poetic on such occasions. Perhaps it's just my way of celebrating our good fortune? Good onboard cooks are rather hard to find but very important to the well-being of my boat crew and their physical state of mind. All fighting men march better on full stomachs.

Our maritime chef has three wives back home in Singapore, so it's rather obvious that his liking for long sea voyages is tied in with recuperation from his extended family. It is also surprising the number of loud plops and splashing that goes on around a boat moored in the open sea at night. Now, my Malay crew are superstitious and don't pass any opinions or even comment on these strange noises at night. They believe that such comment in the darkness would make them vulnerable to the many demonic shoreline or sea spirits that prowl the night. Me, I am more concerned with the task at hand and my return to Singapore.

Thursday, 16 January 1947

It had rained during the night and was one of those rather humid mornings when the sun was late and the mist covering the sea was rather like a white hospital blanket enveloping everything as far as the eye could see. Idris and I agreed about putting on our wetsuits for our first dive, for probably it would be rather cold down on the wreck at this time in the morning. Our descent to the wreck was routine. Idris took up his position on the deck while I went through the hatch in the hold. Using the dragline, we quickly recovered four more ammunition boxes for dispatch topside.

I returned through the hatch in search of the last box. Torch in hand, I searched the cargo remaining in the security cage and eventually found the last ammunition box, jammed tightly between the bottom of the hold ventilator and other cargo. Fortunately, the handle of the ammunition box was accessible, and I hooked it up to the dragline before swimming clear, whilst giving Idris the necessary signal. I then stayed clear of the towline path and waited for the dragline slack to be taken up by the winch crew on the surface ships.

I watched the dragline take up the slack, draw tight, and yank the ammo box towards the deck of the wreck. But then, suddenly, all hell seem to break loose! Now sound carries very well in this three-dimensional world 120 feet below the surface of the sea. For a moment, due to all the banging and thrashing around me, I thought the side of the wreck was about to cave in on top of me. The problem seemed to be a large ventilator shaft. All at once I was completely enveloped in an inky-black darkness, which even my bright sub-aqua lamp couldn't penetrate. Then the banging and thrashing ceased.

Scared? Too damn bloody right I was scared! I could even taste the fear building up within me. But I could not afford the luxury of panic in this liquid environment; no diver can. It took all of my self-discipline, together with most of my military training, in order to produce the self-control required to think clearly at that moment. Slowly I went through the blind diver's drill—air okay, bodyline okay—and I felt the responding tug on the line from Idris. Hand over hand, I proceeded along my own bodyline towards the deck of the wreck and the open sea, even though he had wasted no time in his ascent.

The sight of his legs swimming well above me towards the surface brought comfort and reassurance. The inky black cloud had dissipated quite a lot in the open sea, and the crews of the Chinese Wang-Tows, together with my own crew, were shouting encouragement when I finally broke the surface. Liu Wen-Ming was all over me, the expression on her face a mixture of joy and deep concern. Something the clan master had said back in Fakfak suddenly came to mind: "A man accomplished in falling through the air would have no fear underwater."

"Have you killed it?" she asked.

"Killed what?" I said.

"The sea dragon, of course," she answered.

"You knew about this?" I shouted at her, somewhat annoyed at her non-disclosure.

"Yes," she admitted rather sheepishly. "We lost two of our clan divers here last year. They never came up again."

"*Sotong?*" Idris said, but he made no other comment on the subject.

Sotong is the Malay name for cuttlefish. Fishermen in this region recognize four kinds of cuttlefish; *sotong torak* and *sotong comek* are the most common. These cuttlefish swim in a large shoal, of which there had been no evidence around the wreck. They are all members of the genus *Loligo*. Their black ink is a kind of defence mechanism. The octopus, on the other hand, is far too small for such a large inky cloud as I'd encountered in the deep. Could I have possibly disturbed a giant squid at rest in the shaft of that large ventilator?

"We dive again at midday," I told Idris. He nodded his head in recognition and then went below deck without another word. One of the large Chinese Wang-Tows had come alongside, and Liu Wen-Ming had arranged the transfer of the ammunition boxes to her vessel.

"You are going down again?" she asked.

"Yes, we must dive again as soon as possible," I said. "If we don't, then Idris will never dive again, because he will be too afraid."

"Are you afraid?" she asked, concerned.

"Apprehensive!" I said. "Just bloody apprehensive for being caught unawares and off my guard!"

The weather currently is fine, with just a gentle wind and not much of a swell running. The sun is once more high in the sky. Apprehensive—sure I am apprehensive. But there are two kinds of fear: the fear you run away from so that you never walk that road again, and the fear you face up to and overcome. The one makes you a coward in the eyes of those who would judge you, whilst the other creates legends and heroes.

Idris carries with him all the local superstitions and supernatural lore of the Malay people, but my own ancestors were also superstitious in their day. I am strongly depending on the logic of reason here rather than buying into the myths of sea monsters and their terrible deeds. If logic prevails here, the mass of black ink was a defence mechanism, and whatever it was that we disturbed down there would have moved on before going to ground again. Idris and I kitted up in our wetsuits again and checked the air supply. I was to be the first to dive down, and I would signal him once I was on the wreck—and he would follow.

This was another moment of truth, when boldness would be my friend once again. Adventurous I might be, but courageous? Well, that was something else. I needed this dive like I needed a bullet hole in the head! So I jumped into the water before I had time to change my mind. The descent took an unusually long time, perhaps because I felt much more aware of the immediate surroundings than ever before. There seemed to be much more realism, however, as I was gaining more of my old confidence and ability during this second dive to meet the threat. The strong undercurrents had taken care of that black inky substance and the surrounding waters were as clear as ever.

I had a strange kind of feeling, and it was as if nothing untoward had happened here in the deep. The ammunition box lay on the deck in plain sight, as it had before my encounter with the giant squid had forced our hasty retreat to the surface. The ammo box containing the last of the Chinese triad gold was hard up against the block and dragline to which it was attached. I gave the signal and waited for the winch line to come down. Idris soon arrived at the wreck, and I gave him the diver's thumbs-up to show him all was well. If we were going to do this, it was now or never. Once again, slowly, I made my way through the hatch and into the hold of the wreck. The place seemed the same, and even the ventilator shaft was empty. There were no long, snakelike tentacles or decomposed Chinese divers.

We went about our business until Idris had dispatched the last ammo box to the surface, and then I returned to the deck of the wreck. Together we removed the block and dragline and, finally, the mooring rope. We broke the surface together, but there were sharks around this time when we were getting back into the boat. I noticed that Idris had more talismans on him than a Malayan witch doctor as we got out of the wetsuits. Perhaps it was a good thing. But then we were none the wiser when it came to the push. Liu Wen-Ming was sad yet happy at the same time; she had loaded her cargo in quick time.

I had fulfilled my side of the contract, delivering all the missing triad Chinese gold from the wreck and thus completing my obligation to her satisfaction and that of the Tong. She handed me a red envelope containing a cheque for the agreed sum, drawn on the Lee Wah bank in Singapore. She stepped onto the big Wang-Tow junk moored alongside my boat and cast off immediately. She was gone from my life, and I never saw her again. My whole encounter with this unique woman seemed a surreal dream, sailing on the winds of two soul ships passing through the night.

Friday, 17 January 1947

I set a new course for Dill in Portuguese Timor. It was good to feel the steady throb of the boat engines as we made headway through the water. My thoughts went to the ten weapon boxes I had in my hold, containing 100 pristine heavily greased WWII American .30 M1 carbines. These I will need to convert into cash at some point in the future, preferable sooner rather than later. The ammunition for this weapon system is not a problem with the huge post-war era booming ammo black market surplus from my firearm dealers' contacts.

It had also crossed my mind to retain a few of these M1 carbines for my own personal use, so I withheld two carbines for a rainy day. It was a good bonus from my venture with the Chinese clan master (but especially his representative female consort, who had showed me the way into the unknown). It was due to my helping out the old elder with this assignment to recover the gold that a level of notoriety became attached to me, in the way of respect and possible future monetary advantages. I became one of the very few white men able to move around inside the Chinese communities in Malaya and Singapore unmolested by the gangs. Respect has no price tag on it; it has to be earned.

We live in deeds, not words,
In thoughts, not breath,
In feelings, not figures on a dial.
We should count time by heart-throbs.

He most lives who thinks most,
Feels the noble, and acts on his own intuition.
Where imperfection ends, so heaven begins.

We are ageless and on course,
Running with the seasons for eternity
Beyond the neverness of dubiety,
Two paths diverged by the green.

I took the one less walked and passed unseen.

From the depths of our hearts,
Drowned in the solitude of sorrows,
Came the longing to be loved,
To be held by others' arms.
Just once more to be fed with tenderness
Or seen again as our true selves,
By our words, our actions, and our deeds.

Chapter 5

Captain William Carr

Saturday, 18 January 1947

There was quite a swell running once we were back in the Sawu Sea, and my boat was beating up and down due to the wind. Perhaps this was also due to the inclement and often unpredictable weather in the South Pacific, but I have heard told also of the *coriolis effect*, whereby a mass moving in a rotating system experiences a force called the *coriolis force*. This acts perpendicular to the direction of motion and to the axis of rotation. This coriolis effect tends to deflect moving objects to the right in the northern hemisphere but to the left in the southern hemisphere.

Rain squalls were frequent at this time of the year, and we ran into our fair share around Occusi in Ambeno, a district of East Timor. (Occusi is a coastal exclave in the western part of the island of Timor, separated from East Timor by West Timor.) We maintained a distance offshore of approximately ten miles. Our headway was good, and the bilges were pumped dry. With no change of headwind, we expected to make Dili by first light the next morning. I managed to establish radio contact with Cecil and found that they were now at Vila Salazar; they would also make Dili first thing in the morning.

They had called in at both Nova Sagres and Vila Nova de Malacca. It was good to hear from them again. On the way, we passed the *Plate Explorer*, a Liberty Ship of some 7.185 tons, a one-screw steam reciprocating cargo tramp. The Liberty Ships—officially the Maritime Commission standard EC2-S-C1 (EC stands for emergency cargo) ships—were one of the great production triumphs of the Allies during the Second World War. Liberty ships were constructed as quickly and cheaply as possible, with an intended maximum service life expectancy of just five years.

Many of these Liberty ships far outlasted their intended lifespan. The idea behind Liberty Ships was that they could be produced in the thousands much more quickly than the German U-boats in the Atlantic could sink them.

We reached Dili, on the northern coast of Pulau Timor (Timor Island) just before dawn and watched the sun rise over the wind-tossed palms of the sleepy town. But the remains of Japanese landing craft still lay on the beach, reminiscent of those dark days of the war in the South Pacific. The Japanese occupiers had wasted no time and immediately set men and women to work for their war effort. Little backyard factories of varying sizes sprang to life whenever there was a village that could be press-ganged into working for their Nippon occupiers.

These backyard factories produced everything from paper to forged steel. For the first time since the arrival of foreigners, Timor had been self-sufficient. Factory work had never been the custom of these island peoples, so once the war ended and the Japanese had left the island, the natives tore down all the factories and returned to their age-old custom of just sitting around. Timor is a "Portuguese Overseas Province", and the Timor natives are in fact regarded as Portuguese citizens. There is only the occasional police check on inter-village transport along with a few other manifestations of bureaucracy.

Contrary to all the lies being spread in Sukarno's old accusations, the common people of Timor were neither exploited nor oppressed by their Portuguese masters. But then, neither were these people educated to Western standards. Through a process of assimilation over the many years the Portuguese held sway on Timor Island, it was natural that the local islanders adapted Portuguese dress and customs into their culture. But apart from this, the local natives of Timor Island generally carried on a lifestyle that stretched back in time 450 years or so.

Timor is strangely fortunate in its isolation, for this is a rather sleepy dependency of Portugal. It is fragrant with sandalwood and many tropical fruits along its coast, as well as coffee and tobacco in its mountains. But then, only one half of Timor is Portuguese. The other half of the island, being Dutch, is called Ambeno and boasts five large towns: Atapupu, Occussi, Niki Niki, Pariti, Kupang, and of course Bad, on the tip of the island. The town's name arises from the Dutch word for bath, but it does make you wonder: How in the heck did this town end up being called the Dutch term for bath? The Chinese are also here on the island, but then the Chinese are everywhere throughout South East Asia.

Cast adrift by mutineers, attacked by cannibals, and pounded unmercifully by 300 miles of open sea, thirteen British seamen found this white-sand forgotten island back in June of 1789. It was Captain Bligh of *HMS Bounty* fame. There are conflicting stories as to whether Captain Bligh's mistreatment of his crew led to the mutiny which occurred on the Royal Navy vessel in the south Pacific on 28 April 1789.

Most of the older Chinese here on the island are from Macao and were brought to these islands by the Portuguese during the time of those fabulous Black Ships. That was the name given to Western vessels arriving in Japan during the sixteenth and nineteenth centuries. In 1543 the Portuguese initiated the first contact with the islands of the Japans, establishing a trade route linking Goa to Nagasaki. The large carracks engaged in this trade had their hulls painted black with pitch, and this term came to represent all European vessels in the area of the Japans at that time. Down in the Southern Pacific region of South East Asia, the main port of trade back in those days was Vila Nova de Malacca, named after the Portuguese city of Malacca sited on the west coast of Malaya.

Portuguese Malacca remained under Portuguese control as a colony for 130 years (1511–1641). The port city of Malacca was of strategic importance, as it also controlled the narrow straits of Malacca, through which all seagoing trade between China and India had to traverse. In some ways it could be compared to the strategic value of Singapore to the colonial British. Now, the island people of Timor are rather easy-going, not unlike the Malays in many ways. But then they are of the same ethnic group. The island is divided between the Portuguese, who call their side of the island Timor, and the Dutch, who call their part of the island Ambeno.

The Ambenese make up a large part of the Dutch Colonial Army in the Dutch East Indies. They are rather good fighters, with no love for Sukarno and his Javanese.

I found Cecil and Roy in a Chinese bar on the main street of Dili, had a drink, and told them I was pulling out on the evening tide, headed for the Indonesian island of Bali on my way back to Singapore. I also had a talk with a Chinese merchant who agreed to take the M1 carbines off my hands at a good price, providing I deliver them directly to his agent at Rindjani, on the island of Lombok. The merchant also gave me quite a comprehensive list of known Sukarno agents in the area and warned me concerning the Dutch gunboats.

Roy had not arrived as agreed at the bar, so at 2200 hours PST we cast off without him and put to sea. I fail to understand the stubbornness of this man! Roy had been my co-conspirator from the start of this adventure, chasing after both our dreams, but I was not uneasy about Roy's decision to tag along with Cecil for the moment. I could pick him up later, after our arrival at Singaradja in Bali. The sea swell had eased a little, and with a good steady breeze blowing from the south-west, we were making good headway. I decided to spend the night up on the bridge, thinking mostly about Liu Wen-Ming, who was heading for Nam Dinh (upriver from the Gulf of Tonkin) and then overland to Limchow and on to Nanning.

At 0200 hours, I switched off the boat's navigation lights and changed course to a new heading, which would carry us to the rendezvous point with Tauke (boss) and his bunch of gunrunners. At 0445 hours we were six miles off the coast of Pulau Lombok and saw their signal. Moving in towards the other vessel, we came alongside.

"How do I know you are not a Belanda?" the Chinaman challenged.

"I've not blown you out of the water yet!" I shouted back at him. "Just you," I called. "Come on board!"

He did just that, jumping the gap between the boats with the agility of a cat. "Do I look like a bloody Dutchman?" I asked.

"You people all look the same to me," the Chinaman replied.

"Lee Fatt," the gunrunner Chinaman introduced himself. "But you have something from a lady to show me first?"

I handed him the badge and watched him carefully inspect the small brass dragon that Liu Wen-Ming had given to me not so very long ago. I was awaiting his reply with unusual calm, in anticipation of his stream of questions. Lee Fatt returned the little dragon to my right hand. "I know you now," he said.

At this point I could not resist the feeling that I might be selling all the M1 carbines back to their Chinese clan owners, but a deal was a deal. The transaction which followed was quick and very efficient. It took approximately thirty minutes to transfer all the weapons from one boat to the other. Payment on this occasion was in hard cash and in Malayan currency, but correct down to the last cent on the dollar. I was quite relieved once it was all over with both parties being satisfied. Both the British and the Dutch had a rather nasty habit of hanging people for gunrunning in these waters. My wisdom tooth was playing up again, probably due to the change of weather we were having. I hated dentists, professional or otherwise, but I made myself a promise to see one when we arrived back at Singapore.

It is very unlikely that Lee Fatt would do business with Sukarno or his Javanese Communist PKI cut-throats. PKI stands for the Partai Komunis Indonesia or Communist Party of Indonesia. The Javanese hate most of the Chinese in business throughout the islands, due to their business acumen. Where the Japanese are concerned, the Chinese are much more successful. For now, there is much local gossip on Sukarno's extreme nationalism in these islands, which doesn't go down very well with the Chinese.

Nationalism is the feeling of belonging to a group of people united by a common racial, linguistic, and historical tie. But usually it is also identified with territory. Nationalism is an ideology which exalts the nation state as the ideal form of political organization, with an overriding claim on the loyalty of its citizens. Developing first in Western Europe with the consolidation of nation states in the nineteenth and twentieth centuries, nationalism brought about the reorganization of Germany and Italy and the breakup of the old Hapsburg and Ottoman Empires. This same nationalism had also been the prime force in the political awakening of Asia. Nationalism

91

is a powerful source of inspiration in many of the arts but also in the development of historical and language studies.

This has proved to be as true of the new nations of Asia, as it was in nineteenth century Europe that nationalism formed one of the dynamic elements in romanticism. In the first half of the nineteenth century, nationalism was associated with democracy, liberalism, and the demand for civil and constitutional liberties. The Mazzini interpretation of nationalism was seeing the individual nations as subdivisions of a larger world society which ought to live together in peace. Joseph Mazzini (1805–1872), a native of Piedmont and his parents were deeply influenced by the French Revolution.

It was Mazzini who first give a cultural definition of nationalism. The central theme of nationalism for him was the sharing of language, customs, historical tradition, hope, and geographical continuity. But nationalism and imperialism also assumed aggressive, intolerant forms of integral national expansion during the late nineteenth century, at the expense of other non-indigenous cultures and races, particularly the Zionist and other races considered "alien". These were the scapegoats for all of Germany's ills during the early nineteenth century. Thus nationalism became an essential element in both fascism and other totalitarian movements in the twentieth century.

Nationalism became a moving force in the rebellion of colonial peoples in its resistance of nations and national minorities threatened with the subjugation by much more powerful states. The natives of our former colonies, led by self-promoting, power-hungry individuals, were driven by the idea of independence and self-rule. They embraced violent rebellion, taking up the gun rather than politics to achieve their aims. Their former masters were now seen as oppressors and occupiers rather than benevolent benefactors.

Despite the rival claims of a class war on the other, nationalism as a mass emotion has been and still is the most powerful political force in the history of the modern world.

National Bolshevism was a term used by Germany between the two world wars to describe a policy of national resistance to the

Treaty of Versailles and the West, based on alliance with another pariah power, Bolshevik Russia, against their common enemies. It had adherents among both extremes of the German political scene, but it never really emerged as one well-defined doctrine with the same meaning for all its ideological supporters. Instead, it remained a series of nebulous generalities to which each side provided its own interpretation, which suited a doctrine of argument, a kind of spin-doctoring.

The idea was first promoted by Karl Radak in 1919. Its paradoxical appeal attracted groups on both extremes of the political spectrum—Nationalist on the right and dissident communists and socialists on the left.

The dawn today was the most beautiful I have seen for quite some time, with the sea sparkling in the sunlight like a million glittering gems. The sky is clear and blue for as far as the eye can see. It is a great day! We seem to have caught a rather strong current, which is carrying us on towards the Indonesian island of Bali. The current has in fact increased our speed by approximately two knots, which is quite a good thing, and we are making good headway. We are still out of sight of land, but there are several sea birds in the sky above us, and we know land is not all that far away.

A captive bird longs for the woods of old;
The fish in the pond dreams of its native river;
A dog barks deep in the long lane;
A cock crows from the top of the mulberry tree.

There is no confusion here out in the open sea,
But ample space to spare, with my boat in the sunlit breeze.
How could I venture still deeper into the dusty world of cares?

Dim, dim in the distance lies the island;
Faintly, faintly you see the smoke of chimneys.

When the tide rises, I slip the mooring,
And I am once more on my way.
As the ebb tide falls, I shall return home, singing.
It is the portal to freedom and the beginning of self-knowledge.

The coastline this morning

Sunday, 19 January 1947

I felt it was good to be alive. I thought of many things there on the bridge of my boat. I thought of the old sea dog, my great-grandfather, and the old, smooth Malacca cane he always carried with him. My great-grandfather had picked it up during one of his many sea voyages before the mast, back in the early 1800s, in Malacca, of all places. Captain of his own ship, William had sailed out of Bristol, headed for any port east of the equator where he could trade and show a good profit. He was a canny Scotsman of the border clan Carr. The surname is of English, Scottish, and Irish origin, taken from three sources, the first being a variant of *Kerr*, which is of Northern English and Scottish origin. It is a topographical name for someone who lived near a patch of wet ground overgrown with brushwood.

The name *Carr* appears to be derived from the Middle English (1200–1500) *kerr*, taken from the Old Norse *kjarr*. The second source is Irish, an Anglicized form of the Gaelic *O Carra*, "descendant of Carra", a byname meaning "spear".

Captain William Carr, Merchant Navy

The third source is also Irish, an Anglicized form of the Gaelic *MacGiolla Chathair*, "son of the servant of Cathar", a personal name derived from *cath* or battle. My great-grandfather William Carr married three times. His second wife was a rather fiery Castilian, full of hot Spanish temper. Yet he outlived both his first and second wives. When he finally sold up and retired, he moved into property at Ebbw Vale in South Wales and married once more, into the Redman family, much to the consternation of most of his children from the two previous marriages.

William Carr is on my mother's side of the family, but if any of the stories told of his exploits at sea and on land should give credence to strength of character, his last shipwreck should do the trick! Apparently, he refused to abandon ship placing himself in perilous dangers until all his crew were safely off the vessel as a true sea Captain should. He was to all intents and purposes a hard man with a rather soft centre, a young boy who ran away to sea, worked hard all his life for his captain's ticket, and made good.

I Rex was born in Ebbw Vale, a small mining village in South Wales and from my youth I knew I was never made for the common life. My nature was ever to love the hills and mountains. By mischance, I fell into the dusty world and being gone stayed their captive in the ways of a decadent monetary society. Had it not been for the love of my parents and the tender devotion of my mother, I would have undoubtedly expired with meningitis in 1930, at the tender age of six years old. My mother, Beatrice, had been a nurse at Pembroke Hospital in Wales before her marriage to my father. It was her own reasoning and steadfast devotion that saved my life. She refused hospitalization for my illness and nursed me at home with daily attendance from Doctor Lloyd. Of the eleven cases of meningitis during that 1930 outbreak in Ebbw Vale, only two children survived, and I was one of the two.

At 1600 hours PST we came across an outrigger some three miles off our port side and made towards the craft. *"Orang Bajau!"* Zainal shouted as he unsheathed the twin machine guns to put them at the ready. Sea-gypsies, pirates, swamp men, or sea-nomads—these creatures inhabited a vast area of sea and island coast, stretching from Southern Burma to the Sunda islands of the Dutch East Indies, Malaya, and the Philippine islands. The term *Bajau* has two different meanings. Firstly, it is a collective group label, designating all these tribes of itinerant water men who still share a common language, which takes the form of ancient Malay. By that I mean their speech contains many proto-aristocratic Malay words of the old royal courts.

The language also assimilated many words from Burmese, Dayak, Buginese, and other neighbouring peoples with whom they have bartered and traded over the centuries. The Bajau actively aided the Allies during the war, sabotaging the Japanese occupation forces, raiding their installations, and ultimately driving them out of the southern islands through hit-and-run raids and other acts of sabotage.

"*Orang Kaya Mat Salleh*", came the call continuously from their boat, like a broken record or often-repeated tune. *Mat Sallah* is a Malay nickname for European men. But in the case of the Bajau, it is a little different. "*Orang Kaya*" is the Bajau term for a chieftain; it means "rich man". *Mat* is short for Mohammed and *Salleh* means "child of Sarah", the wife of Abraham. The most famous figure in Bajau history is a chieftain by the name of Mat Salleh. He was a man of both Bajau and Sulu stock, who came from a village at the mouth of the Sugut River, on the east coast of Sabah in Borneo. Mat Salleh married a cousin of the Sultan of Sulu, a witch who never set foot upon the earth but travelled through the air instead. Legend has it that they had several children, so I guess they must have made out high up in the tress—or on the wing, perhaps?

The four men in the outrigger were from Sulu in the Philippines, where they are called "Bajau". They are members belonging to a chieftain called Mat Awi, who I understand is in the area on one of his lightning attacks on some coastal village on the island of Balabalagan. Balabalagan Islands, also known as Kepulauan Balabalakang, is an archipelago located in the border province of East Kalimantan and West Sulawesi. The raiders usually come ashore at night, unobserved, just after the village people have settled down and gone to sleep. They carry out their raids and are away again with a hoard of the villagers' jewellery, sewing machines, and handwoven cloth, as well as anything else they fancy and their boats can carry off.

In the spirit of the nomad, we gave the four Bajau a meal and sent them off in the right direction, with our greetings to Mat Awi. I try never to make enemies unnecessarily; we all have our own way of making a living on the high seas. A good deed is indeed remembered, as is a hostile act on these people.

"A few sore maidens on Balabalangan this morning," Zainal said.

I told him, "Keep an open eye for the Dutch gunboat we were warned about operating close to these waters!"

I rechecked our course heading and found that we were running true for Bali. Mat Awi and I were friends of old, but the last thing I wanted at this moment was a run-in with this group and an invitation to Sulu! *"Mendayu-dayu!"* Zainal said at the rumble of distant thunder. The wind had picked up quite a bit, and a sudden *sumatra* seemed inevitable—one of those rain squalls that lasted anything between thirty minutes and five or six hours at a time in this part of the world. The boat crew got busy battening down anything that could possibly move on and off deck. The ocean swell had grown quite a lot by the time the first drops of South Pacific rain hit us an hour later.

"Ayesha," (Arabic form meaning "she who lives referring to the sea"), Zainal said, meaning the Bugis pirate chieftain Mat Awi's favourite daughter, who also sailed these waters. Ayesha was in her time a formidable fighting woman, a pirate of legendary status who sailed with a female-only crew. She was blessed with a drop-dead-gorgeous body that exuded a femme fatale presence wherever she went. She also possessed an uncanny business sense mingled with her feminine eccentricity. Her crew were loyal to her and as lethal as she was. Should you survive an encounter with this woman of the sea, she would leave an indelible mark on your memory. This was one female pirate you simply did not mess with—not if you wished to survive in her territorial waters.

Ayesha, Bugis pirate Mat Awi's daughter, at Pulau Manis

The squall was a bad one, so I was right to have had my twin machine guns removed and secured below decks. There was no need to defend the boat from raiders in this tempest. I had to turn my boat head-on into the huge oncoming waves for the next few hours. We battled against the elements of this storm—which took me off course from the island of Bali—a needs-must action only to keep us afloat in the heavy seas. Then it was gone suddenly; the sumatra left us just as quickly and seemingly without warning. The night skies turned pitch black.

Some days I feared that we would all be either killed in a Dutch gunboat naval engagement or—worse still—taken into the deep blue waters by a raging storm on the high seas and erased from history with no record as to what had happened to us all. This remained our reality alone while on the ocean and was always a looming thought in the backs of our minds. My enterprises very often carried a degree of risk-taking to make the journey or gain an advantage. We could disappear without a trace, but luck and good fortune seemed to be on our side for the moment. The best I could do was try to stack the odds in our favour. But I would rather be doing this than clocking in and out of some factory back home, working for the masters who help perpetuate the rat race.

I have always maintained that nobody is born a leader, for real leaders are trained. On the matter of respect, well, that must be earned, not just taken. For the most part I find that people are sheep who co-exist in the world with wolves and other predators. The mass of sheep will always need someone to follow. They need to be told what to do, when to do, and how to do it. I find this very sad and the total opposite of what I believe in concerning how to live life.

Only you can decide whether you prefer a lifetime of mediocrity or being—for at least one day in your life—the hero of your own story, taking control of your destiny. You can decide how it continues and how it must end, rather than just sailing along oblivious to opportunity and new adventures, particularly those with the fairer sex.

My role as skipper was to keep the odds in our favour so that I and my crew could make it back to home waters unscathed.

We do not merit ayes and nays.
Was I afraid of life before I was born?
Like the fear of death before I die,
Is it worth it all from the moment of birth? I am alive,
For, at the moment of death, I die but ponder: Why?

Chapter 6

The Island of Bali

Monday, 20 January 1947

I decided to get a new fix on my current location, forced on us by the tempest. In the darkness, I made sure that all my crew was there and all right and then checked with torches for any visible damage on my boat. At 0315 hours I received a radio signal from the Dutch authorities, concerning Cecil, who had put into Balabalagan an hour before the Dutch gunboat that was investigating the Bajau act of hit-and-run piracy. I confirmed his destination as Foochow, ex-Dili in Timor, and my own heading of Singapore. No, I had not seen anything of the Bajau. And that was that.

It seemed that Cecil had put onto the island in search of fresh drinking water. I checked my nautical position on the sextant and worked out the projection. We had completed a total of 955 nautical miles since leaving Fakfak in Dutch New Guinea. At dawn we sighted the island of Bali. The sea around for miles was quiet and calm. It was 1300 hours PST when we finally arrived at the port of Singaradja—if you could call it a port! I made the judgement call to anchor my boat in deep water rather than run her up on the beach, with its incumbent tidal problems. But perhaps I should have swung around the islands and gone ashore at Denpasar (a Balinese city whose namesake suggests a northern market town).

There is a legend on Bali which tells of a time when the island was flat and barren. When the island's larger neighbour, Java, embraced the Islamic faith, Hindu gods entered Bali and created the mountains, on which they lived. Thus these mountains became sacred to the Balinese people, home to their gods and a source of fresh water that made the fields fertile, so that everything around them was green and good. A chain of volcanic mountains runs along the length of the islands from east to west.

The island of Bali, Monday, 20 January 1947

At its widest part, the island of Bali is approximately ninety miles across, and it is fifty miles north to south. It is separated from Java by a strait less than a mile wide. Bali owes much of its lush green vegetation to its mountains, from whence come the heavy rainfall and fresh water. The monsoon rains fill the rivers draining from the highlands, and combined with the mineral-rich volcanic soil, this produces trees and flowers in abundance and profusion. For the Balinese this is reflected in a passion for decoration and elaboration for both their houses and their gateways.

Attached to every Balinese Hindu temple are troupes of dancers. These are the *Nautch girls*, whose duties consist of dancing in honour of their gods and providing physical satisfaction for any worshipper who can afford a generous donation to the temple. Nautch girls don't come cheap; the higher the dancer's station in the temple eroticism the higher the donation required. These dancers are protected and at the same time restricted to the wealthiest clients only; the common man is outpriced. Azuri is the top Balinese dancer for the moment. She can perform every page in the *Kama Sutra of Vatsyayana* with much graceful eloquence.

Azuri the dancer

There are very strange and stringently severe ceremonies to go through, and the oracle is often sought. This is an ancient Hindu who is thought to be wise and able to give the best advice. But often he speaks in words too hard to understand, almost as if the answer were cocooned within a mystery that the querent can only solve in time—if it is his fate to do so!

Then there are the ceremonies of the ritual bath followed by the feast. At the most hospitable moment, the dancer leaves the floor, dancing her way through the crowd into the bedchamber, and the door slams shut. Still dancing, Azuri discreetly disrobes with much skill, and with feminine finesse begins her nuptial dance.

I had the good fortune to experience this. It was bliss itself, rather like something from *Tales of the Arabian Nights*. I felt the way former ruler Harun al-Rashid the legendary caliph portrayed in 'The Thousand and One Nights' must have felt a long time ago. Better known as the Arabian Nights, in Arabic it is called Alf laylah wa Laylah. The tales consist of Middle Eastern as well as Indian stories which there remains no verifiable date or authorship. The oracle predicted that I would return to Azuri again—well, perhaps!

Three Balinese women

Life in Bali is dominated by the perpetual contest between the supernatural forces of good and evil, so that the Balinese are in constant appeasement of evil in order to seek the blessings of their many gods. Balinese dances are composed of stylized movements that use not only the body and limbs but also the hands and eyes.

Music and dance can never be entirely separated from their religious beliefs, and every performance is ultimately directed to the gods of Bali. The *ketjak* is a form of Balinese dance and music drama that was developed in the 1930s in Bali. This "monkey dance" is performed predominantly by men after sunset, with more than a hundred dancers sitting in concentric circles. They sway back and forth, bending and stretching out their hands; they hiss and bellow with remarkable precision.

Life in Bali

Tuesday, 21 January 1947

Johannes Vanderbilt, the Dutch official who ran the marine office at Singaradja, was a stodgy middle-aged man who had spent most of his life in the Colonial Service and was quite addicted to schnapps, the Dutch equivalent of gin.

"Didn't expect you!" he said jovially when I arrived. "Heard you were spending the night with one of our temple dancers." He certainly was rather well informed.

"There are no restrictions on your stay in Bali," he informed me, "but I would advise you not to put in anywhere along the coast of Java."

I raised an eyebrow quizzically at this and waited for him to elaborate.

"Insurgents!" he said. "That troublemaker Sukarno." He continued. "We had Ahmed Sukarno in exile on Sumatra, but then the Japanese arrived and made him president of the Java Central

Council. I suppose they wanted a Japanese sock puppet for a front man. Sukarno got away in 1945 and declared himself president by default."

"The coast of Java is dangerous?" I asked.

"Quite so," he said. "The Javanese insurgents would shoot you on sight."

"What about the Balinese?"

"Oh, they don't like the Javanese, much less Sukarno," he said. "Anyway, you're quite safe in Bali."

My main objective now was to ensure a good supply of fuel, fresh food, and water. The Dutch rupee [Netherlands Rupee] was at the time not worth the paper it was printed on, and the local merchants were hungry for any foreign currency they can get their hands on. This was a point in my favour. I did a deal with one of the Chinese merchants and obtained the full complement of requirements. I then spent the remainder of the afternoon taking inventory of the goods being delivered to my boat.

I was also more than a little surprised to learn of my sudden notoriety. It appeared that the top Balinese temple dancer, Azuri, made periodical visits to the Dutch Residence. Would I go down in Balinese history as the man who seduced the Dutch Resident's Nautch girl?

Zainal and the rest of the crew made short shift of the work and by 1800 hours PST had it all stowed away. With all the necessary preparations in hand for our next put-out to sea, the crew and I settled down for the night.

Wednesday, 22 January 1947

I was busy studying the chart of the Java Sea when Ng arrived on a sampan during the early hours of the morning to where my boat was moored in the deep water of Bali. Just when I'd thought it had gone quiet, things were starting to hum again as regards business. Ng carried out the typical greeting jargon in Chinese fashion before finally broaching the true subject of his visit. It seemed that his dear old grandfather was living in a rather small Chinese village, approximately three miles from the coast and between the town of Tuban and Rembong, on the island of Java—which happened to be full of insurgents.

The Indonesian rebels had taken over control of Jogjakarta, Surakarta, and Madium as well as Pasuruan but were now moving their forces on Surabaja. Ng wanted me to go in and get his grandfather out before it was too late. There were other groups in the Dutch East Indies who were opposed to Ahmed Sukarno, and Surabaja was the stronghold of one such group which, while being opposed to the Dutch, also wanted an Indonesia free of Sukarno and his Indonesian communist cronies. I told Ng that I needed time to think his proposition over but would give him a definite answer at the same time the next morning. My original game plan had been to leave Bali the next day on as direct a heading as possible for Singapore, via Pulau Bawean, Kuala Pembuang, on the coast of Borneo.

Then I would head into the Karimata Strait and on up through the Riau Archipelago. My present route would take me and my crew far from the coast of Java and essentially out of harm's way. Don't get me wrong here, I am not danger-shy nor a coward in any fashion. I had already taken some great risk on my voyage thus far, and I needed to take into consideration whether I should yet again place my boat, myself, and the men I was responsible for in dangerous proximity to hundreds of murderous insurgents who would cut all our throats without any hesitation! Did I need the extra cash? Did I need the prestige of rescuing a loyal friend's family member? Did I need the adrenalin rush of being in harm's way yet again?

The answer was, Probably not. But flashbacks of my Second World War combat battles for my very survival against the Nazis and then the Japs still haunted me, as did thoughts of the good men we'd had to leave behind to perish. We all carry our own ghosts that come back to haunt us many years later. Ng's proposition appeared straightforward enough—just a three-hour job. Run in to the coast, do an hour's hard march to the village, pick my passenger up, and lastly, do the two-hour march back to the coast with the old man on tow. This seemed at the time the best course of action with the least risk.

For the safety of my crew I decided that, no matter what, my boat was to stay away from the Javanese coastline throughout this whole rescue operation, only coming in to drop me off and to pick us up. The chart of the drop-off coastline showed sandbars, but my fast patrol boat had a shallow draft, so this should not be a problem. I listened to the *Voice of Free Indonesia* broadcasting from Surabaja on the boat's radio. This was the group opposed to Ahmed Sukarno, using an underground radio station, and there were no reports of Sukarno's rebels at Surabaja. I decided to sleep on it! The answer always comes to perplexing questions in the morning.

Thursday, 23 January 1947

At 1100 hours the next day I received a radio signal from Cecil on his Pearl Lugger. Seems Cecil had lost one of his boat's masts in that last sudden squall and was headed for Pelaihari, off Cape Selantan in Borneo, for a replacement. At that moment, Cecil was making do with a jib headsail and a foresail, which would slow him down considerably. At 1200 hours a Netherlands Evertsen-class destroyer came through at noon. It was the *HNLMS Van Ghent*, an Admiralen-class destroyer built for the Royal Netherlands Navy in the 1920s. Her sister ship, *Evertson*, had been sunk by the Japanese back in 1942.

The 1730-ton Dutch destroyer had a top speed of fifteen knots and a main armament of four-single mounted 120 mm naval guns; she was probably the last of her kind. As far as I knew, all the others had been sunk by the Japanese during the Second World War. The ship was on a heading for Batavia but most likely had been sent to investigate the Bajau piracy incident at Balabalangan Island. But on the other hand, she could also be heading for Surabaja. I figured, *We shall see what we shall see*. The Dutch claimed it was a police action, but then war is war in any language when armed conflict is involved. I have no faith or trust in the Dutch colonials or their naval presence in this region. I know from past experience with them that it will end badly for them during this conflict.

I am he who causes,
No other beside me.
Upon me these worlds are held,
Like pearls strung on a thread.

I am the essence of the waters,
The shining of the sun and moon.
Know me, eternal seed of everything that grows,
The intelligence of those who would understand,
The vigour of the active.

In the strong, I am strength,
Unhindered by lust
And the objects of craving.

I am all that a man may desire
Without transgressing the law of his own nature.

The first mention of the word *varna* is found in the Hindu book *Rigveda*, the most important of the *Vedas*. One of its Hindu hymns describes the creation of the world through primeval sacrifice. The gods offer a primeval being, identified as Prajapati (lord of all creatures), as a sacrifice to himself. From his body are born the four great classes of society: from his head the *Brahma*, from his arms the *Kshatriya*, from his thighs the *Vaishya*, and from his feet the *Shudra*. The prime duty of the Brahman is to study and to teach. The Kshatriya is the warrior, and the duty of Vaishya is to keep cattle. These three classes are the twice-born of Hinduism.

The Shudra are the servants, to be disposed of at their masters' whims. The Shudra class itself is again divided into "pure" and "untouchables". When the warlike Aryans invaded India in the second millennium BC, they brought along with them a well-developed religious system. Gradually the fierce gods of those conquerors fused with those of the conquered, and there emerged the dazzling complexity of ritual and belief and the rigidly stratified society which characterize the oldest living religion in the world. There is Brahma, the Creator; Vishnu, the Preserver; Shiva, the Destroyer.

Below is a Shaivite temple. Shaivite Hindus believe that Shiva created the world through dancing and that his wild rhythms will destroy it at the end of the Cosmic Cycle. The Cosmic Cycle spans four thousand million years.

Vishnu is asleep on the cobra, Sesha, who is the symbol of eternity. Note the white dot on the centre of the dancer's forehead. This is the pineal (or third) eye.

Shaivite temple dancer

According to Hindu mythology, each man has a third eye, the channel of his occult powers; it is supposed to be situated in the centre of the forehead. In fact, the "third eye" is an anatomical reality; it is the pineal gland, lying roughly in the centre of the brain. In birds and animals whose cerebrum is at the top part of the brain, it is either very small or non-existent.

The pineal gland lies immediately under the skull and is sensitive to light. Its existence has been known for centuries; René Descartes believed that it was the point at which the mind and body were joined together, a kind of mystical "principal seat of the soul". The pineal body is a tiny grey mass one quarter of an inch long, weighing one thirtieth of an ounce. It has always intrigued anatomists, because while the rest of the human brain is "double", the pineal body has no duplicate. As far back as the fourth century BC, Herophilus described it, considering it the organ which regulated the flow of thought; he compared it to a sphincter.

Melatonin is manufactured by the pineal gland through hormonal action upon serotonin, a chemical messenger which transmits nerve impulses across the synapses. It looks very much as if melatonin and serotonin could be connected to man's higher functions—which would certainly confirm the Hindu belief that the third eye is man's spiritual centre.

Life is full of happiness, each instance with its own, very special, significance. The boat is underway, and I am curled in my favourite seat on the bridge. I drink the peace of early morning and let my mind reminisce one times forelock which means for me to act quickly and decisively but not let slip an opportunity as this is how I make my living out here.

Small snippets of sense are gleaned in those quiet moments among the whirlpool of my daily events and experiences. Each individual consciousness is stripped down and analysed to disclose its concealed worth and separated—subject from language and moral behaviour. I picture the cockle picker, sifting through wet beach sand at ebb tide, in search of shellfish and the fisherman ankle deep in the receding water, gathering his catch from the throwing net attached to his left wrist by a long length of cord. In the quiet light of dawn, I see the fulfilment of prayer; there is a deep religious significance in "Give us this day our daily bread." From my viewpoint, westerners simply mumble off these words in recitation without any real grasp of what hunger is.

What it is like to go without the basic essentials, such as food, water, and shelter? A good catch and both those men would have enough to sell in the marketplace. A poor catch, and would they still be able to feed their families? Perhaps this was the way that God intended mankind should live.

A simple life as a fisherman in Bali

I set course in the direction of Pulau Bawean in the Java Sea and settled back in my seat to await the consequence. No, I am not a fatalist who believes that somehow our destinies are carved out in stone for us from the day we are born! We have choices to make along the way, some leading us to better avenues of possibilities and others not so good, should you take a wrong turn. I decided long ago that every step I took would be of my own calling. But of course, there are times when fate also seems to take a hand and things become a little uncertain.

I took over the boat's wheel from my helmsman, Zainal, while he went off to *bacha wirid*, his morning ritual prayers. Bali was a kind of *keyangan*, the abode of the old divinities of Hinduism. This part of the world was Hindu long before the Arab spice traders arrived on the scene. Bali remains the last enclave of Hinduism in the Dutch East Indies.

The island of Java fell to the Islamic influence of Arab traders around the time of Mirza Nur-ud-din Beig Mohammad Khan Salim, better known as Jahangir, Mughal Emperor of India, as well as Ustad Mansur (1590–1624) a seventeenth-century Mughal painter and court artist. That was long before Portugal found the sea route to the Orient.

We are not infallible—yours truly here included—as we always make mistakes and learn from the experiences, some of which hurt both physically and emotionally. I guess my scars never really healed. This had been a strange and exciting journey up to that moment, full of adventure and sometimes dangerous activity.

Zainal smiled knowingly when I changed course. In a way I had known all along that the challenge has been quite a bit to my liking. The Azuri temple dancer affair back on Bali had taught me that at long last I could have a physical relationship with another woman without thinking about Pam, my wife back in England. The aftermath of ending that relationship was not quite so painful as it had been, though deep down in my heart it could never be painless. Pam, after all, is also the mother of my daughter, Sandra, and the connection of the past through blood can never be completely severed. I took the bundle of old letters I'd received from well-meaning people back home and threw them into the sea.

It seemed that Pam had been having an affair with some manager in Dudley. One or two of the letters had been rather explicit in detail. I decided not to return home to England. Of course, I would still love my wife Pam back home. But at this very moment, she would be in more danger from me or what I might do in the heat of the moment. With noble people like those who wrote me such detailed, informative letters, who needed friends! Pam, I doubt I will ever get over her! Well, the die was now cast! I was going to make a rather quick run into insurgent territory in Java to see if I could pick up one rather old Chinaman!

Chapter 7

Grandfather Ng
Friday, 24 January 1947

It was 0630 hours when Idris and I waded through the water, across the sand, and into the cover of the pervading palms. Zainal had taken the boat out to sea and would come offshore again in three hours, waiting for my signal before making a quick run onto the beach to pick us up. We walked at a leisurely pace, taking steps of equal length at a steady rate. Half a mile on we found the dirt road Ng had described to me back in Singaradja. There was no sign of any military activity, and we saw no other travellers along the way. We were a day late, though timewise we were on schedule. This was deliberate; we had given considerable thought to both Dutch punctuality and Javanese impatience.

We shirted the Javanese village, which was unusually quiet except for a group of women working in an adjacent field. The absence of men in this area was quite strange, but then again, Javanese men were notoriously lazy and preferred to sit around talking while their women did most of the work. We located the Chinese village and the house we required. Yet again, the absence of young men was quite noticeable. Checking the area for any insurgents lurking in hiding, Idris and I moved quickly into the compound of the house. *He who dares wins the fight!* The possibility of an impending ambush within the house itself or on the road back to the coast could not be ruled out.

Any sudden burst of gunfire on our part would probably bring the Javanese insurgents out of the woodwork post-haste. There were bound to be security patrols in the area, even if we had seen nothing of them on our way into the village. Keeping in the depths of the shadows, Idris and I sprinted across the compound and through the open door of the house. Idris seized one of the two Javanese insurgents we came across by the hair and held his knife across his throat with the other hand, while I covered them both with my Webley .455 pistol. We'd caught the two terrorists having their jollies; they'd been taking turns raping one of their female captives before we'd charged in and coitus interruptus had taken place.

The young Chinese woman seated at the table with the two military-dressed men stared in wide-eyed disbelief at the way the tables had suddenly been turned against them.

"*Ampun tuan belanda, meng-ampukan kita?*" The Javanese wind was bleating like a couple of sacrificial goats.

"British!" I snapped back at them aggressively. "What have you done with the old Chinese *tauke?*" I demanded.

A *tauke* or *towkay*, refers to a Chinese employer of labour or financier behind an enterprise. It's a descriptive title given to Chinese people of good position.

"In the back room," they bleated in chorus.

Idris and I immediately set to work binding and gagging the two Javanese. The Chinese woman had recovered most of her composure and was hurriedly climbing back into her trousers, which had been forcefully removed from her by her two assailants. She spat contemptuously in the face of one of her Javanese antagonists whilst directing a string of expletives at him. She then led the way to a small door in the rear of the house and unlocked it. The spry old Chinaman was discussing what had transpired with his wife, a Chinese woman in her sixties, when we entered the room.

The old Chinaman then gave the younger Chinese woman his full attention, listening while she related the sequence of events leading to our sudden arrival on the scene.

"You have arrived at a most opportune moment," he said in English. "Had you arrived yesterday, then the situation would have been most difficult. The Sekarno insurgents are moving on Surabaja, and a group of them surprised us just before dawn yesterday morning. Locked me in my room with my wife and held my second wife against my good behaviour."

"Can you walk?" I asked with concern.

"Of course I can walk," he replied indignantly.

"Good!" I said. "We are taking you out now, as we have no time left in which to argue or pack."

The old man stared at me with astonishment in his eyes.

"Ng sent me from Singaradja," I told him.

The old man nodded his head in agreement and then spoke rapidly to his two wives, who left the room immediately. There was nothing Idris or I could have done to circumvent the commotion that occurred in the front room of the house during the next few moments. The two Chinese women set upon the Javanese men we'd tied up with *parangs*—long, single-bladed Malay/Javanese machetes—literally hacking them to death.

The old man spoke. "The honour of a woman is her most valued possession." There was no hatred in his voice, just the quiet statement of fact, spoken for our benefit.

A matter of honour, not retribution? I wondered. If I had been just a little more fluent in the dialect the old man had used when speaking to his wives, I might have been able to prevent the killing. Of course, prisoners were rather a problem in such a situation, behind enemy territorial waters. My original intention had been to force my two prisoners to carry the old man if he was infirm and unable to walk to the coast. Then I would put out to sea with two prisoners on board.

When out in the deep blue waters, I would toss the two Javanese overboard and let them take their chances at swimming for shore. I was, of course, assuming they could both swim.

Never confuse my compassion for life as a weakness. I was more than willing to kill when necessary and have done so when the situation merited it.

The two Chinese women scouted the territory ahead of us on our journey back to the coast. The old Chinaman was quite agile, considering his age, and kept up with us all the way. I suppose both determination and nature gave that little something extra, enabling us all to get up and go.

We made the coast and the rendezvous point with time in hand, ten minutes to spare for our pickup from the sea—which seemed like an eternity. The boat was just a speck on the distant surface of the horizon, growing steadily larger. Zainal was making his run with the boat, and we were home free.

When he arrived, I settled the three Chinese passengers down in my own cabin, aware of the quiet care and attention the two women fostered upon their husband. These two women who now appeared so domestically docile were also capable of extreme hostility, as I'd seen earlier on during their rescue. Perhaps when all is said and done, the female of the species is far deadlier than the male!

I set course for Pulau Bawean, where I intended to drop off my three passengers and put back to sea immediately. The island was in Dutch hands, and grandfather Ng and his wives would be quite safe. But one of my pumps was playing up and required attention. On inspection, I discovered that the pump was functioning but pumping at a slower rate. So I spent the next busy hour changing the pump's diaphragm from my on-board repair kit, bringing that pump back to full capacity.

Saturday, 25 January 1947

It was now 0500 PST, and my boat lay off the coast of Pulau Bawean in the Sea of Java. Pulau Bawean is located approximately 150 kilometres north of Surabaya in the Java Sea, off the coast of

117

Java. My papers were in order, and we anchored off, waiting for dawn to throw some light on the scene. We had sufficient fuel to reach Pulau Badas in the Lingga Archipelago, though I decided to top up my tanks and have extra fuel on hand in case of the unexpected. At 0800 hours PST, Ng and his two wives took their departure to stay with relatives on the island. The job was over where they were concerned, and I had completed my part of the commitment.

I up-anchored at 1200 hours PST, and we were once more on our way. I set a new course for Pulau Belitung and the Karimata Straits, which is the wide strait that connects the South China Sea to the Java Sea, dividing the islands of Sumatra and Borneo (Kalimantan), both of which border the strait from Indonesian territory. The crew were happy, and I wanted to reach Singapore without any more of those devilish diversions. Below, my cook, Ali, was singing an old Malay folk song called *"Rasa Sayang, Hey!"* *"Rasa saying, sayang, hey! Hey, lihat nona jauh, Rasa saying, sayang, hey!"* It translated roughly to "I've got that loving feeling, hey!"

Sunday, 26 January 1947

It was 0300 hours PST, and we were off Pulau Karimundjawa, in the sea of Java, heading for Pulau Belitung, on course and making good headway. We passed the *SS Schiedyk* at 0430 hours PST, a 9,592-ton Dutch cargo liner heading for Bali. At noon I shot the midday sun with the sextant and calculated the position of the boat. We had 526 more miles to Singapore. At 1300 hours we passed well clear of Pulau Belitung and entered the Karimata Straits.

The dolphin is always an impressive sight to watch, made more so by the way dolphins join in each other's games. One moment they will be swimming alongside the boat inline, then one will leap into the air, and a second later they will all be bunched together, rolling and twisting about the sea and splashing each other. They will roll over on their backs but then leap vertically out of the water, landing back on the surface in a kind of belly flop and leaping out of the water in a perfect line-abreast formation. These are the common dolphin The Common Dolphin (*Delphinus delphis*), much smaller than the bottlenose dolphins of the South Pacific who inhabit tropical and warm temperate seas. Dolphins prefer deeper waters and shelf regions.

Common dolphins possess some 82 to 108 sharp, pointed teeth on each jaw; they eat a varied diet of squid and most varieties of fish. The weight of a common dolphin is approximately 160 pounds, and they can grow up to 8 feet in length. Their beaks are narrow and sharply cut off from the forehead. Their jaws have in my estimation perhaps 40 to 50 teeth on each side. They have a dark stripe running from eye to snout, and their backs are dark grey. This school of playful dolphins was with us most of the day, and we enjoyed having them around the boat. No sharks will be in the area when dolphins are around, and of course, they are good company.

We checked the oil and coolant levels of our engines and topped to the maximum where necessary. Our engine's health remained always my top priority; we would not get very far in any diesel/aviation fuel fully motorized boat without it, not in this former Motor Torpedo Boat anyway.

The weather at the moment was fair to fine, with a little headwind, but we were making good headway again, with everything on board being shipshape and in good working order. I scanned the horizon with my binoculars, but there was only the rolling sea.

Down below, all the men appeared to be busy either reading old newspapers, preparing food, or removing from the boat unwanted products or stale food. Hygiene in these waters was as important as dental health. We had no medical help on the ocean, and a toothache would be very difficult to treat.

I set myself to task cleaning our .303 Bren guns and lubing them in preparedness, should we ever need them in a hurry. I took in turn emptying some of my Bren gun magazines, to allow the springs to rest. It appears that even ammunition magazines on light machine guns have a memory.

A common mistake made by the lesser trained is to retain fully loaded ammunition magazines week in, week out. This historically has led to stoppages, something I can ill afford in a firefight. So my gun magazines got rested regularly. I placed new magazines in their stead on a rotation basis.

Once all the work was done and my boat was fully shipshape, I returned to the bridge of my craft to relieve my coxswain, Zainal, who then went down below for his rest period. I sat down on the bridge, daydreaming of home back in Britain and imagined a much brighter future for myself and my crew in the days to come. There is always that one final big score every soldier of fortune dreams about, the one he believes will set him and his family up for life. But that was not to be, at least not in this itinerant life I have carved out for myself.

Chapter 8

In a Previous Life
Monday, 27 January 1947

My wife, Pam

The name Pamela was apparently invented by Sir Philip Sidney for a character in his *The Countess of Pembroke's Arcadia* (1590). Samuel Richardson adopted it for the heroine of his first novel, *Pamela; or Virtue Rewarded* (1740), and the fashionable book led to its being used as a Christian name.

The name Sidony was formerly used by Roman Catholics for girls born around the date of the Feast of the Holy Winding Sheet of Christ, the Sacred Dendon of Turin. She prefers the name Pam to that of Sid or Sidony, the name tattooed under the two lovebirds and heart on my right arm. It is the only tattoo I have, and Sidonia Pamela will always have a place in my heart. The photograph was taken back on 18 January 1943. Of course she is a redhead. It is strange how in these quiet moments, she returns to haunt me. No, I could never truthfully hate her, and I doubt very much if she could ever hate me.

Barry Island, 1934

This photograph was taken at Barry Island in 1934 and 1935. From left to right at the back are Auntie Maud in her wheelchair, leaning on the arm of which is my mother, Beatrice. In the front we have Cassandra and Belinda, two friends of Nancy, who is seated next, with her arms around me. We are on the annual chapel outing, a day by the sea at Barry, and it was indeed strange and a little frightening to suddenly hear a trainload of Welsh chapel people singing hymns as we passed through the darkness of the Severn Tunnel on the Great Western Railway.

The length of the Severn Tunnel in its entirety is about four and a third miles, with some two and a quarter miles under the River Severn. The remaining length of about half a mile remains in Gloucestershire, with the rest in Monmouthshire, making a total length of approximately seven miles.

Nancy and I were first cousins. The minister, Mr Griffiss, was forever preaching the wrath of God and the wages of sin. He was the one who publicly denounced courting couples from the chapel pulpit; this seemed to be one of his delights. "Burn in hellfire, they will!" he would shout at the top of his voice.

Tuesday, 28 January 1947

The soft breeze was out of the south-east at the time, hardly above a gentle whisper, and we had no great rollers to worry about. We were between two islands, Pulau Lingga and Pulau Pedjantan, in the Lingga Archipelago. This was pirate territory and we were again running without our navigation lights.

Catnapping on the bridge of my craft, I remembered as vividly as if they'd happened yesterday moments from my past, and in such moments my wife, Pam! I then quickly turned my mind to other things.

Annie was five years older than me and I was ten years of age when I saw my first vagina. I was literally amazed, though not impressed. It was hot but nice to the touch. It was 1938 when I finally lost my boyhood. Annie had trained to become a nurse and was down in the Midlands on holiday. It was one of those indigo starlight nights, when the moon was in the last throes of its monthly wane.

Annie used to wear a camisole! This was a kind of undergarment young girls wore when they were growing up, a rather close-fitting combination of bodice and drawers all in one, with a flap fastened in the appropriate place by two buttons. Annie married a chap named Jones back in 1940 and returned to the valleys with him. Annie was my very first sexual experience.

It was one of those family get-togethers back in 1939, before the war broke out. We were at our house in the Midlands. I remember Annie at that time was wearing a pair of French knickers; she had told me that camisoles were out of fashion. She took my pillow and lay down across my bed with both her feet on the floor. Seeing her take her knickers off was quite a thrill for me. Her vagina was no longer the bald thing she had let me feel and finger all those years ago. Like Annie, it had grown up, and her mound of Venus was now carpeted in fine black, silky hairs. I could have sworn it was winking at me! I thought it funny how she called her clitoris "the man in the boat". I thought it looked like a hairy bird's nest. Were there hungry fledglings waiting to be fed?

"Now, put it in gently, dear, just below the man in the boat," she said. Annie then told me, "When you feel you are coming, for God's sake, pull it out quickly!"

When I entered, her vagina was warm with a moist stickiness. I felt it grip, like a small terrier gnawing at a bone. It tickled and felt silky soft, with a smooth, slippery kind of tightness. I could feel it drawing me in with every breath she took, breathing heavily in the sexual embrace. However, I didn't pull out as she had asked me to. Perhaps it was rather neglectful of me? But then Annie was nineteen and I was fourteen at the time. It was, however, my first and last time with Annie, and we did it proper! Despite the fact that the whole experience was more mechanical than erotic, it remained memorable nonetheless. People say that you never forget your first sexual encounter. Perhaps this is true, as I have found that you tend to recollect best the first time you venture out into the unknown.

Church Street Ebbw Vale, 1940

This is Church Street of Ebbw Vale in 1940. Down the hill into High Street and to the left was, of course, Eureka Road (not the place where Archimedes uttered the word *heureka* when he discovered means of determining specific gravity and thus the proportion of base metals in Hiero's golden crown). The Tabernacle is the

Congregational Church, or chapel, in Ebbw Vale. Congregational churches are Protestant Christian; they practise Congregationalist Church governance, that is to say, each congregation runs its affairs independently and autonomously.

Ebbw Vale is not without its colourful characters, like William Williams, who is called "Billy whole-half an egg". When asked what he wanted for breakfast one morning, Billy replied, "A whole-half an egg." Of course the name stuck! Yanto was another character. He was called "Yanto full pelt". Late for work one morning, he took to his heels, sprinting all the way, but arrived just as they were closing the gates. "I ran full pelt!" he exclaimed rather breathlessly. Of course that name stuck too.

Wednesday, 29 January 1947

I had decided against Pulau Badas, and we were well into the Riau Archipelago, a core group of islands within the Riau Islands Province in Indonesia, south of Singapore. We expected to pass Tanjung Pinang on Pulau Bintan around noon, with any luck. We had sufficient fuel to reach Singapore and were making good headway. One of my first priorities was to beach the boat for general maintenance as well as an engine refit, renewal of spare parts, and repairs where necessary. I didn't expect to do much to her other than an engine refit.

I am always meticulous when it comes to the well-being of my boat. Good, fully operational engines are a must in my game, as there would be no Royal Navy rescue vessel to save us should the worst happen at sea.

We reached Pulau Badas at 1000 hours PST. The expression on the face of my helmsman, Zainal, was quite something when he found that I was not about to change course and put into the island. I could read his mind like a book. He was always aware that I might pick up the odd job and change course on some other diversion.

But then, I was just as anxious to reach Singapore. At noon I shot the sun with my sextant and took the necessary reading from the decimal micrometer, the dotted lines indicating the direction of light from the sun (or if at night, a star on the horizon). I plotted the course on the chart and was rather pleased with the result. We should reach Singapore at dawn the next day.

At approximately 1600 hours PST, Zainal spotted a submarine on the surface approximately half a mile off our port side. I took a damn good look at her through my navy binoculars. The submarine appeared to be a Netherlands K XV class; she was capable of a good surface speed. Now, Dutch submarines of the Second World War appeared similar to the German U-boats that had been responsible for so many Allied merchant ships ending up on the bottom of the North Atlantic. This diesel-powered submarine, however, had a U.S. Pacific Fleet flavour to her; she was most likely a former United States Navy Balao class that had been converted for the Dutch Navy here.

She was moving fast in the opposite direction, and I breathed a sigh of relief. The last thing that I wanted now was to tangle with the Dutch so near to my home port of Singapore. The Dutch Pacific submariners had a formidable track record of destroying Japanese merchant ships during the last war, more than both the British and American Navies at the time. This made them to me a most battle-tested and dangerous enemy. Had she seen me? Of course she had seen me, but again, I could outrun her should the need arise. I had every intention of trading in these waters, and with the old Red Duster fluttering from our ensign staff, we went on our way unmolested.

Lynn Pireara, Roy's mistress, thought Roy was at the *kelong*, which is a large offshore fishing platform. These have several compartments; the fish are hustled from the outer compartments into the innermost and caught in a large net. I reassured her that there was no real cause for concern and explained that it would take us a few days to clear up the problem. Roy was wanted by the Singapore port authorities for trying to escape a board and search by the Singapore customs and excise people. In the meantime, I'd keep Roy safe. After dinner that evening, I talked the problem over with my housekeeper and suggested that it was a question of a safe house for a few days.

She thought it unlikely that anyone would be looking for Roy at her old place near the harbour, and of course her brother could use a little extra cash in hand, as he was financially embarrassed at the moment. She talked it over with her brother and later that evening gave me the front door keys of the safe house. She suggested that I pay her brother at the office at Tanjong Pagar at 0830 hours the next morning and that we check the back room of the house before taking Roy there.

The kelong

I dropped in at the fishing stake of a mutual Chinese friend off East Coast Road, and there I saw Roy.

"I saw you coming in this afternoon," he said. "What took you so long?"

"Plenty!" I told him. "I suppose you know they impounded your boat! What happened?"

"Well, it was like this," he said. "We were off Pulau Bukum at 0300 hours on Saturday, the fifteenth, when our port engine suddenly packed in, and I went down to the engine room to see what was wrong. Of course that silly Malay bastard was asleep! He had forgotten to switch over the fuel tanks, and it took me another ten minutes or so to bleed and restart the engine. By this time we had drifted close in towards the island. I had just managed to get underway again when the Excise boat took up the chase. Well, I decided to make a run for it, ran her up the beach at Pasir Panjang, and took off with my crew, every man for himself!"

"What about your machine guns?" I asked

"Overboard in the usual way, off Pasir Panjang," he replied.

"So your boat's clean then?" I said.

"Clean!" he replied.

"What's the cargo?" I asked.

"A bloody full load of batik sarongs," he replied.

"If you stay here," I said, "there is a good chance of you being picked up by Excise during one of their spot checks. I am going to move you to a safe house near the harbour first thing in the morning. Where your impounded boat is concerned, I will get the necessary Dutch export papers from our usual source, pay the import duty, and recover the boat and cargo."

"What about the charges against me?" Roy said.

"Any Bugis *praus* in the area at the time?" I asked.

"No!" he replied.

"Pity!" I said. "We would have claimed that they followed you up from Java and that you were attempting to outrun them."

"I guess we will have to do a little horse-trading with the Excise people and top up their rainy-day fund." *Everybody has a price*, I thought. *The trick is knowing exactly what their needs are and what that price is.* I am not talking about money here, in case you are wondering.

"Give them information, and they will keep coming back for more," Roy said. Live intelligence was after all a priceless commodity, especially where the drug trades were concerned.

"Oh, by the way," I said, "some friend of ours are in the market for penicillin. Any ideas?"

"Try T. S. Clark," Roy advised.

Thursday, 30 January 1947

Roy Walton, my partner in this Southern Pacific Ocean

island-hopping venture, came from Manchester and had seen active service with the Manchester Regiment as they deployed against the invading Imperial Japanese Army landings during WWII in Malaya. But as the British lost the Malayan Campaign (8 December 1941 to 31 January 1942), Roy was taken prisoner by the Japanese during the fall of Singapore. How he survived his internment under brutal Japanese occupation is another story! But we all do what we must under such circumstances, don't we?

Survival through adversity is one of the most basic instincts in any human being. Roy and I first met each other at Princes Bar in Orchard Road, early in 1946. He was then living with a Portuguese–Eurasian girl, Lynne Perera, at a rather large rooming house in Sophia Road. Roy and Lynn had met just before the Japanese had decided to invade Malaya. Lynn was a young woman with a small child, who had been turned out of her own home by her parents. I suppose the stigma attached to their daughter was too much for them to bear; she was an alleged rape victim and unmarried mother who'd caused them shame. So, for appearance' sake, they'd made their daughter homeless.

The English father and alleged rapist had been quickly shipped out of Singapore by his firm, and the child was taken into care by the nuns at the Convent of the Good Shepherd at Bras Basah Road. It is rather strange and a little ironic how circumstances seem to throw the unfortunate of this world together in the same melodramatic melting pot.

Lynne Pireara, Roy's mistress

Lynn was homeless, and Roy was AWOL—absent without leave—from his unit when they first met each other. Roy found her a place to live, and she made life more bearable where he was concerned. Then, of course, the Japanese arrived on the scene, but she still managed at great risk to herself and Roy to keep in touch with him whilst he was in the prisoner of war camp at Changi Prison. It would have cost them both severe punishment or even brutal death under the rules of the Japanese had they been caught carrying out contact with Japanese prisoners of war by secret rendezvous.

For once in all the bloody and brutal mayhem that was occupied Singapore, fate was kind to them both. Roy was already acquainted with Thomas Story Clarke and his manager, who traded under the name of AB Company on a large plot of land in Henderson Road. Their premises boasted several large wooden and *attap* dwellings and warehouses that Clarke had suddenly acquired when the Japanese left so hurriedly when the British returned to the island in 1945.

An attap dwelling is a kind of traditional Malay house found in the kampong villages of Brunei, Indonesia, Malaya, and Singapore. It is named after the attap palm that is used as wattle for the walls. Attap leaves are used to thatch the roofs. Attap-style houses range from huts to large dwelling houses.

T. S. Clarke was a Liverpool Irishman who spoke Cantonese; he had been a sanitary inspector in Hong Kong prewar. He arrived in Singapore in 1940, having received the order of the boot from the Hong Kong authorities, for corruption. When the Japanese arrived in Singapore in 1942, Clarke claimed he was an Irishman and member of the Irish Republican Army (IRA), an illegal paramilitary organization whose aim was to unite Northern and Southern Ireland by means of armed conflict against the British Empire.

This ruse found favour with the Japanese, who bought into his anti-British story and left him to his own devices. Clarke immediately set up home with a Portuguese–Eurasian woman and her small son and went into the business of acquisitioning every electrode he could get his hands on.

At 0400 hours PST we were well clear of Pulau Ayer Chawan and travelling admidst many Malay fishing boats inwards bound after a night fishing the Straits of Malacca. These fishermen equally disliked the Customs and Excise people and if questioned would give them the three brass monkeys: seeing no evil, hearing no evil, and at all costs, speaking no evil. There are two points of contention on this route in and out of Singapore.

Friday, 31 January 1947

The Shell Oil refinery with its very high security on Pulau Bukum and the road bridge over the narrow point of the estuary in West Coast road.

This is so near to home, would not those bright sparks in Customs and Excise think it way too obvious? We made Kampong Tanjong Penuru when the brandy-ball made its first appearance in the morning sky, my boat running dead slow under the bridge in the early dawn light. A little less than ten minutes later, we had tied up to our moorings, and our journey had ended. At 1200 hours PST I paid off my crew in full and decided that, come what may, it would be seven days or more before we put off to sea again. We had arrived during the tail end of the monsoon season, when those sudden swells would sweep in from the sea. It was the only place I knew where it could rain on one side of the road but at the same time remain quite dry on the other.

This was also a time for dragonflies. These come in swarms with the monsoon rains. The ocean-going dragonflies have orange bodies and bright-red eyes. They are known as globe skimmers *(Pantala flavescens)* or wandering gliders and were first described by Johan Christian Fabricius in 1798. As the name might suggest, this dragonfly species is found pretty much around the world. Globe skimmer dragonflies thrive throughout all the tropical oceans, the Americas, Africa, Asia, Australia, and into the Pacific, wandering far and wide. Some say they wander thousands of kilometres in their lifetime. I find these dragonflies on the wing fascinating to observe, as they in some ways remind me of my true itinerant free-spirited self.

I telephoned a marine engineer friend named Yan Jensen over in Tanjong Rhu. Yan operated a boatyard, and I needed his services to ensure the seaworthiness of my MTB but especially to perform the necessary repairs and full servicing or replacements of all three of my power-horse marine engines. I regularly serviced and maintained well my boat engines, so my best guess was that, despite the recent hammering they had taken on the high seas during our last voyage, they couldn't be too far off maximum efficiency. But I could not be too careful. If there was the potential for something to go wrong with them, I needed to know well beforehand, in this game.

Jansen told me that this would be no problem, as a client had recently cancelled maintenance on one of his boats, which would allow him to fully service my engines at the preferential mate's rates. He and I went back many years; I always used only trusted people in this game. That arrangement being concluded, I set about my business whilst still in town to find more work for myself and the crew. Despite the slowdown in specialist jobs out there, the kind nobody else wants to take on due to the high risks involved, something always turns up for me.

Rain clouds breaking over Singapore

The dark area immediately below the cloud belt is one of those sudden downpours of heavy rain. All we needed at that point was high wind and we would have had a *sumatra*.

This photograph was taken from Fort Canning Road. On the immediate left you can see St Joseph Secondary School in Bras Basah Road. The school was run by the Portuguese Mission. On the right is the French Cathedral of the Good Shepherd.

The Portuguese Cathedral of St Joseph is the one in the centre with the black roof. In the front right-hand corner is the French Convent of the Holy Infant Jesus. Waterloo Road, to the left of St Joseph's School, was where the Jewish community of Singapore lived. Then, in the background, you see the infernal streets of brothel houses; Albert Street, Bugis Street, and the night market, where you could buy anything you'd like to name—at a price.

Saturday, 1 February 1947

Malacca Street was always a busy place, with its traders, wholesalers, ship handlers, and brokerage firms of the Indian Chulia community. This was where the brokers' fees or commissions were made by wheeling and dealing, most of which was honest money. But as always, there were a few human sharks in the game, out for a quick killing in the spice trade and the other nuts and bolts of Asian cuisine. Black pepper, white pepper, cloves of garlic, coriander, ginger, cayenne, cumin, almonds, macadamia nuts, coconut, cilantro, limes, and dark-brown sugar were among the goods traded here. The Lee Wah bank was in Chulia Street, along with a number of Chinese brokerage firms in the rice game.

The Chinese financiers also dealt with any other commodity that would bring back a quick return on the money invested. Again, most of the traders were honest, with only a few sharks. But then, these sharks exist in every community under the sun, don't they? Where the Chinese Khek [means guest people] who migrated from South Eastern China to Malaya was concerned, they were just a little more apparent. Kheks tended to keep to themselves distrusting outsiders and were considered a displaced people with no citizenship status in Malaya back then.

The G.H. Café, in Battery Road just off Raffles Place, was the centre of all kinds of wheeling and dealing. In 1947, the manager was an Armenian with a rather bad limp and a dubious reputation for shady dealings with the wrong sort of people. He had been knocked down by an ambulance full of wounded during the Japanese invasion of Singapore. He was quite a useful person contact-wise, though I would never trust him with anything big. I managed to pick up another job at the G.H. Café over a Tiger beer. They wanted me to lift a Dutch–Eurasian family from one of the islands in the Straits of Karimata. It was a family that had to get out of Sunda in rather a hurry, and I was to run them across to Johore in Malaya. I told them it would take a week for me to put another crew together, and I suggested a couple of other people for the game. My clients replied that they wanted the best and were prepared to wait. Flattery at my time of life? But it was nice to know!

An early painting I photographed at Raffles Museum back in 1945, entitled "The Esplanade from Scandal Point" (1851), by John Turnbull Thomson, showing the people of Singapore in its younger colonial days, when Raffles was top man.

John Turnbull Thomson's painting is kept today at The National Museum of Singapore. When I first viewed the painting, it was at Raffles Museum, which has now closed down. It depicts the period when John Turnbull Thomson (1821–1884) was the government surveyor for the Eastern Settlements. The painting represents the residents of Singapore relaxing at the *padang*, which is a Malay word for a flat field. Singapore's founder under the British was Sir Thomas Stamford Raffles (1781–1826). It was Raffles who wanted this padang to be reserved for recreational use.

The painting also shows the colonial part of old Singapore town during a time when the British ruled here, in 1851. Scandal Point is a small hill located at the edge of the padang Its name probably came about over many years of being used as a gathering place for local chit-chat. A family group is shown, with one man holding a spear. This is most likely one of the *orang-laut* or sea gypsies. These sea gypsies may have been earlier inhabitants of the island, immigrants who had settled along the coastline of Singapore island in precolonial times. The orang laut community typically lived off a long dwelling boat, known colloquially as a *sampan panjang*.

During the late nineteenth century, Arab traders from Yemen migrated to Java and Sumatra. Raffles, the lieutenant governor of Java, met these Arab traders and encouraged them to trade and to stay. A plethora of Muslims traders from Java, Sumatra, and Borneo stayed as a consequence, while waiting for boats to take them to Mecca. There are also Chinese shown in the picture. The Chinese followed Farquhar, Raffles' right-hand man and former resident of Malacca, to Singapore. Because of their ability to speak Malay, Hokkien, and English, Muslim traders were able to find productive and well-paid work as middlemen for both Chinese and English traders.

Singapore's first Indians were soldiers and sepoys who came with Raffles and Farquhar. George Drumgoole Coleman (1795–1844) was the principal architect of all the buildings shown in this painting. Coleman was responsible, as advisor to Raffles, for the draft layout of Singapore in 1822, and he planned the centre of the town, created roads, and constructed many fine buildings. Coleman, who was appointed the superintendent of Public Works in 1833, realized that more labourers were needed in Singapore.

Coleman used convicts from British India extensively on the island to shore up the shortfall of labour and of course to save money; this was in essence slave labour. Most of early Singapore's public roads, buildings, and bridges, many of which have stood the test of time, were built by Indian convict labour during the colonial days of the British Empire.

I was looking for a good radar set uniquely designed for a small boat and came up with just the job over another beer. It was compact and used a very light radome which, of course, meant it used very little power. A radome is a structural, weatherproof enclosure that protects a radar system or antenna. It is constructed of material that minimally attenuates the electromagnetic signal transmitted or received by the antenna. Above all, it has a variable range marker and electronic bearing marker. When you press the button until the ring intersects the target, the distance is shown on the digital readout. A target that continues to approach on a steady compass bearing is on a collision course with you, and you can take positive steps early to avoid action. That meant no more having to run my boat through poor visibility!

Dinner was on the *thali* when I arrived home: chicken curry, curried meatballs, green pea and curd cheese curry, spiced lentils, milk fudge sweetmeats, stuffed pastry envelopes, yogurt salad, mango pickles, fresh coriander chutney, unleavened bread that was flaky and buttery, and raisin rice with peas. Incidentally, a *thali* is an Indian and Nepalese meal made up of a selection of various dishes. Its actual meaning is simply the round platter used to serve the food. The idea behind a thali is to offer all the six different flavours of sweet, salt, bitter, sour, astringent, and spicy on one single plate. According to Indian food serving customs, a proper meal should be a perfect balance of all these six flavours. A fruit is often served at the end of meal.

Gloria, my housekeeper, provides an exceptionally good table but always keeps fish off her list of dishes. She does so when I am home in appreciation of the fact that fish is our main source of fresh food while we are at sea. Of course, spiced food should always be offset by bland, wet by dry, and soft by crisp, but if you happen to eat with your fingers, as the locals do, never eat with your left hand. Try to remember that in this part of the world your left hand is considered unclean, probably because it is used for the more basic bodily functions like using the toilet.

But enough about food and the formal rules of proper culinary behaviour at the moment. I am more concerned with the science which deals with moral principles. I am, of course, a free spirit in every sense of the word.

Echo sounders were my immediate problem. I needed a good echo sounder with both an accurate depth range while the boat was cruising and an audible alarm in variable shallow water. I had a little contraband that was bound for one of the islands plus a contract to lift a Dutch–Eurasian family out and back to Johore. This meant I would have to run the gauntlet where the opposition was concerned. Running a coral reef, even with a shallow draught boat, is not easy at high speeds. The echo sounder would make such a journey just that little bit safer and allow us to literally see in the dark.

A large, brightly coloured dragonfly in full flight flew into the room through the open window and hovered over the glass top of the coffee table in the reflected beam of a shaft of sunlight. Caught in the weft of a gentle breeze, it flowed out of the room through the other window. Strange though it may seem, the dragonfly in nymph form is rather a predator.

Yah my housekeeper is twenty-one days overdue with her menstruation, which should have arrived around the eleventh of January. She doesn't seem concerned for now, because at forty-three, she is in control of her own life. But of course, conception can occur even after the age when menstruation should cease. The menopause part of ageing usually occurs between 45 and 55 years of age as a woman's oestrogen levels decline.

I took Yah and her adopted daughter into the better part of Chinatown for a meal of Szechuan food, which tends to be rather hot and spicy. Their favourite dishes included prawns and chicken fried in oil, with dry green and red chilies along with lashings of smoked duck. There is nothing spectacular about Singapore Chinese restaurants; you can hardly call an atmosphere of steam noodles being hoisted from a seasoned wok elegant. But the food is indeed good and is served in what is best described as some adventurous surroundings.

Chinese dishes in this region are always perfectly cooked in their respective regional styles; you do not have to eat Szechuan. You can go Cantonese, Hainanese, or Teochew whenever you wish to spice up your options for oriental culinary delights.

There were Chinese women, clad in black *sampoos* with red headdresses, working on the construction sites close by and in full view. These were the Samsui sisters, who had chosen this lifestyle in preference to marriage. Believe me, they were strong and could do this kind of heavy work better than most men. The Samsui women, from Sanshui of Guangdong (Canton) Province in China, came to Singapore to work as cheap labourers from the 1920s to the 1940s and mainly worked on construction.

Chinatown is one of the places where Europeans could attempt to immerse themselves in the culture of Old China with all her traditions. They were building a war memorial out at Kranji, Singapore, to honour the men and women from the Commonwealth who died in the line of duty during World War II. It's so very little for the many who gave all they had to give, including their young lives and their tomorrows cut so short.

Romulda de Castro, a relative of my housekeeper gave birth to a boy at 1000 hours PST today. The newborn weighed in at six pounds four ounces, and she had an easy birth. This is her third child by John Peutra, who is still on the run following his working and collaborating with the Japanese during the war.

Sunday, 2 February 1947

Yah and her daughter, Teris, went to St Theresa Catholic Church this morning in Kampong Bahru for morning mass. But this old barbarian here did not go along with them. It is not that I do not believe in the one God—or the old gods, for that matter. My God has gotten me out of one or more difficult, life-threatening situations, and yes, when necessity warrants it, I pray for divine intervention in my fate at that time. Perhaps that is selfish of me, but at least I am honest about it.

The Jingbang

After all, have we not all been gifted with the free choice of what we believe or choose not to believe in? Who else but God would give us our free will? The *jingbang*? One of Yah's many expressions [referring to the made up word jingbang]is down at her place in Nelson Road, on a visit from Kuala Lumpur, so I am told. The Ottiagor family, in the form of Enjang's mother and her sister Pat Benang; her brother Bernard, along with his Chinese wife, Bunny; as well as Enjang's firstborn, Joseph, who lives with old lady Ottiager in Kuala Lumpur. The lad is six years of age. Barbara is two years of age and Enjang's second child. The two children are to be seen in the photograph below with Enjang, who is to the left of her sister Pat.

Enjang gave birth to a son at three this afternoon. The boy is called Daniel and was adopted by her brother Bernard and his wife, who have no children of their own. It seems that Manong who is the brother of my housekeeper Yah, gives his male children away? Bernard is a musician with the band at the Great World Cabaret now, and they are staying at Nelson Road while he looks around for a house of his own.

It will soon be Thaipusam, which is an important Indian festival for Hindus. They gather at various temples to participate in their rituals of penance and thanksgiving. The highlight of this festival is the awesome *kavadi* procession, during which devotees carry yokes of steel skewers embedded in their own flesh while in a state of trance. At darkness, the temple deity is taken in an illuminated chariot through the streets of the city from Hindu temple to Hindu temple. Come Thaipusam this year, I hope to be on my way from Singapore back to Burma.

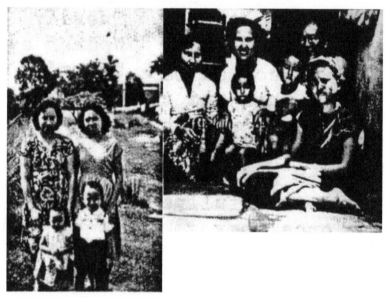

Top left: Enjang and Pat. Top right: from left to right, Enjang, Bunny, Bernard, Barbara, Joseph, and Enjang's sister Benang.

My home at Seri Menanti in Singapore

Monday, 3 February 1947

The Malay word *seri* is taken from the Sanskrit and means charm, beauty, glory, or the best of everything. The Malay word *menanti* means to sit waiting. *Tupai nandong* is "at play in the trees", or the large squirrel, and then we have *nangka*, the jackfruit. My home at Seri Menanti in Singapore is a place of peace, *niat*, from the Arabic word meaning desire, wish, longing, or aspiration. *Niatkan* means to will. Strength of will, or willpower, to use a better word, is something to be reckoned with, provided you are prepared to be a pragmatist and are not preoccupied with lesser things. This requires a lot of commitment in personal time management and single-minded effort if you are to be effective. You must take the problem in question and subject it to scrutiny from every conceivable angle of approach, allowing for the pros and cons.

Now, once you have established the essence of the problem, split it down into its various components so that the weakness of the problem becomes fully apparent. Focus on the weakness, and the structural elements of the problem can be resolved one by one without difficulty. It is just a question of willpower or mind over matter!

The bungalow on the side of a hill overlooking the village was the home of a Japanese official during the war. He did the honourable thing and committed seppuku, or ritual suicide, when the British arrived in 1945. Seppuku, sometimes incorrectly vulgarised by the West as hara-kiri, is the brutal and bloody Japanese ritual suicide by disembowelment, originally reserved for samurais, who sometimes appointed a second to oversee the procedure.

The house was supposed to be haunted, but up to then I had seen no Japanese appearing out of the woodwork in strange forms! I was the only one haunting the place, but that was just as well, for it kept the inquisitive ones away from the place. The local people didn't dare come anywhere near it, and this was quite a good thing. The dead harm no one; it is always the living we need to concern ourselves with.

Tuesday, 4 February 1947

But what I did find here instead was his 1925 design Type 14, 8x22 mm Nambu pistol, complete with several boxes of WWII Japanese 8 mm bottleneck brass cartridges. The Japanese Nambu pistol—although way underpowered with the smaller 103 grains (6.67 gram) jacketed bullet filled with the 3.5 grains (0.23 grams) of smokeless powder—produced muzzle velocities of about 1065 fps (325 m/s).

By comparison, the Allies' more rugged and harder-hitting 1911 Colt Government .45 was, in my opinion, a very reliable pistol in her class. Her semi-auto action never failed me.

But my 8 mm Nambu pistol was also remarkably accurate. The Nambu pistol designer was Lieutenant General Kijiro Nambu, circa 1925, during the fourteenth year of the Taisho emperor. It was adopted by the Imperial Japanese Army and widely used during all South East Asia campaigns and through the Second World War as their standard military sidearm. This Type 14 Japanese Nambu pistol has kept me from harm's way in a few awkward situation throughout my life. But then after all, accurate bullet placement in the kill area is everything!

Autumn Leaves

Autumn is a season passing,
Children playing, crying, laughing;
Yellow, brown, and crinkled leaves;
Winter's nearing smells the breeze.

Curled up on the outer edge,
Like a leaf discarded by the tree,
Breath worn with age and summer,
Gone forever the glory that was spring.

Now at rest and gently floating,
Gently floating, gently floating,
Blown on the breeze, away, away,
Crinoids tree, wintering.

Existence and non-existence,
Life without suffering,
Glowing embers on the pyre;
Yet still my desire. Pray, tell me,
Why do we have to die?

Wednesday, 5 February 1947

The evil of this world of ours centres around three things, according to Penghulu Muhammed Shebbears, friend and quite a philosopher. The three things are money, power, and women. I rather tactfully suggested greed could be added to the list.

"Ah, yes!" he said. "A strong desire to obtain a lot more than our share of money, power, and women! We are, for want of a better word, gregarious, living in groups and enjoying the companionship of others."

"But you have three wives," I pointed out. "Is that greed or gregariousness?"

He smiled, accordingly choosing his words carefully. "It is not either," he said with a laugh. "I am allowed four wives by Islamic law, each of which must be treated with equity. I have only three wives—to have four would be greedy!"

"Which one of your three wives is your favourite?" I asked.

Penghulu laughed, responding, "You Europeans know so little about such things! They are all my favourites, each wife with her own very special quality. No two women are ever the same; each one is unique. I married my first wife back in 1932, and we were happy together, but she was barren. We both wanted children, and under the law of Islam, I am entitled to take another wife. I married my second wife in 1936, and she gave me children."

"Didn't your first wife become jealous?" I asked.

"Of course not," he said. "She was just as much the mother of my children and shared the responsibility for their care and upbringing with my second wife."

"But your second wife must have become jealous of her?" I said. "After all, they were her children."

"That is why I took my third wife," he said, "so that they would each have nothing to be jealous about."

"So, when are you taking your fourth wife?" I asked.

"That is the threat which ensures the good relationship between all my three wives," he said with a laugh.

Throughout the Islamic world, from Morocco to Java, Muslim men could have up to four wives, and many among the ruling class boasted a far greater number. Similarly, a Hindu man was allowed as many wives as he wished, and all the children they bore him were legitimate. Traditional Chinese society favoured a family system in which a man married a principal wife but also had a number of secondary wives, or concubines. Polygamy has always been a feature of the most populated religions in the world. It was only the Christian nations that constantly rejected the multiple marriage arrangement as a permissible alternative to the union of one man and one woman.

Still, in the greater part of Asia, polygamy remains the most prestigious form of marriage, and men of wealth or political power normally support many wives. But even so, in those societies which place a premium on the possession of many wives, the normal balance in the number of men and women has compelled most men to content themselves with just one wife. Indeed, where powerful chiefs monopolized too many women, others might be unable to marry until they were well into middle age.

Polygamy, specifically the marriage of one man to several women, is the most common form of multiple marriage, while polyandry, the marriage of one woman to several husbands, is rarer. It is restricted to certain tribes, wherein it is common for two brothers to marry one woman. Indeed, the desire of brothers to keep their inherited estate intact is often the primary motive for their taking of only one wife between them. Most Islamic communities allow men greater freedom in sexual matters; this has always been the status quo and it remains so to the present day.

Interestingly, there always remains a puritanical and most rigid insistence on the chastity of women equalled by few other societies. Unmarried daughters are strictly guarded by their parents, and any sexual lapse on their part dishonours the whole family; it may even be avenged by the killing of both the girl and the seducer. Under Islamic doctrine, once married, a woman remains under the complete control of her husband. If she is unfaithful to him, the wronged husband can restore his honour by the simple device of divorce. The obligation to punish her then lies with her brothers, and amongst the Malays there are many cases of brothers killing their own sisters for having sullied the family's honour. Harems are for the powerful and are guarded by eunuchs, who deny any woman in the harem the right to act as free agents. These women are placed under the total physical control of men to whom their kinsman handed them over as brides or concubines.

Singapore waterfront

This is a painting I photographed at Raffles Museum back in 1945. It shows the Singapore waterfront during the days of Raffles. The large eye on the front of the Chinese junk are so that it can see where it is going in a mythical sense—either towards danger or good fortune.

I spent the evening at the Club in a party for old George Apple, who is retiring from the Singapore Harbour Board. George on this occasion was with his mistress, Fame Alvares, a very charming Filipino woman, with a figure like a Spanish guitar and well-rounded hips that swayed tantalizingly with every step that she took. Fame Alvares danced around with George most of the time but was quite the able conversationalist during those moments between dances. This was "Fame the flame", a renowned courtesan of stature, and I felt rather attracted to her. However, George was quite attentive and monopolized most of the evening—but then, she was his mistress. But George was going back home to England on his retirement. I had at this point formulated a plan of action in my mind. One way or the other, I was going to have this woman!

Singapore River from Fort Canning hill

The large building on the left in the background is Mansfield's Blue Funnel Shipping Line, with the lighthouse on top. The other lighthouse is at the end of Clifford pier, on the right. The bank of the river in the background is called South Boat Quay, and this side in the foreground is North Boat Quay.

The river itself is tidal, with a rather strong current running during its ebb and flow. You did not want to ever fall into this river—not so much because the water was dangerous but because you never knew what you would come out of the water with. This included every known disease plus a few you have never heard of. The Singapore Sweetwater River was so damn contaminated and stinking that sharks wouldn't swim in it, even though they are scavengers!

Thursday, 6 February 1947

Yan Jensen had checked out all the marine electrical systems on my boat, replaced the oil and fuel filters, done the sea water pumps, checked the crankshafts of each engine, replaced a dodgy bearing as well as servicing my bilge pumps, and finally declared the boat ready for sea again. "She will outrun any revenue boat!" Yan said with a laugh on his face.

"It's not the revenue boats I need to concern myself with!" I told him. I paid Yan off with cash for his diligence in bringing my boat back to seaworthiness and spent the next two hours at the Department of Fishery, concerning my lease on the Pulau Darah abalone beds.

Now *darah* is a Malay word meaning blood, and *Pulau Darah* therefore means Blood Island. The Japanese had a prisoner of war camp on that island, and of course the local fishermen all believed that the island was haunted. C. H. Koh, a friend and eminent barrister, shook with laughter but agreed to draw up the necessary legal contract between Fame Alvares and myself and have it served that afternoon.

C. H. and I had been friends during the Force 136 days of World War II in the Far East, and we were both noted for our sense of humour. When the Imperial Armies of Japan entered the war towards the end of 1941, they swooped all over South East Asia, cutting through British, Dutch, and French colonies like wildfire. South East Asia was different: infiltration teams, such as the Special Operations Executive (SOE) based in Europe, of necessity had to blend in with the local population. White Caucasian officers would not fit the bill, as they would be spotted almost immediately. As well, former white colonists might find it difficult to gain the support of the locals to form armed resistance against the Japanese.

A new approach was needed, and it was decided by the British High Command Far East to target sizeable groups of local Chinese who were vehemently opposed to the Japanese Occupation of their island homes. Then the idea of using Chinese Canadians came into play—they could easily blend into the local populations of the Far East, speaking Cantonese, but most importantly they were loyal to the Allies and could be trusted. Between 1944 and 1945 some 150 handpicked Chinese Canadians, keen volunteers, were recruited, sworn to secrecy, highly trained up to commando standards for jungle survival, and secretly seconded to SOE South East Asia. They were known as Force 136.

These handpicked men were trained in silent killing, stalking, demolition, wireless operation, parachuting, and unarmed combat. In short, they were highly motivated, well-trained, dangerous men, whose sole purpose was to disrupt and hurt enemies inside their own strongholds as well as to provide vital live-time intelligence to the Allies on Japanese strengths and movements.

"You are aware that this woman is much older than you?" C. H. asked me.

"Yes, of course," I replied. "Most likely it is just some manifestation of the mothering instinct!"

That remark had been the cause of all the laughter. The usual crew had been assembled in the G.H. Café when I arrived, and the chatter took on a class of its own. This was where quick business dealings were done and commodities changed hands over lunchtime drinks. Low Seack Chuan had a deal for me, if I was interested, a trip into Burma the next March. The commodity was secret for the moment.

"I don't run drugs!" I informed him and asked who had recommended me.

"The word came in from a reliable friend," he said. "Lee Fatt. The tauke of Pulau Lombok and his bunch of gunrunners."

"I am not running up the coast of Malaya with any commodity like that!" I told him.

"Let me set up a meeting with my principles," he said.

I agreed to further talks sometime is the near future and again emphasized that I would not run that commodity. I would have nothing to do with the peddlers of human misery who dealt in hard drugs or human trafficking. That was where I drew the line.

Friday, 7 February 1947

It is strange how there are always these chancy challenges set upon my life's game plan, regardless of how I try to avoid them. Perhaps my reputation by default as a gunrunner (which is a hanging crime in these waters) spread because of those crates of pristine M1 carbines I'd salvaged from the bottom of the giant squid's lair and sold. The story had gotten out via the usual channels, and now it seemed I was stuck with this reputation, a man with integrity and scruples who actually could get the job done, no matter how great the risk. Of course, it was a matter of initiative on the one hand and conscience on the other.

One listens to one's own conscience, that inner sense which knows instinctively the difference between right and wrong. If you cannot make a living honestly and with integrity, don't bother. Yes, it's a kind of gut feeling, for want of a better name. If you are honest to yourself and always act according to what your conscience tells you, you will not go far wrong. The notion of "I was only following orders" is a feeble excuse used by men who lack the courage and moral compass to take responsibility for their own actions. This can be seen by the huge scale of atrocities carried out during the last war by both the Allies and Axis military forces.

I like to think that this quality, the ability to make the right or wrong choices and take responsibility for his own actions, is what distinguishes man from the animals. Though in the case of some people I personally know, there is not much of a difference. But then, we all have a conscience, and likewise, something or other to feel guilty about, depending on personal values. The Malays have an old saying concerning those people who delight in flouting some moral or social rule: "*Sa belum jadi manusia*" or "not yet a human being"! Perhaps this quiet small inner voice within each and every one of us, this inner wisdom, is the voice of the guardian—the good spirit, if you like—that protects each one of us. This I do believe in.

It was 1700 hours PST when I boarded the P&O liner the *SS Carthage* at Tanjong Pagar and joined the party. George Apple was homeward bound on his retirement after twenty years of service in Singapore. There was almost a forlorn look about him, seated there in the lounge of the *SS Carthage*, surrounded by his friends and other well-wishers who had come for a last drink with him. He shook hands with most of them and the occasional tear in his eye passed without comment.

Fame appeared sad, and her customary wiggle was gone as she fussed around him. She was the mistress he was leaving behind, his goodbye girl. I took my leave of the crowded lounge at the first call for visitors to leave the ship and waited unashamedly on the quay for that hoped-for moment. At 1800 hours PST the wharfinger blew his whistle, and the linesman cast off. The SS *Carthage* was on her way, bound for England. Fame turned and walked towards her waiting taxi, but this time there was no wiggle in her walk. I saw a young Chinese approach her, say something, and then hand her a large envelope.

Clutching the envelope in her right hand, Fame turned, gave me a fleeting glance, and was gone! C. H. had sent his man, who had done the job required of him rather well. Now it was just a question of time and perhaps more time. Feminine curiosity would do the rest. I doubted very much that this contract offer I'd made would be easy for her to decide about. But I knew that she would reach her own decision in due time without any pressure from me. In the meantime, I would keep my ear close to the ground and go about my own business in the normal way, playing the waiting game, which I am very good at.

Saturday, 8 February 1947

My partner Roy arrived back in Singapore with the morning tide, apparently none the worse for his mad moments of adventure with that delinquent bunch of Australian pearl divers. According to Roy, they had been under full sail and heading for the island of Bali when a squall had come out of the blue and caught them unexpectedly. Edward was below deck, high as a kite due to his opium pipe addiction, but Cecil was also stoned with sly grog. That left Roy and the two Chinese on board to deal with the damn situation.

Buffeted by very high winds and seas, the pearl lugger had lost its mizzen mast while Roy was attempting to turn her into the large waves to try and stop the boat from sinking. Fortunately for Roy, a Dutch gunboat was in the vicinity and answered his distress call. The Dutch gunboat, my enemy, rendezvoused with the stricken boat in troubled waters and managed to tow it back to calmer seas at Pulau

Balabalangan, where Roy was able to carry out some emergency repairs. Roy was in rather a hurry to get home to his Portuguese–Eurasian mistress, Lynn Pireara, to whom he had a lot of explaining to do.

He promised to give me all the details later but left post-haste. To be fair, I did not envy him his task, for Lyn was a very jealous woman where Roy was concerned. She had a quick temper, which would explode suddenly but soon cool off after reaching its emotional apex. The truth was that Roy was somewhat of a sexual hobo, with very little honest-to-goodness horse sense, and Lynn was fully aware of his sexual misdeeds when he was not at home. But then, love and passion always seem to make for stranger bedfellows!

Low Siak Chuan got back in touch with me again. He set up a meeting with his principles at 1000 hours the next day at a shop near the junction of Middle Road and Bencoolen Street. I again pointed out to the fact that no way would I be running up the coast of Malaya with a boatload of guns—they were talking about lots of guns, from what I'd gathered—even if these weapons were meant for deliver to Burma! Gunrunning carried the death penalty; it was a hanging offence should I or any of my crew be caught in the act by the Dutch or British authorities. I felt a deep responsibility to all my crews and their families; we were a family when at sea. Gunboat patrols were frequent along the haunted Straits of Malacca with the likelihood of detection very high. Thus I took all measures necessary to reduce that danger.

I love a challenge, but only when it is balanced, with the risk factor and reward taken into full consideration. I never rush into a situation, always staying calm and cool throughout any dangerous venture. However, there was another contraband boat-run on offer, down to one of the Mentawai Islands in the Indian Ocean, but off the coast of Sumatra in Indonesia. Perhaps Roy would take the run in a day or so? I myself was in no immediate hurry. I saw Zainal at Kampong Amber and instructed him to assemble the crew at 1700 hours the next day. We had another little trip to make into the Riau

Archipelago, a small job that would take two to three days at the most.

I heard nothing from Fame herself, though any inquiry she cared to make concerning my activities outside of Singapore would draw a blank. The information out there about me was at best conjecture on the part of people who thought they knew me, since I kept a very tightly closed circle. Where Fame Alvares was concerned, I felt sure that her own curiosity about my interest in her as a contract mistress would eventually do the trick. But I was no drunken fool; the power from money and success meant very little to me. When the rich amongst us live and apparently seem to prosper off the backs of others by their financial investments, both good and bad, while the poor die poorer and meaninglessly, their gods seem not to care.

I have never kidded myself about having a green thumb, but I had brought back with me during one of my forays in the Karamata Straits a dirty, smelly old coconut with a bunch of young green leaves sprouting from a small stem. I dropped it into a hole I had previously prepared in the garden at Gloria's house, firming the ground around the little palm. Teris, Gloria's daughter, had taken care of it, and under her hand it had flourished for posterity. The planting of a tree is symbolic in these parts. It signifies putting down roots or perhaps even a sudden declaration of incomprehensible permanence, a kind of subconscious desire for the establishment of a point to return to. Call it home if you like.

Chapter 9

Guns for Burma

Sunday, 9 February 1947

I have made my will. The bulk of my estate will go to my daughter, Sandra, in the event of my sudden death. But I also made arrangements to take care of both Gloria and her daughter, Teris. C. H. Koh my barrister and former Force 136 operative, had a copy of my will in his safe and would do the necessary should the occasion come about. I am not morbid, just a realist. I do run contraband in uncertain places where anything can go wrong and frequently does! Roy and I made the 1000 hours PST meeting in the back room of a little shop in Bencoolen Street, where we met the two Chinese principles in the scheme.

We spent the next hour listening to their proposition. The commodity they had in mind was guns, lots of guns which they wanted me to deliver to a point in the estuary of the river Salween, near a town called Syriam. The Nu/Salween River is one of the region's free-flowing rivers, shared by China, Thailand, and Burma. Syriam is a port town in South Western Burma that is situated on the Rangoon River, a tributary of the Irrawaddy River, opposite Rangoon. It was once formerly part of the Mon kingdom; Syriam subsequently became a port of the Portuguese and French. But the window of opportunity for this job was closing in, their delivery date being the eighteenth of March next.

"What's the distance like?" Roy asked.

"About 1,160 miles, give or take five miles," Ong Chin Beng replied.

"Syriam is way too hot and out of the question!" I said. "It is much too close to Moulmein, and we have Burmese military all over the place there!"

"You can, however, as an alternative, use the river Salween to Ta Kaw, from which point transporting our goods to the final destination would be a little easier," Ong Chin Beng suggested.

Tan Ho Ching, the other principle, nodded his head in agreement.

"Have you considered using the place between Thaton and

Papun? Where the Salween River runs along the border of Thailand?" I asked.

"*Dacoit!*" Roy said (armed robber bands).

Roy and I decided that our principle's scheme to run guns into Burma was rather prohibitive and most likely to get us caught and even killed in the process. The scheme was filled with far more negatives than we would like in its present form. It required more research, including local up-to-date intelligence before it could become a workable proposition for us. We had a little business at a boat quay where several Chinese business houses were situated along the banks of the Singapore River.

Most of these traders had long-standing dormitory accommodations where they locked up their indentured labour after work each night. They were dealers in large and varied commodities, brought upriver in barges from the ships offloading in the roads of Clifford Pier. I was fully aware that our two principles would come back to us with another proposition after they had rethought in depth their current one, which bordered on the suicidal from my point of view. Hopefully they would return with a more feasible plan of action that was both workable and had the potential for a successful outcome.

Roy and I both loved taking risks, but calculated risks, where the chances of coming through it all remained in our favour. We were not blind fools motivated by the lure of making fast dollars but running straight into great danger! We knew exactly what we were doing in the contraband business.

That was how we had stayed alive thus far in front of others who also played the mercenary game. Neither of us nor any of my men would get paid if we found ourselves dead, would we? In this soldier-of-fortune trade, if you got dead whilst carrying out the business in hand, you did not get paid. It was that simple in our game of cat and mouse across these dangerous waters of uncertainty.

I stood down my crew and spent the evening with my feet up, reading a good book, having partaken of a good supper and some locally made grog. Yes, I read up a lot and for the most part educated myself. I read as many good books as I could lay my hands on during the quieter times in my life out in the East.

I have plans yet to make and my next job to set up. *Kuching* is the Malay generic name for cats, or if you like, the smaller *Felidae* or family of cats. *Kuching hatan* is the Malay term referring to a leopard cat (*Felis bengalensis*) and *kuching jalang*, a name given to the flat-headed cat. *Kuching negeri* is the domestic house cat.

The cat following Yan's daughter, Teris, in the photograph is rather unique, because it is a jungle cat and a true descendant of the golden cat of Malaya. Note the kink towards the end of its tail. This kind of cat is said to be very lucky and, of course, the legendary enemy of the tiger. *Harimau* is the Malay word for a tiger and *rimau* the word for a leopard or any of the larger *Felidae*, though the golden cat (*Felis temminckii*) is also called *harimau anjing* and *harimau telap* by the Malays. Teris calls the cat Princess, and it follows her around wherever she goes. It is quite tame for a jungle cat. Cats to me have always held a special association with their human counterparts, especially when love is shown between them. They remain magical creatures and are capable of keeping death away from your door as well as keeping illness out of the household—at least according to legend!

Jungle cat and Teris

A story goes that once upon a time, a long while ago, a Malay princess was in the habit of taking a bath in one of the cool jungle streams during the heat of the afternoon. She would remove the gold rings from her jewelled hands and slip them onto the cat's tail for safekeeping. On one such afternoon, when the princess was busy enjoying herself in the cool stream water, a rather large tiger suddenly appeared out of nowhere.

The jungle cat gave the alarm and immediately sprang at the tiger in defence of her mistress, with such ferociousness that the tiger ran away. But all of the princess's jewellery was lost during the sudden affray, so it took a long and diligent search of the immediate jungle undergrowth before all the valuable rings were at last found. The princess was said to be very wise. She put a kink near the end of her cat's long tail so that her valuable rings would never fall off again whilst she was taking a bath.

Monday, 10 February 1947

It was now 0100 hours PST, and we had left the estuary on a high tide and were mingling with the Malay fishing craft pushing out towards their fishing grounds beyond Pulau Bukum. The young crescent-shaped moon was high in the heavens, and there was little or no cloud cover. I set my boat on a course for Pulau Tambelan, and we were once again heading towards the uncertain. My friend Roy would be leaving on the next night tide for his run down to Pula Nias, off the coast of Sumatra, near the small town of Talak Dalam. It was not that we operated individually always, but rather it remained a ploy we used to help gain an advantage over our adversaries.

We had always considered ourselves to be professional specialists in the field of smuggling contraband, medical supplies, military weapons, and sometimes people as well. We were able to slip in through most ports, including that of Singapore and the islands off the Indonesian archipelago, at will. Recreational drugs or human young female trafficking I would never do, for I had witnessed first-hand the many broken people in opium dens and other such horrid, seedy shitholes that these peddlers of human misery have introduced to our already broken planet. Our enemies never know where or when we are likely to be at any given moment, which remains our saving grace, so to speak.

Gunrunning with two almost identical high-speed motor torpedo boats could be very confusing to our pursuers, with conflicting reports of sightings all over the Java seas. We had been sighted as one boat but in two different places at the same time. This had become almost a legend, with reports that the whole operation was being run by a disappearing Dutchman, which added significantly to the mystery! Think of *The Flying Dutchman*, only on a much smaller but faster craft. Nobody seemed able to catch the flying spectre from Holland either, but stories abounded, as did sightings.

Realistically, I suppose there remained the possibility that my enemies would catch us someday, but I was prepared for that with a complete change of tactics if and when it happened. For the moment, however, our adversaries were stuck with playing their guessing games, much to our advantage. My crew on board the boat all believed that we were on a heading for the Louisa Reef off the coast of Brunei in Borneo.

The weather held good, and at 1200 hours when I shot the sun with my sextant and correlated our position on the charts, we were well set on course. It is approximately a 1343 nautical miles' journey from the island of British Singapore down to Manila in the Philippine Islands. However, on this occasion our true course was the Anambas Islands, which we were making for with good speed. We should have been off Terema on the Anambas Islands at first light in the morning. I would make the drop and then alter course immediately for Pulau Tambelan.

We would soon have to make an 805-mile journey up into the Gulf of Siam. This new undertaking was on the cards for the next month, but at that point I had not yet decided which one of us would make the actual run. The other would feign the run with the second boat, in yet another location, to keep the authorities guessing. Roy at the moment was making his way up the Straits of Malacca and around Kutaradja, on the tip of Sumatra, to Pulau Nias rather than through the Sunda Straits. I personally would have liked to take a boat run up to Krakatua, between Sumatra and Java in the Sunda Straits. It had been a rather quiet run up to the moment, uneventful and calm—smooth running, which was the way I liked it. My boat was running like a dream, and we had good, clear-visibility night running, with nothing around to concern us in line of sight or on the radar. At 0200 hours, I was forced to reduce my boat's speed to maintain and keep my schedule.

Tuesday, 11 February 1947

The quiet, almost gentle pitch and roll of the boat, together with the continuous low-pitched hum of her engines, has a contemplative, relaxing effect. It is a feeling of soul peace and contentment, a kind of passiveness, if you like. But the sea is not always predictable, for all she can be gentle as a mother quietly rocking her child to sleep in its cradle. Like most women, she is subject to her wild and woolly moments. That is the time when the *perahu penjajap*, or boat cruisers, make their ghostly appearance, faint and uncertain shapes in the early light of dawn. They are the ghost ships of the old Malacca fleet.

Like most Malays, my crew are a rather superstitious lot, and anything not explained by natural law is thought to be supernatural. Zainal was convinced that if an object could not be seen on our radar then it must be ghostly. The waters we were in were probably the most haunted ones for those who choose to believe in legends or are superstitious. For my part, I know what I have seen and cannot rationally explain away. Widely circulated reports between June of 1947 and February of 1948 suggested that multiple ships traversing the straits of Malacca between Sumatra and Malaya picked up a series of SOS signals. The unknown ship's message was as simple as it was disturbing: "All officers, including captain, are dead, lying in chart room and bridge. Possibly whole crew dead." This communication was followed by a burst of indecipherable Morse code and then a final grim message: "I die."

This cryptic proclamation was followed by tomb-like silence. The chilling distress call was picked up by two American ships as well as British and Dutch listening posts. The men manning these posts managed to triangulate the source of the broadcasts and deduced that they were likely emanating from a Dutch freighter.

This was the *SS Ourang Medan*, which was navigating the straits of Malacca. Like all mysteries, a lack of records makes this either a grand hoax or a ghost ship story with no real evidence going for it. Neither *Lloyd's Register* nor the *Dictionary of Disasters at Sea … 1824–1962* shows any record of this incident and probably no *SS Silver Star*, which sailed the Strait of Malacca to answer the distress call.

I tied up with the anti-Sakerno insurgents as they arrived in several narrow fishing canoes in the early dawn and came alongside. Their headman stood at the side of the hatch while the contraband was quickly offloaded. At 0700 hours we had got underway again, a feat we would never have accomplished had the sea been anything but a flat calm. Our cook was slicing *pinchok*, sour fruit and vegetables, and he fell off his stool in the galley due to the sudden surge of our powerful marine engines. I set a course for Pulau Tambelan, where we had been assigned to make a pickup. Pulau Tambelan is one of a group of several small islands on the edge of the Lingga Archipelago and the beginning of the Karimata Straits. I reckon we'll hit the island around 2200 hours, all being well, of course. I will know better at noon today when I shoot the sun with my sextant and carry out a bit of reckoning on my charts.

The word *kari* is Malay for curry and *mata* means eye—if you like, the point of focus or "curry eyes"? For dinner we had fish curry and the cook's pinchok, which went down well. Anyway, both the fish and the vegetables were fresh, and the black coffee good. Now if I could only finish it off with an icy-cold pint of Australian lager, served fresh from the bar tap in a chilled tall glass, I thought. But it looked as if I would have to settle for bottled Tiger beer, chilled in an ice box. Cheers!

Anti-Sakerno insurgents

Wednesday, 12 February 1947

At the moment we were running a little late, because I'd decided to approach on a semi-circular course and swing out towards Cape Datu, on the tip of Sarawak and Dutch Borneo. The Tambelan Islands are a group of eight rather small islands and two medium islands; it was a rather smaller island on the edge of that group that we were heading for. We passed the Dutch East India trader around 0100 hours on her way to the Borneo part of Pontianak, en route from Medan on the Island of Sumatra. Of course, we were running without the required navigation lights so that the Dutch trader passing in the early hours would mistake us for some kind of native craft should she pick us up on her radar at all.

We arrived off the island at 0215 hours and immediately picked up three small blips on our radar, which could have been native fishing craft. At that point they were too far away to be seen through my night glasses, so I reduced my speed by half. The three blips were still stationary when I searched the screen again at 0300 hours.

I decided to stop my engines and pause in the darkness to wait for their next move.

There was no point in being speculative at this juncture; the three small blips could have been fishermen going about their trade, pro-Sukarno terrorists, or even Bajau pirates. But if they were pirates, my local knowledge of them in these waters and their way of operating told me that there should also be close by a *perahu-ibu*, a parent boat. For the unacquainted, the mother ship would be filled with cut-throats, in all probability waiting on the blind side of the island for the break of dawn and the commencement of their piracy business on my boat—their intended prey!

My instructions had been implicit, that is to say meant though not plainly expressed. I was to wait for a signal flashed seaward to my location at 0530 and then to go in. At 0430 hours I checked the drift of my craft and put my engines into slow forward to correct our position. The three blips on our radar were still stationary; they must have been anchored in shallow water. They say that patience is a virtue—it is also bloody tiresome!

Dot dot dot dash; dot dot dot dash; dot dot dot dash came the signal flashed in the darkness. The tension picked up tenfold; my stomach tightened and my throat dried up. It was an old British Navy signal lamped to me at 0525 hours. This was the right signal but some five minutes early, and worse still, not from shore as expected but rather from one of the three fishing boats I'd detected anchored in shallow water. I immediate changed the position of our craft and waited for them to make their next move.

Bajau pirates

Then I remembered that the Bajau pirates had actively aided the Allies, particularly the British, in the Pacific war against the Japanese, sabotaging their resources at every opportunity. The Bajau, for the record, have been a nomadic, seafaring people throughout most of their nautical history and are sometimes referred to as "sea gypsies". They charted particularly the waters of the Sulu Sea, off the southwestern coast of the Philippines, and the various seas that surrounded the Indonesian island of Sulawesi.

These seas remain among the most dangerous waters in the world, with sporadic policing at best and a very high incidence of open piracy. The five minutes that followed seemed like an eternity. My next move would decide the outcome of this cat-and-mouse play on the ocean in the dark.

At 0530 hours sharp, whilst the island and the seas afforded me the cover of darkness, I took my chances and made my move, positioning my craft on a slow but direct course towards the three fishing craft. I brought all of my 100-octane Packard 41.8-litre, four-stroke, V-12 4M-2500 aviation engines to full power and let my boat go! She leaped forward at full throttle in a circular sweep, with the target at six o'clock. If I drew their fire now, my intention was to rake them with machine-gun fire in passing, complete my run out, and turn back at high speed to complete the kill. We were almost in range of my pair of .303 Bren guns when they began signalling frantically.

Dot dot dash dot; dot dot; dash dot dot signalled FID or Fox Item Dog. I held fire and completed my turn, reduced speed, and came towards them slowly. Bajau pirates they were—Mat Awi's lot? They had been waiting for two days, but the news they had to give me was not good. My passengers had been delayed and would be arriving on Saturday 15 February, three days late! Did I want to change the pickup point to another island?

They were quite adamant concerning their behaviour. These Bajau pirates had not put a foot on the island, raided any village, or impregnated any of the island women. This was a safe island, and they were all on their best behaviour. So I decided to take a chance and wait rather than have to go through this morning's deadly game with the unknown again on some other island paradise, which might well cost me the lives of my men and myself. My first consideration was fuel, and we got this priority out of the way first.

Thursday, 13 February 1947

Rex's Law says you always deal with the most important priority first! After all, there are no second chances for a private contractor out there in the open seas or anyone to come to the rescue should the worst happen. We refuelled from the 100-octane aviation fuel drums we carried in the hold.

I checked the oil and coolant levels of each engine, topping up to the maximum level where necessary. These engines were the hearts of my boats, and I owed it to my crew and my boats to service them well and regularly. I cannot stress this enough! One must always maintain foremost one's weapons, kit, and craft. One's life depends on it!

Now the first light of dawn in this part of the world comes very quickly, like a thief in the night, unmasking her veil quite gloriously at times. The sun came out fiercely shining, bright above the lush green foliage of the jungle canopy, giving the island the appearance of a beautiful emerald jade set in the deep-blue sea.

We had obviously come through the reef rather than over it but at one point had only had about four feet of water under our keel. After kitting up for scuba, I dove overboard and inspected my boat's hull underwater for any signs of damage; there was none to see. I was quite pleased when I found nothing to speak of. My craft was shipshape and ready for the open waters again.

The islanders here were Karimatanese. Rather like the Sundanese, they were hard-working and fun-loving, making a game of life rather than a chore. They had little care for money; they didn't need it. The men caught fish in the sea, kept a few domestic animals, and grew a little rice.

The women had perfectly moulded bodies, lithe and graceful to a degree that brought envy to the eyes of many white women. They were all naturally excellent swimmers and would come to meet an incoming boat of their men friends. At harvest time, men and women toiled together side by side in the rice fields, the women in their sarongs with perhaps a thin cotton cover over their breasts. They wove their own material and dyed it with various vegetable dyes in a special waxing process to produce the end product after completing the dyeing process *kain batik*. All of these things were found in the forest, the cotton from the trees, or fibre from the nipa palm (*Nypa fruticans*).

I paid my respect to the headman of the village and was rather surprised to learn that the island was a transit haven where the Bajau pirates were concerned. They had come to this arrangement a long time ago and would not molest each other in any way due to this arrangement. It seems there had been a small Dutch signal unit on the island back in 1942. This had been bombed and machine-gunned by the Japanese during a rather bad air attack, and several Dutch citizens had been killed. The Dutch had left the island immediately, leaving three badly burned bodies behind them at the bombed radio station on the hill.

The next morning the islanders had been in the process of preparing the dead Dutch soldiers for burial, when the Japs arrived and quickly searched the island for any remnants of the Dutch. The

Japanese officer saw the three badly burnt bodies wrapped in *keladi* leaves and questioned the headman in Japanese. But the headman did not understand a word the Japanese officer said, and when he became very angry and drew his samurai sword, the headman trembled with uncontrollable fear. The Jap officer said one word that the headman understood: *"Batak?"* In fear for his life and not wishing to infuriate the angry officer further, the headman nodded his head in agreement. The Japanese left the island the next morning, and apart from the occasional Jap gunboat, that was the last the islanders saw of them.

The Batak were noted for being cannibalistic, having eaten the occasional missionary. Ritual cannibalism was well documented among precolonial Batak people, being performed in order to strengthen the eater's *tendi*. The concept of tendi is central to the Batak old religion. The Batak believe that tendi is given to their people by their gods at birth and determines the fate of all their new born children throughout his or her life. In particular, the blood, heart, palms, and soles of the feet were seen as rich in tendi. Marco Polo recorded stories of ritual cannibalism among the "Battas". His stay was restricted to the coastal areas, and he never ventured inland to directly verify such claims. Through second-hand accounts Polo describes in some detail how the victim of the Batak was eaten:

> They suffocate him. And when he is dead they have him cooked, and gather together all the dead man's kin, and eat him. And I assure you they do suck the very bones till not a particle of marrow remains in them … And so they eat him up stump and rump. And when they have thus eaten him, they collect his bones and put them in fine chests, and carry them away, and place them in caverns among the mountains where no beast nor other creature can get at them. And you must know also that if they take prisoner a man of another country, and he cannot pay a ransom in coin, they kill him and eat him straightway.
>
> —*Polo*, Vol. II, Chapter X, p. 369

Perhaps the burnt bodies were wrapped in the leaves of the water hyacinth?

These people were not Batak, and I had no fear of being eaten by any of them! The Batak were Proto-Malay people living on Samosir, which is an island in the middle of Lake Toba in central Sumatra.

The Karimatanese were extremely superstitious and believed in a variety of evil spirits. Quite a number of their women were in the habit of smearing glutinous saffron rice behind their ears to keep the evil spirits away. There were five villages on this island, and like many remote islands of this region, the people's lifestyle was polygamous; that is to say, a man here would have many wives but never in the same village. Just imagine all that walking between the five villages! The walking should keep them fit and out of trouble, if nothing else! As a man with an eye for new business potential, I thought there would certainly be a good market for bicycles. With this two-wheeled mode of transportation, a man could make love to each of his wives in each of the five villages and be home at his favourite wife's village for supper—if that did not drain the life out of him!

It is rather easy to romanticize a place like these islands; they are part of the Western imagery of paradise. Sun, sea, beautiful women, and lots of carefree multiple sexual adventures would sound to many like heaven on earth. But the politicians would one day come there and bring with them their false promises and lying ways. The Christian missionaries would force the native women to cover up their breasts for the sake of Western modesty and morality. Neither politician nor missionary would ever take into account the fact that these island peoples already had a good, moral way of life.

Whether you believe in the one God, a supreme being, or have a need of many gods, as some do, it seems to me that higher beings than us made this world in great perfection! I find it strange that Western people seem to prefer the artificial to everything that is natural. They like to re-invent the wheel, so to speak, to suit their own way of life and culture. Such is the white man's burden. A toast to those poor Western fools who are the tools of the industrial revolution that brought us mechanized warfare, putting the subservient under the control of the money people sitting in their unreachable ivory towers back home at Mount Olympus and plotting how their next millions will be made at the expense of poorer people.

Friday, 14 February 1947

But perhaps this is not of their own choosing but imprinted by their birth lines and upbringing, being born slaves of their mundane society because they have always done it that way. I could never see myself working deep in a rut from nine to five. I guess it's the itinerant soul and free spirit in me. *Itu nassib!* This means, "That is fate." I don't for one moment believe it is their true destiny any more than they do.

Perhaps it is just their bad luck. Like all colonial powers, the Dutch placed a kind of poll tax on every village on the island and called in to collect the price of colonialism twice a year. However, the islanders here made a point of being out whenever the taxman arrived, returning only after he had left!

It seemed that we were having curry fish and barbequed wild pig for dinner. One by one the island women, with their soft golden complexions, along with their quietly dignified men, set out the food and directed everyone to his or her appropriate place at the feast. This was served on green banana leaves to the music of the village *gamlan* in the background.

The word *gamlan*, meaning to hammer, refers to a sort of collective Indonesian orchestra made up mainly of tuned percussion instruments.

I had a quiet morning's work hunting the wild pig in the forest, and I managed to bag five of them for the feast. You must remember always that a wild pig or boar is a seriously dangerous game animal. Bush wild pigs possess a mix of phenomenal strength, two razor-sharp tusks, and an extremely bad hard-knock attitude that makes them a real hazard. This is especially so when you choose to hunt them on foot, so you are at your most vulnerable. If a sow has young ones close by, beware. Wild bush pigs will charge fiercely, so whether you are using a rifle or a spear, you cannot afford to miss your mark. You must always hunt in armed pairs, never alone!

Once we got back to the village, the women took over and did all the necessary gutting, skinning, and cooking for one and all. The curry they served there was akin to *korma,* not too hot as some of the Indian curry sauces are. Rice and fish are the staple foods here, so meat is always a luxury reserved for feasts and other special occasions.

Buginese traders came to the island from time to time, made contact, and traded Indian *patola* and *cinde* cloths imported by the Dutch East India Company.

Most important to this group was the juice of the palm, which was gathered by inducing a flow of juice from the crown of the palm tree. Tappers climbed the trees twice daily to obtain large quantities of sucrose-rich liquid. This could be drunk fresh from the tree and made quite a pleasant, refreshing drink. The juice was also cooked to a dark-brown treacle that could be stored for quite a considerable time. This syrup was a part of the staple diet there. The people also fermented and drank the syrup in the form of beer and made fine sweet gin out of the distilled mash.

Each of the islands in this group had its own oral history and tradition, with many tales about the exploits of their ancestors. Like all cultures, of course they had a trickster protagonist whose cunning could outwit their enemies and bring success to their own tribe. Occasionally they would kill members of a tribe from neighbouring islands as a kind of self-defence against villainous sorcery of that group, but murder within the tribe itself was unknown. The closely knit community was held together by the headman of the island, though some authority rested in council, which was drawn from the five villages on the island. The taking of women here was a crime, though adultery as it is acknowledged in the West was alien to their concept of crime.

Saturday, 15 February 1947

It is quite accepted should a woman come to join you of her own free will, as the single women here frequently do. It's their way of life, with its own sense of morality—in my view far superior to that of any Western country as morality goes. Married women, on the other hand, don't. They are for all intents and purposes taboo. Neither should an outsider ever consider doing so. There are rules in every game, codes of conduct to be honoured in each and every culture or peoples.

The party on the island broke up around 0200 hours, having run its course of consuming all the food and available drinks at the feast.

I returned to my boat, where I checked in with the crew I'd placed on watch duty. Then I got my head down for a few hours needed sleep on board. The *keladi bunting*, or water hyacinth, are extremely beautiful where the hill stream runs quietly down to the sea, at a point just above the salt water. I was determined to unobtrusively obtain a good specimen for my garden in Singapore. The village was sleeping off the effects of the previous night's feast when I walked through it shortly after daybreak. I was quite surprised when Maya who was a very attractive young tribal women arrived as if out of nowhere to greet me amorously a few moments later, while I was busy quietly digging out the plant I had chosen. This was their custom as the women here on these islands went with whatever man they wanted or took a liking to. This was their lifestyle and not immoral at all.

Maya stood, hands on hips, with her back to me. Her head was half inclined towards me and her eyes downcast in a sideways glance. I suppose I should have realized the significance immediately when I saw her sleeping mat thrown carelessly over the plants in front of her. But I was busy at the time and not paying attention. The next moment she dropped her sarong and stood naked before me. There was no mistaking her intentions, and of course I had no misgivings. Maya went quietly down on her sleeping mat as I walked towards her. There is an honesty to sex and life or death out there that we in the West would do well to learn from.

Here I was, on my quest for the water hyacinth, but I had also obtained the legendary flower that gives life to everything it touches into the bargain. No words were spoken, but what ensued was a timeless piece of unconditional loving from one human being to another. It took my breath away, all this freedom from sexual taboos; it was far outside the norms we observed in Western society. Life and death was simpler out here. But probably ownership of what is considered yours regarding sexual liaisons is universal. People have fought and died over women the world over. Fair Helen of Troy comes to mind, in *The Iliad*, by Homer, the Greek poet and legendary author. It is said that Helen of Troy had a face that launched a thousand ships.

Sunday, 16 February 1947

At 0200 hours, whilst I was on the bridge, I saw the flash and then heard the thud of heavy naval guns in the distance. This brought everyone who'd been below deck up to see what was going on. The firing was nothing like those naval bombardments during the Second World War, softening up a beach before landing troops. It sounded more like twin 4.5-inch (105 mm) naval guns from a Dutch destroyer and they were firing illuminators into the night over the shoreline. But there was no sound of small-arms fire, the absence of which was helpful in determining the approximate distance of the fracas to my boat.

In my estimation this was about thirty miles. The firing ceased after about twenty minutes, and that was it. All that early morning mayhem of starlight shells made my crew rather apprehensive, including myself. Our first instinctive impulse was flight rather than fight, to take off at high speed in the opposite direction. It took a good thirty minutes of arguing the case against putting immediately to sea before the Bajau were finally convinced to remain at their current anchorage close by in the shadow of the island. The fracas was in all probability between a Dutch destroyer and Japanese insurgents.

The Dutch destroyers were armed with an array of more powerful, sophisticated electronics, including all-seeing radar technology. The last thing I required now was a number of boats all heading in the opposite direction and drawing the attention of that destroyer and every other gunboat in the area to my location. If it was true that curiosity killed the cat, then I was not going to be stupid and let it kill me! I had calculated the risk and made my choice in the face of the circumstances. Our anchorage was within the shadow of the island because the solid land would shield us from being detected by radar.

It was relatively quiet for the next two hours. But then we picked up three small images on our radar screen, running on a convergent course with these islands. The blips on our radar screen appeared to be a little more than one hour away on their current heading. They were coming from the wrong direction, and this made me rather apprehensive. If I slipped mooring now, the Bajau would put out to sea in an uncontrollable panic. I would have to wait for the appropriate moment, slip mooring, and race around the island to take up a position in the immediate rear of these incoming craft.

The Bajau would panic, so that the incoming boats would be caught up in the confusion, giving me the advantage. I had a pretty fair idea that the Dutch gunboat would otherwise be engaged on a follow-up at the moment. At least I now knew from which direction the bloody thing would arrive, if it did. This was only an assumption on my part, just another calculated possibility or degree of likelihood. We were able to ascertain from the shape, size, and approximate rate of progress of the three vessels that they were indeed native craft. The larger of the three suddenly changed course, diverting to approach the island from the starboard side.

This action would bring them to our rear, while the other two continued in direct approach. It was time to make my move, to warm up and meet halfway the vessel bound for my rear. We dropped our mooring, moved out at half speed, and rounded the northern tip of the island, picking up to full speed in the straits. The vessel in question was a large Bajao *perahu*, the crew of which was busy trimming her sail to reduce speed—hardly an act of aggression. I cut my boat's speed to half but then brought her down to slow ahead on my initial approach.

"Ayesha?" Zainal said.

I was sure he was right on this occasion. It was Mat Awi's daughter.

I turned my boat, following the craft, and eventually they threw us a couple of lines. Once we had secured and my craft had reversed engines, this slowed us both to a quiet drift in the early light of dawn. Ayesha came onto my bridge from her own craft, cursing Sukarno, the Dutch authorities, and General Douglas MacArthur and his American forces. She blamed all of these for her delayed arrival.

Ayesha's all-female pirate crew at Pulau Manis

A group of Sukarno Javanese had been en route to Pulau Badas when they'd been intercepted by a number of Bugis *praus* on the rampage. The Bugis and the pro-Sukarno Javanese were sworn enemies, but of the two the Bugis were the more skilled sailors, with a notorious reputation for piracy. It seemed that the Bugis had gained the upper hand and been looting the Javanese boats when a Dutch gunboat had arrived on the scene. Ayesha had been forced to make for the cover of Pulau Singkawang and wait for things to quiet down.

Ayesha had brought my passenger from Semarang in Java—no, not a family, just one woman passenger! The Dutch gunboat was blockading the coast of Java and investigating anything that moved in those waters during the hours of darkness. The Dutch Navy were meticulous in their sweep patterns, searching for pirates and insurgents in the dark. They maintained a search-and-destroy policy as far as we were concerned; that they did not take prisoners was well known in these waters. Being captured was never an option for us. If and when the time came, we would all make a run for it or die trying to escape.

Monday, 17 February 1947

Words—still we go learning them! We need them to describe new discoveries and new inventions, new ideas and fashion, new social problems and new crimes. All of these demand new words, and the wonder is that they are always forthcoming! We may run a little short of fuel, food, and water but never words. The word *prau* refers to any of several Malay or Indonesian boats powered by sails or by oars and paddles. The word is Malay, *perahu*, which is the correct Malay Romanized spelling.

Ayesha was 27 years of age and quite arrogant where men were concerned. But then she was Awi's eldest daughter and the apple of his eye. Awi was a chief to be reckoned with, who gave no quarter in a fight and expected none in return. Ayesha's perahu was something special in the way of Bajau craft, a 65-foot outrigger with twin Grey diesel marine engines, so that she was not dependent on sail alone. This gave her a definite advantage over the many sail-dependent ships when the winds suddenly calmed. Twenty young women formed her crew, each a member of her clan and loyal to a T. Woe to any man who attempted to set foot on board her ship without a proper invitation. He would answer for such an indiscretion!

Ayesha was now bound for her home base at San Miguel Island in the Sulu Sea, by way of Cape Datu and along the coast of Sarawak, Brunei, and Northern Borneo to Cagayan Sulu. Cagayan Sulu is an island south-west of the Sulu Sea in the Philippines. The island is low lying, surrounded by thirteen smaller islets and coral reefs, with a geographical land mass of twenty-six square miles or about sixty-seven square kilometres. Ayesha took all the other Bajau praus of her small fleet along with her, and likewise they would behave on their journey home. The transfer of my solo Eurasian female passenger had been completed in quick time, so the business of my meet with the pirates completed, I immediately set course for Johore and the east coast of Malaya, glad to be homeward bound once again.

Tuesday, 18 February 1947

Soon we were back on the old shipping route which runs between Kuching and Singapore, which is the best way through to the Riau Archipelago and as safe as houses to navigate, providing you are not in a rush to get there. You must be careful that you do not appear to be legitimate, which makes you fair game for pirates on any seas. In this part of the world, it pays to take your time! My passenger kept to herself most of the time, maintaining a rather low profile whenever we were in the main shipping lanes and other vessels larger than a rowing boat were around.

I spent most of my time on the bridge, which suited my requirements of the moment; it was where I was supposed to be, anyway. The last island in the Tembalan group was some fifty miles astern of us now, and we were making good headway towards Pulau Bintan. We would be off Tanjong Pinang in approximately five hours at this rate, which was a slower pace than my boat was capable of. It had been a quiet trip, highlighted with the occasional unprovoked roll in the hay.

I did not consider myself promiscuous, but on the other hand, when at sea I accepted whatever was offered in good faith. What happened in the sack stayed in the sack. I had never thought it necessary to show off where women were concerned. My emotional encounters I never made public, other than to commit a few notes to my journal. From my standpoint, women were not objects to be taken, touched up, and seduced. Each woman was something special, each one with her own exact differences, the equal of man, who must never be abused or dominated.

Fishing boat, with Rajah Brooke in the background

The sea around us was full of *ikan bilis*, better known as anchovies, a small, common, salt-water oily forage fish belonging to the *Engraulidae* family. Ikan bilis was a Malayan culinary delicacy, with around 144 species found globally in the Atlantic, Indian, and Pacific Oceans, as well as in the Black Sea and the Mediterranean Sea. We had run into a rather large shoal of these small fish feeding near the surface. Anchovies were abundant in these tropical seas, and if you watched them closely, you would note that they formed a kind of pattern, with the larger individual fish swimming below the yet-smaller ones, which is important shoaling behaviour.

The anchovy swims straight forward with its mouth open, thus taking the plankton indiscriminately, and then it turns aside. If a shoal of anchovies swam straight forward, those in front would of course capture food whilst those in the rear would go hungry. As nature would have it, the leading individual fish turn off to either side when full but return quickly to the rear of the shoal, keeping within the safety of the fish formation. That way each individual fish gets its turn to feed itself, and in this manner the shoal assumes the shape of a rather large teardrop in the sea.

Chapter 10

Special Intelligence Far East
Wednesday, 19 February 1947

My Eurasian passenger came up at 0635 hours onto the bridge and watched the shoal of anchovies feeding in the water around the boat. She remained silent and uncommunicative, which was all right by me, as one does not ask too many questions in the game of smuggling people about whom you know little. From my perspective, she was cargo which I was paid well to transport to a given destination—minus the questions.

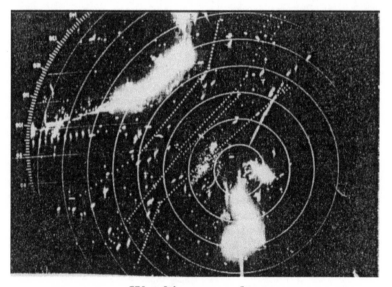

Watching my radar

"You are always on the bridge!" my elusive passenger suddenly burst out, in an apparent attempt to start conversation.

"Yes, of course!" I replied, wondering exactly where she was going with this. Perhaps she had gotten bored of exclusiveness.

She watched the anchovy fish shoal dancing about my boat in silence for a while but went below again soon afterwards, as soon as the wind began to pick up a little speed.

The sumatra came suddenly, with heavy rains together with a

good, strong gale-force wind, which tossed us about quite a bit for the next few hours. This made my Eurasian mystery female passenger rather seasick, so much so that she vomited up all the contents of her morning breakfast on my deck. But then, without explanation, the storm disappeared as suddenly as she'd come.

It left a good groundswell in its wake. At this point we were about an hour away from Tanjong Pinang, and it was time to change course again and set up a new heading. Tanjong Pinang was a trading port between islands in the Riau archipelago, located south of Pulau Bintan. Darkness came quickly at sea in this tropical climate, where twilight was always a marginal thing of little or no consequence. The old brandy ball, that is to say the sun, had done its thing—now you see it, now you don't—and it was gone for the night. It was amazing how time could fly in this part of the world, but for the moment I did not anticipate any further problems.

The crucial point would be between Tanjong Pinang and Singapore, where all the tall ships were to be found. My plan was to arrive at the main shipping lane well after darkness had fallen, which would allow me the advantage of not being observable with the naked eye, although there was the threat of detection by radar from the ever-menacing Dutch gunboats. It was obvious to me that my elusive passenger was a most-wanted woman, though her crimes were unknown to me for the moment. My best guess from my gut was that she must be an agent provocateur or some sort of hated political activist whose life and safety was now in my hands. But I always looked after my human cargo well. I had a reputation to keep up regarding the safe and speedy delivery of all my cargo, human or otherwise, unmolested.

My new heading would take my boat through the reefs in darkness, a risky venture but one of necessity if I was to evade detection by prying eyes.

Thursday, 20 February 1947

At 0230 hours we are running the reef at low speed and in near darkness. There is a new moon so no moonbeams to aid our way through the darkness. Boldness is my friend, even if the coral is not! At 0400 hours, I pick up a strong image approaching fast on my radar screen. I immediately think it could be a Dutch gunboat. I opt to take the only realistic choice available to us at the moment, in the hope that they will believe we are a fishing craft after the anchovy. With any luck, if I can dodge them, we will be back in British territorial waters inside an hour or so.

I am now back in British territorial waters and ready to run the shipping lanes through to Johore in Malaya. The last thing I want at the moment is to get the boat stuck on some coral reef.

Coral reefs are formed by repeated budding of the parent stock and new growths formed from it. A colony, sometimes numbering hundreds of thousands, is formed, building a common skeleton several feet high, which keeps growing. Corals feed like the sea anemones, their tentacles armed with stinging cells which paralyze small fish and other free-swimming sea creatures and pushes them into the mouth at the centre of the ring of tentacles.

Should my craft get stuck on a reef, then a few well-placed HE (high explosive) charges should do the trick to free it, but only small charges, mind you—otherwise I end up sinking the boat!

My female passenger has gone to her bed below. She has no family with her, just one Dutch–Eurasian female around my own age. All I know about her is that her given name to me is Mille and that she is a wanted woman.

Do the Dutch and the nationalists under Sukarno have a bounty on her head? It seems she worked as a dancer in Batavia for a time but also became deeply involved as an activist with a group opposed to Sukarno. Mille was wearing a sarong and *kebaya*, which is a sixteenth-century Malayan–Portuguese costume still used in Malaya today. My passenger is rather like a famous dancer from Batavia called Dewi Lashmani. I wonder if they are one and the same?

Dewi Lashmani

The line between disagreement with authority and treason is very minute indeed, for once you have taken up the gauntlet for a cause, you may suddenly realize that your predicament is due to your own political anti-government stance. This may well cost you your life in parts of the world that do not practise freedom of speech or the right to legal defence. At best you will be made a scapegoat or end up publicly arrested and imprisoned for alleged crimes against the state. If you are a female activist in a detention camp out here, you may end up brutally gang-raped to degrade and humiliate you as well as tortured by your captors during interrogation.

Alternatively, those in power may choose to make you disappear from the face of the planet, your body unceremoniously buried like garbage down some unmarked grave. Either way, you will end up dead and soon forgotten about. It is only by fully grasping the full measure of your opponents, their weaknesses and strengths together with their predictable disciplined routine, that you may beat them.

We have run the coral reef gauntlet through the darkness, contrary to the popular belief that this cannot be done, although my heart was in my mouth most of the way. This was a necessary evil, the choice between being caught or staying free to roam these waters as I please. At 0530 hours we are off the southern tip of *Pulau Blackang Mati*—meaning "death from behind island"—on the edge of Singapore harbour's outer shipping roads. Running legitimately, with my navigation lights on, in the authorized lane, I alter course for Kampong Tanjong Ramunia, a village lying on the tip of the east coast of Malaya. Taking a wide course at this point would draw unnecessary attention to my boat and arouse suspicion from the British port authorities. But by running my boat slowly and in close to the coastline, I give myself a sixty for/forty against chance of not being stopped and boarded by the local authorities.

The night has soon passed into day on the bridge of my craft, and at 0700 hours we are off the marker buoy at Tanjung Ramunia. I then set a new course for Kuala Terengganu, which is located on the north-east coast of Malaya. The name can be roughly translated as "the confluence/estuary of Terengganu", referring to the broad estuary which empties into the South China Sea. On my present heading, I estimate that we will reach this destination during the early hours of the next morning. Although we are not yet home and dry, we are almost there!

My elusive Eurasian passenger has eaten her breakfast below decks and then showed up on the bridge for a while, making light chit-chat. She seems very pleased with herself. But then there is still quite a way before we reach our final destination—nothing is over till the fat lady sings! At 1600 hours we are making good headway, at a steady ten knots per hour, with a groundswell running. I always make a point not to thrash my engines, which are capable of twenty-one knots over a sustained period. But as with all things running at speed in these waters, you are more likely to draw attention when charging around like a bat out of hell. High speed remains my ace in the hole. I only use it when necessary, but it is always there as a last resort during an emergency.

Barracudas are all around us, and it is likely that they are running down from the Gulf of Siam, heading for the South China Sea.

Barracudas are a pike-like fish, although not related to the pike. They have a similar long-bodied form, with a jutting lower jaw plus a wicked set of fangs. Fisherman treat even the dead barracudas with respect when handling them. The length of the fish is approximately eight feet, and believe me when I say that they have a rather evil reputation for merciless attack against anything in the water around them.

Barracuda shoals tend to scare off most of the other fish in the area, scattering them during their relentless feeding. In short, the fish-catching in this area will require several days before it gets back to normal. The Malay fisherman don't eat barracuda, but the Chinese folk will eat anything that won't eat them first. It's hard luck on any fisherman with nets when they are around.

There is quite a lot of *Laminaria digitata* around this part of the east coast of Malaya. That's kelp, in case you wondered. *Fucus vesiculosus*, or bladder whack, is what the Malays use to make agar-agar, a kind of jelly made from seaweed—or is it *Gracilaria lichenoides* or perhaps *Eucheuma spinosum*? Anyway, it's rather nice to eat.

Malay fishermen employ a *pawang*, a man who practises some primitive industry such as hunting, fishing, or agriculture by the aid of the black arts—sorcery, in plain speaking. He is a witch doctor, a man who combines magic and skill in the exercise of his profession. A *pawang pukat* or even *pawang kelong* is a practitioner of magic in connection with various types of fishing.

Pawangs always seem to know when the fish are swarming, but more to the point *where* they are swarming in multitudes. They take the first of any catch in payment for their services. These witch doctors of the sea use a kind of rattle to attract the *parang-parang*, the wolf herring. *Ikan* is the Malay generic name for fish and *ikan you* for sharks, dogfish, and rays resembling sharks. According to Hindu mythology, Varuna is the god of the ocean as well as of water and all the laws of the underwater world.

Today we have fish and *pauh* curry for dinner; that is a kind of wild mango. *Pauh janggi*, the great ocean around the bank, which is all that is left of a submerged continent. Apparently, a Malay legend,

Pauh Janggi Lake is said to be very popular among Malays because of its unexplained mystical things. At the base of Pauh Janggi Lake, around the area of the navel, it is said there is a government ruled by seven powerful jinn. It is also said to be the center of the supernatural beings around the world regardless of the genie of Islam or non-Muslims. Pauh Janggi refers to the name of the coconut fruit.

Doyak riau is a large gold-coloured cuttlefish found in these waters.

The annual rainfall in Malaya varies from place to place but averages around 100 inches each year. The year is commonly divided into the south-west and north-west monsoon seasons. The average daily temperature throughout Malaya varies from seventy degrees Fahrenheit up to around ninety degrees, though on higher grounds, such as the Cameron Highlands, temperatures are lower and can vary widely. The Malay states each have their own ruler, and each state has a British advisor. Islam is the official religion in all states. The Malay states are as follows.

Johore: Johore Bahru
Kedah: Alor Setar
Kelantan: Kota Bahru
Negri Sembilan: Seremban
Pahang: Kuantan
Perak: Ipoh
Perlis: Kangar
Selangor: Shah Alam
Trengganu: Kuala Trengganu
Malacca, Penang, and Singapore are British colonies.

The Malays adhere to the Moslem calendar, the basic date of which commemorates the *Hejira* or flight of Muhammed from Mecca to Medina. The corresponding date of this is AD 622, or July 16 in the Julian calendar. Hejira years are used primarily in Iran, Turkey, Arabia, Egypt, parts of India, and Malaya. The Hejira months are as follows.

Muharram: 30 days
Sufar: 29 days
Rabia: 30 days
Rabia II: 29 days
Jumada I: 30 days
Jumada II: 29 days
Rajab: 30 days
Shaaban: 29 days
Ramadan: 30 days
Shawwal: 29 days
Dhu'l Qa da: 30 days
Dhul'l Hijja: 29 or 30 days

The length of the Hejira year is 354 days, 8 hours, and 48 minutes, and the period of lunation is 29 days, 12 hours, and 44 minutes.

We rounded Pulau Yu (Shark Island) and were approaching Pulau Tinggi (Tall Island), off the east coast of Johore, just before sunset. We had been running in darkness again for a little over an hour when we picked up an image on the radar screen, between us and the coast. The image was moving fast, on a steady bearing of 25 degrees off our port bow. I held our course and made ready to turn quickly to starboard in order to head out to sea at full throttle.

"It's my friends!" my passenger said. "Watch for a green light. They are friendlies."

Sometimes during situations such as this it is better not to ask too many questions. As far as these "friendlies" were concerned, this remained to be seen. I always played my cards close to my chest, keeping my ace hidden away. When it comes to secret liaisons on the high seas, it's best to assume and prepare for the worst but hope for the best outcome.

***Pulau Yu* or Shark Island**

"Javanese?" I shouted. The adrenalin was running high once more.

"Of course not!" she shouted back at me. "Watch for the green light."

A small motor launch then loomed out of the near-total darkness, flashing a green signal light at us. I throttled back, feeling the craft shudder as I placed the engines into reverse so that we lost headway quickly before going into idle on standby.

The motor launch came alongside us, and two of my crew made fast the lines thrown on board from the launch. A young, extremely fit English gentleman in a tropical white suit clambered aboard.

"I will relieve you of your passenger now, skipper," he said with confidence in a quintessential Oxford English accent.

"If that is what she wants?" I said gruffly, pondering exactly who this Etonian gentleman "spook" might be.

Mille smiled, nodded her head, and got her things together, making ready to leave.

"Sorry for the inconvenience, but we were not in a position to make a definite pickup point when we first made these arrangements," he said. He placed a small briefcase down on top of my chart table.

"The rest of your fee," he said.

"Open it," I said, and when he complied, I instructed him to move the material around inside the case with his own hands, turning it over. I was not taking any chances, as this clandestine meeting had all the hallmarks of some nation's Special Intelligence unit; I did not dare to risk a bomb on my boat.

"You don't trust us, skipper?" he said in his rather eccentric posh English accent. I should add that he could be a Cambridge man, but Oxford University halls came strongly to mind.

"Just insurance!" I replied, and we all laughed the matter off.

Mille shook my hand, and then they were gone into the night. My gut instinct told me that I had been coerced via third parties and paid off to do a job for my own damn country. That made me think that certain eyes-only military intelligence departments back home in England had been aware of exactly how I made a living out here for some time now. I stowed the cash in my duffel bag and threw the empty briefcase overboard into the sea, just in case.

At 2000 hours PST, I put my craft into slow ahead and rounded Pulau Tinggi before opening her up and heading down the coast towards Singapore and home. I wanted to round Tanjung Ramunia before dawn and go upriver to Tanjung Surat, where I would trade for *ikan kering* and have a cargo of dried fish for my return to Singapore, no questions asked. I had approximately fifty batik sarongs, which would go well with the Malay kampong (village) women, in exchange for the dried fish, which in turn would bring a fair price back in Singapore.

It would give those Singapore Excise people something to think about. No doubt they would soon be on the telephone to Johore, and when Johore Excise found out that I had traded batik sarongs for dried fish, there would be a few red faces back in Singapore. It was often a struggle to keep up the appearance of being just another honest trader of goods. The lucrative jobs were in running guns or contraband, or special one-off rescue or delivery missions.

Every now and then I would be asked to deliver cargo, but I always had to know up front exactly what the nature of that cargo was. Then I would factor in the risk I had to take with my boat and the lives of my crewmen, which in turn determined my price to carry out such a run. I always charged a reasonable and realistic fee, with a small mark-up, never wishing to appear greedy. I was in this for the long haul, not just to make quick dollars.

Friday, 21 February 1947

Tanjung Surat, Sungai Johore estuary

At 0530 hours we were off Tanjung Surat, in the Sungai Johore estuary, having first rounded Pulau Tekong Besar. We were now on course for the fishing village of Panchor, further upriver. I had a license to trade with the Johore authorities and an old Magelang bill of sale from the island of Java, which would lend authority to my scheme to appear on the up and up. We arrived at Panchor at 0700 hours, and I immediately declared my small cargo to Johore

Customs and paid the duty required. That side of the business being concluded, I gave a couple of sarongs to the officer concerned. It was a little insurance that would make his wife happy and ensure his conjugal rights were always forthcoming. It was a sort of quid pro quo that would keep him in in a more benevolent frame of mind the next trip around.

Ahmad Ibrahim agreed to take the sarongs and use his influence to oblige me with a cargo of dried fish, provided I would allow him the consignment of batik sarongs on credit. This would net us both a fair profit. Most of the Malay fishermen in this area of Johore had an agreement with the Chinese fish traders, who advanced them cash against their catches before they were even caught. This gave the Chinese the full monopoly of the fish at the retail end of the market. As I was in a strong position cash-wise, I could have paid on the spot for the dried fish, but this would have had to be done on the quiet. I left Ahmad Ibrahim to make the necessary arrangements, telling him he had just two hours to have all the fish loaded.

Jani, our boat's cook, was busy in the marketplace, selling *minyak tangis duyong*, the tears of a mermaid, a potent love philtre, at a dollar a bottle. Indeed, I give credit where it is due for his ingenuity, but perhaps it was time to give our ship's cook just a little more work on board. It was 1300 hours when we finally completed the loading and got the boat underway again, heading downriver towards the estuary and into the Straits of Johore en route to Singapore. By 1500 hours we were off the east coast of the island, and thirty minutes later we had come alongside the fish market at Beech Road.

As expected, Singapore Customs and Excise people went through everything on my boat, but it was good, exciting fun to watch them go through all that hard work and not find any contraband. The look on the face of the officer when he handed me the necessary clearance papers was well worthwhile. Chan Bee, a trader and friend I knew took the consignment after a little haggling, and we came up with a reasonable price that left me with a modest but fair profit.

A reliable source from my underground informants had told me that a certain party was in the market for penicillin and I had promised to see what I could do. I'd also heard on the grapevine that the Customs and Excise people were after Roy concerning his last trip, when it was alleged that he'd outrun an Excise boat near Pulau Bukum, the Shell Oil Refinery. To me this was not a major problem at the moment; I was confident that we could clear it up and settle it once I had been made aware of all the facts relative to this case. A little horse-trading where the Excise people were concerned could work wonders—providing the horse concerned delivered the necessary result on time.

Saturday, 22 February 1947

I dropped in at the fishing stake of a mutual Chinese friend off East Coast Road and saw Roy.

"I saw you coming in this afternoon," he said. "What took you so long?"

"Plenty," I told him. "I suppose you know they impounded your boat! What happened?"

"Well, it was like this!" he said. "We were off Pulau Bukum, around 0300 hours on Saturday, the fifteenth, when our port engine suddenly packed in. I went down to the engine room to see what was wrong, only to find that silly Malay bastard was asleep! He had forgotten to switch over the fuel tanks, and it took me ten minutes or so to bleed the fuel lines and restart the engine. By that time we had drifted close in towards the island. I had just got on the way again when the Excise boat took up the chase. Well, I decided to make a run for it, ran her up on the beach at Pasir Panjang, and took off with my crew, every man for himself!"

"What about your guns?" I asked.

"Overboard in the usual way, off Pasir Panjang," he replied.

"So, your boat's clean, then?" I said.

"Clean?" he replied.

"What's the cargo?" I asked.

"A bloody full load of batik sarongs," he replied.

"If you stay here," I said, "there is a good chance of you being picked up by the Excise during one of their spot checks. I am going to move you to a safe house somewhere near the harbour, first thing in the morning. Where your boat is concerned, I will get the necessary Dutch export papers from our usual source, pay the import duty, and recover both the boat and the cargo.

"What about the charges against me?" Roy said.

"Any *Bugis praus* in the area at the time?" I asked.

"No!" he replied.

"Pity!" I said. "We could have said they followed you up from Java, and you were attempting to outrun them. Looks like we will have to do a little horse-trading with the Excise people."

My next port of call was on a backstreet in the Malay part of the city near Sultan Gate, which is where the *istana* is situated—the palace and seat of the Malay Temenggong in Singapore—between Arab Street and Jalan Sultan. Haji Hassan Omar taught the Malayan art of self-defence, called *bersilat*. This Malayan martial art can be divided into two forms: *putat*, which is a dancelike series of movements intended for public display, and *buah*, a realistic combat method rarely openly displayed. Bersilat is also practised in the southern Philippines, along with *langkah silat*, *kuntao silat*, and *kali silat*. Silat techniques vary greatly, from the low ground-fighting postures of *harimau* (tiger) silat to the high-flying throws of *madi* silat. Silat roughly means "skill for fighting".

There are hundreds of different styles of silat, most of which are found in Indonesia, Malaysia, Singapore, southern Thailand, and the southern Philippines. Common to all these styles is a combat-oriented ideology and the use of weaponry, such as the kris. Haji was the best official rubber stamp and document manufacturer in the business, particularly where Dutch export permits were concerned. A well-informed and practical old man, Haji promised me that he would have the necessary documents finished by the morning and suggested I pick them up at 0900 hours. Now, that is my measure of efficiency for a skilled forger—a turnaround of twenty-four hours or less.

C. H. Koh, my barrister, was adamant that the charge against Roy (failing to comply with the lawful challenges of the Excise boat and attempting to evade import duty) would be dropped once the duty was paid. He suggested that I pay the duty required and take it from there. The fact that I had paid import duty to the Malay Excise people at Johore on my own cargo would stand me in good stead, I believed. There was nothing more I could do to alleviate the problem at that moment. If the boat was clean, then why had Roy gone into a panic? Perhaps this was due to the late onset of PTSD (Post-Traumatic Stress Disorder), a mental disorder lesser known back in the day, a result of his internment at Changi Prison at the hands of his brutal Japanese occupiers. Obviously, something had snapped and intensified his fear levels, for the Roy I knew had always been calm and collected.

It seemed that Fame Alvares had accepted my contract to become my mistress and all that it required of her. To start the contract required only her agreement on the start date, which was March next.

Taking a mistress in this part of the world is rather a serious business, in some ways like taking a contract wife, which is another story. There is the diligent in-depth background research to carry out on the person, including a proper medical examination. Health checks in such matters are standard procedure. All my private investigations to facilitate the contract meant that I knew more about Fame than she did about herself.

I'd look up T. S. Clark, with a view to negotiating a deal on his alleged supply of penicillin during the next couple of days. But my principal priority now was to get Roy off the hook with the Excise people. Gloria and I had a long conversation, during which we exchanged our thoughts and feelings on the subject. She was acquainted with T. S. Clark, as she'd worked for him before becoming my housekeeper. Her general opinion of the man was that he was not one to be trusted.

Sunday, 23 February 1947
Singapore is a rather busy port, even on a Sunday. I had an early breakfast and saw Gloria's brother at his Harbour Board office in

Tanjong Pagar shortly after 0830 hours. He confirmed the arrangements and handed me the key of his front door. Nelson Road is a side street of Keppel Road, immediately opposite the harbour Gate 5. There were a few people about the street when I arrived at the house. There was a young Malay boy selling *nasi lemak*, a kind of rice cooked in coconut water, plus a couple of small children playing outside one of the houses.

The house at 121 Nelson Roar was situated immediately behind the fire hydrant. One of the few in the street that stood out from the rest, it was close to the harbour and more or less under the noses of the Excise people. The logic of my reasoning was that you wouldn't expect to find the man you are looking for in your own backyard. Once I had a good look around for all the advantageous approach points, I felt more or less sure that this place would make a good safe house. The front door was locked, so I knocked and waited. I thought it strange, because he'd said his wife would be at home. After a moment or two, I unlocked the door and entered, relocking the door behind me.

I then heard the sound of laughter in one of the upstairs rooms. If my informative was correct, his wife was supposed to be alone. The laughter proved otherwise! Catlike, I took the stairs step by step. The door of the front bedroom had been left wide open so that they could hear anyone coming into the house from either entrance below. The wife, Enchang, was on the bed with both knees held tightly together. A youth, a member of the Joseph family from the next house, was attempting to force her legs apart and mount her. I placed my automatic pistol to his head and threatened to blow his cock off with it if he ever came near the woman again. Trembling, the youth fumbled with his clothes and managed to dress himself.

"Now remember, this woman is mine!" I said for effect, and he nodded his head in agreement.

I marched him down the stairs and out the back door. Enchang was still naked on the bed when I returned a moment later, her eyes ablaze with anger. Her breasts were large, like bronze papayas, full and fleshy, and her buttocks well-formed, falling away into her chunky thighs.

"Open your legs!" I snapped, and she complied immediately, revealing a mass of thick black hair at her crutch, though which her clitoris peeped pink and healthy between the open lips of her vulva. It was the largest vagina I had ever seen. Perhaps I had done the Joseph youth a favour, for she would have drawn him in shoes and all!

"Your husband told you I was coming?" I asked.

"Yes," she said.

"Good," I replied. "Now get dressed, and prepare a hot meal for the man who is going to stay here for a few days. But keep your hands off him while he is here!"

I picked Roy up and saw him safely installed in the back bedroom of the house. Enchang cooked him a good meal, and there was nothing more to be done. Later I called in at Sultan Gate at 1045 hours, a little later than the suggested 0900 hours to meet and picked up the necessary papers for Roy's cargo. I watched the Malay bersilat fighters train hard their skills for a while outside their kampongs. I did not mention anything concerning my encounter with Enchang to Roy. I felt rather sorry for her husband, having to cope with a woman like that.

Practising bersilat

Monday, 24 February 1947

I suppose you could call it empathy, the power of aligning oneself to another person and sharing his or her feelings. Perhaps this is why Roy and I, on the one hand, and Gloria and I on the other, seemed to get on so well. We shared each other's problems, up to a point. We had mutual respect for each other's points of view. Roy, however, often used meaningless expletives like *damn* and *blast* or even curses. Gloria, in contrast, was always very logical in her approach to problem-solving or working out a tricky situation. But you had to be linguistic in order to appreciate the qualities of her logic. It was quite normal for Gloria to switch languages mid-sentence, for a more precise definition, during the course of any conversation, English being her third language.

My encounter with the Customs and Excise authorities was not unpleasant and, contrary to what many here on the island believed about these people, did not present too many difficulties. Paying the duty required for the release of Roy's boat took me just twenty minutes. Breaching the bureaucracy of those officious junior members of staff all bucking for sudden advancement to promotion was another matter. It was another hour before I finally arrived at the headman in the preventative branch. It was an encouraging start to rather informative talks on both sides.

I emphasized the fact that Roy had been the subject of some unexpected difficulties during his voyage home from Tjilatap. During the war, Tjilatap had been the only ocean port of any significance on the south coast of Java. It had a very small anchorage and narrow channel and correspondingly limited facilities. I further argued that Roy had been hassled by the Bugis, who had a monopoly on the sarong trade from Java and were smugglers and dangerous pirates. The chief officer of the preventative branch then agreed to drop all the charges against Roy, but with the same breath he was looking for new intelligence—quid pro quo—on the crux of a rather large problem he was faced with.

"Do you know the fat man," he said quietly.

"You mean Lue Poh Kee?" I asked—and could have bitten off my tongue at that moment. "Yes, I know him," I said quickly, "but we do not move in the same circles. I believe he is into drugs?"

"You are quite right," he said without batting an eyelid. "The fat man's next major drug consignment is due in these waters shortly, on my watch, most likely. I'm going to introduce you to one of my drug enforcement operatives," he said. He picked up the telephone and spoke into it briefly.

Margaret Woon walked into the room, looking her old self and not a day older. She was all gracious smiles. She was not nicknamed St Margaret for nothing. I fully expected her fourteen holy helpers to pop out of the woodwork at any moment. Margaret was a useful criminal underworld information source through horse trading when I first met her acquaintance after leaving the British military at the end of the second world war. She was also a friend.

"Hello, Rex," she said and held out her hand towards me, which I crushed in one of my masterly handshakes. Rex is a term of endearment used by those who know me closely, because of my jungle dog, also named Rex.

"You two know each other then?" the headman of the Excise said. "Good. That makes things a little easier to put together."

"I have got to pick up a boat, plus I've got a little party to go to after that," I told him.

"Come on then!" Margaret put in. "I always enjoy a good party."

I got the distinct feeling that the headman had deliberately set me up, the favour in return for a favour. This was something I had to live with for a while, at least until he had got from me what he was after. I decided to pick up a few of my old teammates from the Royal Engineers to crew the boat. It would be much quicker than attempting to round up Roy's crew, and a night on the town to my former Royal Engineer comrades would provide me with the necessary distraction of a party.

As expected, Margaret tagged along, and once we had berthed the boat alongside my own MTB, she came along with us to the Criterion, at the junction of Oxley Road and Orchard Road. Dutch Ann and her friends kept the lads well entertained with Tiger and Anchor beers, which I paid for round by round rather than running up a large bill for the end of the night. The occasional trips the lads made upstairs with the various pretty working girls were at their own expense. The last party I had thrown at the Criterion had been in 1946; it had turned out to be a rather wild affair.

That one had been paid for with a chit signed by each one of us and drawn on good old Lord Louis Mountbatten of Burma, who paid up like the gent he was when the note was later presented for payment at Government House in Singapore. Dutch Ann had a very good memory, so it was cash on the barrel on this occasion.

"My place or yours?" I asked Margaret, who pretended at first that she didn't understand.

"Your boss told us to get it together!" I said innocently.

"Not that, you fool!" she retorted. "Your place."

Gloria put her up in the spare room for the night.

Tuesday, 25 February 1947

I've always done my little business deals with God—again, a kind of quid pro quo—I mean to say through sincere prayer and exchange of energy. I really do believe it works, because my prayers have been answered on more than one occasion, and I've managed to get home safely when all the odds of coming through the ordeal in one piece were so stacked against me. Again, for the sake of clarity, I will say that I am not a religious man. But all the same, life can be very precarious at times, so it's nice to know there is a god out there who keeps his or her word.

We had breakfast early, at six o'clock, and spent the rest of the morning prancing around in the South China Sea beyond the three-mile international waters limit with Magge, short for Margaret, the drug-enforcement operative in this region who was following me around and hoping to catch the major drug drop-off bound for Singapore. Watching every ship approaching Singapore through our binoculars, I found the surveillance game extremely tedious. Magge kept in touch with a couple of Excise boats on shore by radio, but as she allowed me to listen in to their sitreps (situation reports), I managed to pick up a lot of their drug enforcement coded jargon, which would come in handy later on.

Isn't it strange and kind of funny how boredom seems to accentuate everything around you? Magge was in her element, self-importance, doing what she was most happy doing, which was catching drug gangs in the act. Her boss had twisted my arm to help her get that first big break and chalk up a huge drug bust to her resume. Then she became rather fidgety, the way children do, moving from one leg to the other in a kind of highland jig on the spot when they want to spend a penny. I was against the idea of quid pro quo, but we would have to see where this was going and whether there was a future bargaining chip to be gained by investing a degree of co-operation with the authorities. The locals called them "the eyes".

"I suppose you have one?" she said.

"Most men do, Magge," I said with assurance, making humour by taunting her further still.

"A toilet?" she blurted, her face blushing red.

"Yes," I said. "The boat's head (naval term for toilet) is immediately below, opposite my cabin. But watch out for the redback under the seat before you use it."

"Redback?" she said with astonishment.

"Yes," I said. "It's a little poisonous spider. We have been trying to kill it for months, but don't worry, we will suck the poison out for you if necessary. But if it's an emergency and you don't want to chance it with the redback, you can always put your bottom over the starboard side of the boat. The wind is to port at the moment. But watch out for the sharks." I smiled, straight-faced.

Magge went below in quite a red-faced flutter and was gone for a good twenty minutes. She was quite composed when she returned to the bridge and took up her binoculars again.

It was a little over 1500 hours when a ship of the Liberty-type cargo tramps arrived on the scene, on a heading for the harbour at Singapore. Her course was right, and she had obviously travelled down the Gulf of Siam from Bangkok. She was, of course, United States built, with a short, high superstructure, three masts forward, and one mast aft. Her kingposts were set against the after end of the bridge, and she had a flush deck.

The strange thing concerning this ship was that she was discharging galley waste aft. It was not a lot, and it was quite normal for any ship's cook to dump his waste before the ship berthed. Magge and I spent the next ten minutes at my chart table examining the number of cross-currents running in that area and working out the necessary coordinates. At the next turn of the tide, the surge of the inflow would put most of that galley waste on Bedok beach. The coordinates were spot on with the tidal drift in that area of the sea. Magge got straight back on the radio and set the operation up with the rest of her team. This made me aware that things for me would not be the same; with all these drug enforcement operation stings, I would have to watch out more diligently in this neck of the woods from now on. Her people would probably have a boat out here on a permanent basis, which would rather cramp my contraband-running system a little in these waters. But proving a point is always something else. I started the compressor and filled the two tanks, checked the compression, and kitted out in my wetsuit.

This was going to be a swim more than a dive. I instructed Zainal to hold the boat on course for twenty minutes and then to turn and trace the course, picking me up with the hoop on his return run. I rolled off the deck when Zainal indicated we had reached the spot. There was an abundance of galley flotsam on the surface of the waves, more than enough to draw all the bloody sharks in the South China Sea. I wondered where the sharks were. A lone diver in a sea of sharks is not something I would recommend to anyone!

It was then that I did one of my little business deals with god, for I saw a jute sack, one of a number of sacks floating some three of four feet below the surface of the sea. There was no way I could pick up a large sack and get myself out of the water in one go with that hoop. I decided to chance it and attach my bodyline to one of the sacks. I would trail it behind me and hope like hell the sudden weight would not pull me back into the water when I made contact with the pickup loop. There was also the chance that the trailing line would foul the screws of the boat and drag me down.

Twenty minutes is no time at all. The boat was back for another pass, and I gained the hoop in one this time. Unfortunately I also bashed my right knee badly during the process, but I held on fast and was pulled back on deck. Zainal kept the boat at an angle while we recovered the sack from the sea. It contained eight 4-gallon tins, with each tin three parts full of green, raw, top-quality opium. Magge was overwhelmed with our success. We headed inshore with the necessary evidence, but that was the last I saw of her, because she went into immediate conference with her superiors. She did not resurface again until it was all over the bar, all that shouting. I was glad of the respite this state of affairs gave me. It allowed me to focus on my own little business in hand without hindrance from the Excise people, who were too busy rejoicing over their drug-bust success.

I could now get back to a number of little jobs requiring our immediate assurances. I was rather tired, needing to at least rest after my little dip in the sea. I had one hell of a bruise on my right knee; this was rather painful and left me with a slight limp. Strange though it may seem, the injury did not concern me so much as the absence of sharks in the wake of that ship.

It's surprising what a good meal and a few brandies can achieve where one's morale is concerned, and I was soon feeling my old self again. I have always been a rebel at heart, the kind never to yield under pressure from anybody.

I suppose it is a kind of personal pride in my self-esteem. Perhaps there is something moral in it, the right way of leading one's life, which comes from learning through experience. I am fully aware that there may be far-reaching repercussions from my part in today's actions against the drug lords by helping the Excise people. There is also the possibility of reprisals from the drug runners, due to the amount of corruption in the lower establishment where the Excise people are concerned. I decided to sleep on it. After all, tomorrow must be a better day!

Wednesday, 26 February 1947

It was a bright, sunny morning in spite of the few dark clouds on the distant horizon, a remnant of the predawn squall which had swept in from the sea and uprooted a number of coconut palms along the beach. The bruises on my right knee were more profuse this morning, although not quite so painful as they had been the night before. The knee joint itself was rather stiff and not so easily bent. Gloria decided to use *urat* on the strained muscles. Urat is a type of Filipino and Malayan healing art using physical massage at specific points on the body.

The manipulation of the afflicted muscles and areas on the body is also intended to drive away any spirit that has lodged itself in the etheric level of its victim. When the bad spirit is gone, the sickness will go away, or at least that is the theory. At first the urat treatment felt worse than the injury itself, but then it seemed to do the trick. At least I could walk without much of a limp afterwards. Gloria certainly knew her healing arts, in particular massage, but then her late husband had been a master diver, and she had done it all before.

The Straits Times and the *Malaya Tribune* both had the story on their front page: the Excise people had captured two boats off the coast of Bedok in Singapore and had seven Chinese in custody, together with a large quantity of drugs. Drugs had also been found on the *Sam Holt*, a ship in the harbour, with two members of her crew now in custody. There was no mention of Magge or the part I had taken in the operation, for which I felt most grateful. I dropped in at the G.H. Café later that afternoon and put an ear to the old grapevine. Lew Poh Kee was not one of those in custody. The people they'd arrested were a bunch of small fry. I guessed I would have to be just a little more observant and watch my back. These drug smugglers could be very vindictive, and I did not place much trust in the Excise people, who could be horse-traded.

The immense profits made by selling opium to China in the nineteenth century financed British expansion in the Far East and caused untold suffering. A significant portion of colonial revenues came directly from the sale of opium in those days. When the Chinese and the British signed the Treaty of Nanking back in 1842, at the end of the Opium Wars, the Chinese began to produce their own opium on a large scale. Then the Chinese armies massacred entire populations in an attempt to subdue and tax the independent tribes. Many refugees of the Hmong ethnic group fled into Laos, Siam, and the Shan States of Burma, carrying the technique of opium cultivation with them.

Thursday, 27 February 1947

The bruise on my right knee was less sore this morning than yesterday. I felt a little better when I woke up with some mobility returned to my right leg. Rest and healing arts indeed have an amazing effect on bodily processes.

I can be nagged by a woman, and I can also be coaxed, but no woman will ever tell me what I should or should not do. My mind is my own, and this will always be the way I am. My heart, however, is quite a different matter. After all, I am one of those roguish males who is rather fond of playing tricks.

In life I have found that some people are so strong they do not need anyone else in their lives. Some people are so weak that they need the support of many others.

My injury kept me indoors for the better part of the day, seeking solace within myself and perhaps some answers also in Kahlil Gibran's 1923 book entitled *The Prophet*. I made notes in pencil throughout my copy of that book, which I knew Pamela, my wife back in England, also had. Born in 1883, Gibran believed in universal spirituality, although his private life—he was an alcoholic—was certainly in contrast with the work in his book. But then, all the truly great people in our lives, the ones with mission and purpose, have their own crosses to bear.

"For what is it to die but to stand naked in the wind and to melt into the sun? And what is to cease breathing but to free the breath from its restless tides, that it may rise and expand and seek God unencumbered? Only when you drink from the river of silence shall you indeed sing."

Kahlil Gibran ~ The Prophet

Everyman

Every man is both good and bad,
A portrait just for exhibition;
Vanity recounts that flatter the ego
Quick keep the real self-safe.

Beneath the face mask we choose,
Rather than face what is real,
Do not let them peer behind,
Where shadows lurk or prance in time.

The dance of life needs laughter,
But the dance of death is pain;
Are life and death impostors? Indeed, they are the same.
The end of the cycle always allows a new beginning.

You would never like the real me,
Nor I. for that matter, given food for thought;
For no shadow is ever truly real in the scheme of things,
But alas, in the end of it all, no one truly gives a care.

The pain of life's desire avoids at all costs
That hidden sense of purpose and of good and bad
Deep, deep within us all who dare;
Nightly make your conscience give account to bear.

On what is right and what is wrong
Or wishing hard for things you never had,
Does it really matter all, that clatter?
You can't take it with you, inanimate matter.

So, do live your life the way life is
And not how you think it ought to be;
Those shadows all around us are but limited illusions,
Concealing a higher truth, you see.

Friday, 28 February 1947

My knee is much better today, and I can now walk without a limp again. Roy is finally back with Lynn, and Magge didn't get the smuggler she was after. But knowing Magge, that won't deter her one bit. So, Lew Poh Kee had better watch his back.

Lately I've noticed that Roy is rather too pleased with himself. I think smug is the word for it! I seem to remember the sound of steel springs being sprung at 121 Nelson Road—that sound of bedsprings under the torment of immense strain. I have the feeling that Enchang got her man after all. Roy has said nothing about it for the moment, but then he was never one to keep things to himself for very long.

I would like to attempt another trip and go adventuring in search of the lost world of Agharti, with its network of tunnels linking the continents to its capital city. Myth or reality? The occult secrets of Asia, perhaps, together with the lost continent of Atlantis. But maybe tomorrow will be a better day and next month a better month. For now I will need to focus on my next job, raising a large seaplane from the murky waters where she was shot down during the war by the Japanese and disturbing the dead who perished where she sank.

Chapter 11

The Flying Boat

Saturday, 1 March 1947

We have gained a contract to raise a "flying boat" that crashed during the last moments of fighting before the fall of Singapore on 15 February 1942. With the outbreak of World War II, Australian Qantas pilots bravely kept flying to Singapore to maintain a three-flying-boat link per week with the island colony. But when Singapore fell to Japanese forces, the last Qantas flying boat escaped the beleaguered island by moonlight on 4 February 1942, carrying approximately forty passengers. The wreck of this flying boat is in approximately sixty feet of water on the harbour side of the old breakwater, a thick wall built out into the sea to lessen the force of the waves near the harbour. I initially suggested that we place a couple of demolition charges under the wreck, which would be quick and effective in producing the desired effect, but the port authorities want the flying boat raised whole and in one piece. Roy and I are to make our exploratory dive this afternoon and report back our findings as to the state of the wreck blocking up the harbour channel. I wonder what they expect to discover in the wreck. It's anyone's guess.

I noticed a couple of tiger fighters, Kow Ong (Big Dog) and Kow Sai (Dog Shit) hanging around the wharf. Both these dodgy characters are hatchet men, paid assassins for the 303, one of the local Chinese secret societies in Singapore. It appears the Chinese take pride in their given nicknames, and being called Big Dog I can understand, but why Dog Shit?

About five years ago, the Japanese-instituted atrocity known to the local Chinese as *Sook Ching,* (purge through cleansing) took place, lasting from 18 February to 4 March 1942. These brutal massacres were as per SOPs (standard operating procedures where war crime massacres are concerned) secretly carried out by the brutal Japanese occupation forces at various locations on the island. Our dive site is reputed to be one of them and carries notoriety for being haunted by the hundreds of local militiamen who were machine-gunned to death here alongside thousands of other innocent civilians. So it was not much of a secret after all. There were many first-hand survivors who were left to tell the tale of the horrors committed on thousands of innocent Chinese people, some of whom dared oppose Japanese occupation in the colonies.

At this site, the Japs marched the local Chinese defence force militia along the wall and summarily executed them all at the wall of the wharf, so that their bodies fell into the sea to be devoured by the sharks and crabs. The Japanese repeated this atrocity also on Pulau Blakang Mati. Both Roy and I have seen the large number of skulls and skeletons in the water just off Pulau Blakang Mati, and while we are not squeamish or easily shocked, diving in such an undersea boneyard is unpleasantness itself. But then, it is a violent world which we live in!

The exploratory dive went rather well, but contrary to local belief, there was little evidence of the alleged massacre five years earlier at this place. However, the local crabs were fat and well fed, and the sharks had in all probability done their job well at the time of the massacre. The flying boat was right side up on the bottom, sheltered from the sea and its prevailing cross-currents by the breakwater. We would have to loosen the seabed a little around her, and this would take time. We spent the rest of the afternoon making the necessary arrangements and getting our working pontoon into its proper position above the wreck. The rest was a mathematical problem-solving conundrum to calculate all the equations required to lift the wreck from the seabed and back to the surface.

We also needed to remove a large volume of water to create the necessary buoyancy. We intended to use compressed air as the lifting force but would need another air compressor to supplement out own and give us the required power. The idea was to inflate a number of air bags within the fuselage of the aircraft simultaneously, while maintaining a balance equilibrium and refloat the wreck gradually. Theoretically it was a good proposition, but in practice, as with so many things, there was always the unforeseen factor, a kind of fait accompli or something that has already happened and cannot be changed.

I had my ritual bath and spent the next hour developing the film I had taken around the wreck during the dive. To my complete surprise, an oddity appeared on the developed infrared negative which I simply could not explain. I am not governed by superstition; this place did not give me the creeps, massacre or no massacre! The people around here are a little too credulous, and I will require more proof before I can arrive at any solid conclusion for the moment.

It has always been my contention that you only need fear the living and not the dead. I have witnessed some very strange phenomena in my life where no other possible explanation would exist for the events that had transpired. In any tight or unexplained situation, my way of dealing with it is to stay calm and to remain cool. Conon Doyle once said, "Once you eliminate the impossible, whatever remains, no matter how improbable, must be the truth." Only after you have considered all other possible rational explanations should you delve into the world of the supernatural and ghosts who never rest in this world. I have seen a few apparitions in my time, but the following is the very first time some photographic evidence came to light on the spectre that shadowed Roy, my partner in the deep.

The spectre behind Roy at the wreck site

That's Roy and Idris in the infrared military photograph which I had taken above. If you look closely where Roy's airline is curled behind his head between the air bubbles, you will see another figure, without diving gear, right behind Roy. Indeed, the face is quite clear, and the figure is almost a part of Roy. It's weird, like some sort of ghostly being looking over his shoulder. There must be a reasonable logical explanation. Perhaps it was the infrared military film I am using?

Sunday, 2 March 1947

Air under pressure is a funny thing. The higher the working pressure, the more negative the buoyancy and the greater the inherent risk. We decided to use air lines rather than bottles on this job, due both to the depth of the wreck and the long hours required to set the job up right.

Sharks are the biggest hazard for divers, and up to that moment we had been rather lucky. Perhaps it was because we were working inshore. For years it was believed that the most vulnerable time for a shark attack was when the diver was going down or coming up from the seabed and that sharks would not attack divers working close to the bottom. However, several know fatalities have proved this urban legend wrong! The disappearance without a trace of the occasional solo diver emphasizes the perilous nature of this work.

The front of the aircraft was half buried in the seabed, and I set up a couple of low explosive charges deep on each side of the wreck, which would loosen the seabed under the wreck at the moment of lift, at least that was the theory. We set the large airbags up inside the fuselage of the aircraft and connected them to the airlines in the necessary arranged sequence. This was a long, laborious, repetitive task which took most of the day to complete.

"Well, it will be Monday before we can put her to the test," my boozing partner, Roy, said.

Back on land, we found the coffee shop in Anson Road and had a fresh pineapple with a couple of bottles of Tiger beer.

"Hey, you are divers, aren't you? Want a woman?" the barboy asked.

"You have her!" Roy replied and finished his beer. Tanjong Pagar Road at Anson Road is where most of the Chinese coffee shops cater for seamen, and I suppose they think we are all tarred with the same brush. It was nice to have offers but sad in a way to know the locals here believe all Navy divers are boozers and whore chasers.

Isn't it strange how time seems to fly when you have something interesting to do? Well, the next day would be the acid test where the flying boat wreck was concerned, and we were going to make an early start, just in case. I was going to sleep on it and have an early night!

Monday, 3 March 1947

The explosion was rather mild, just as I had intended; I'd used only low charges carefully sited deep on each side of the wreck. My intention was to loosen up the seabed's grip on the wreck and not damage the flying boat, as our contract required her to be lifted from her resting place whole and intact. Then followed the enforced period of waiting for the murky pea soup that had been stirred up around the wreck to clear up. This seemed to take forever. The air compressors were both running at full working pressure, and we commenced by bleeding the air valves attached to each of the airbags in the fuselage of the wreck.

We checked everything, looking for any faults as the airbags slowly expanded with the steady flow of compressed air filling them to capacity. We found a leak on one valve, so we were forced to shut down the operation while we changed the damn valve in situ. Then it was all regulators on, and at 3,000 PSI working pressure, the wreck started to lift slowly from the seabed and commence her gradual ascent to the surface after some five years on the bottom. I had fully anticipated a number of problems with the buoyancy of the wreck once we got her afloat, but against all expectations, she came right, which meant that I'd got all my mathematical calculations and equations right first time! My old mathematics teacher would never have believed it!

The pontoon at the wreck site

I'd had visions of the wreck popping up to the surface like a cork out of a bottle once the airbags were fully inflated. That is why it is such a slow job; it is necessary to maintain an equal flow of air under pressure at the right capacity. Once we had the wreck on the surface, we brought the air bags up to full capacity in order to keep her afloat while she was taken in tow and the air lines finally disconnected. Then she was on her way over to the British Naval base at Seletar, leaving us to clear up our diving gear and supporting kit.

We headed back home at the end of play, to rest up and relax for the evening. We were quite pleased with the outcome. This was one of those rare times when a job had turned out exceptionally well for me and my dive crew. I spent the rest of the evening in town killing some Tigers. Out in this part of the world we never drank alcohol in the daytime, only in the cool breezes of the evenings. It rained that evening, so I guess that saved me from washing my hands and feet when I got home. Local Malay superstition said that if you'd been to a haunted site, washing the body would keep the bad spirits away.

Tuesday, 4 March 1947
I had seen nothing more of that ghostly apparition which had appeared in the photograph of our dive to the wreck. There is a Buddhist text that describes how the Buddha trained himself to

overcome fear by sitting in a haunted graveyard. All civilizations have believed in ghosts, and there are quite a number of well-authenticated accounts given by some very credible people. Even famous celebrities have claimed they have witnessed ghosts and spirits first-hand.

Spiritualism takes the view that there are many earthbound spirits who are not aware that they have died. They therefore continue to visit the scenes of their past lives in a state analogous to delirium. With all the violence and sudden death during the war, with so many young lives cut off in their prime, this explanation is quite plausible. I now wonder how I would have reacted had I suddenly been confronted with this apparition at that depth. I couldn't write it off as a figment of my imagination, simply because one cannot photograph a figment of imagination!

I had taken the black-and-white exposures with an old German 120 Aktiengesellschaft für Anilinfabrikation which had been rather crudely adapted for underwater photography. The 120 film I was using was ex-British Army infrared with a speed well below the spectrum of ordinary light so that it would pick up heat signatures also. Electromagnetic radiation, having a wavelength longer than that of red light, is invisible to the naked eye but can be detected by photographic and other means that can penetrate haze. My conclusion about this place was that yes, there had been a massacre there five years earlier. The place had a rather macabre local reputation historically. Again, we were all of us aware when we made the dive of what had once happened there, and I suppose each one of us felt a certain amount of trepidation.

Flying boat wreck at naval base in Seletar

You can never quite know what you will discover on such occasions, and that is always a disadvantage on your first dive. I kept the discovery of the shadowy phantom to myself, not wanting to discourage the others in my team, many of whom held local superstitions close to their hearts and would be disturbed by it. Discipline and self-control are very necessary where divers are concerned. I try to keep an open mind, but in fairness, this certainly was not my first encounter with the supernatural nor will it be my last.

We may choose to believe in a higher order of being, call it God or beings out there watching over us, such as guardian spirits. It would be naïve to assume that nothing else can possibly exist outside of flesh. Many of my Malay friends believe in the supernatural; as I've pointed out, they are by nature a very superstitious race.

Wednesday, 5 March 1947

Yesterday was rather busy, and we spent most of this morning over at the British naval base at Seletar recovering the salvage gear we had left inside the wreck. They have got her up on the sloping track for moving boats in and out of the water and have a gang of people working on cleaning her up. She is still rather tatty and will require a lot of hard work if she is ever going to fly again. But we have got her off the bottom with time to spare, a fact we are rather proud of. The base commodore thought we were a couple of ex-Royal Navy divers, or perhaps it was just the way we walked, but more likely it was the speed, professionalism, and efficiency with which we retrieved their plane intact from the harbour waters after it had been there for some five years! There is always an unmistakable look and demeanour to military veterans of combat, something very different about them. Perhaps it's the way they hold themselves, the way they walk or, especially, their way of thinking.

Needless to say, on parade days a real military combat veteran can easily pick out the pretenders who claim the glory for something they never did. Those who were there and saw first-hand would rather forget.

Roy and I spent most of the afternoon trying one of the few bottles of Tiger beer at the G.H. Cafe. We met the proprietor of the East West Traders, a former major in the Indian Army who has a consignment of silk he wants picked up from Bangkok. If we can find cargo for Siam or anyplace near, then he is on. I paid the salvage cheque into the bank next door and returned to my boozing partner to kill a few more Tigers and bravely tackle our next problem. We have had enough of diving for a living, and it was time again to get back to the more lucrative trade of smuggling contraband now that the heat was off for a while.

Thursday, 6 March 1947

Low turned up this morning, and it would appear that the River Salween job is on the table again. But this time it is scheduled for the eighteenth of May next. I just hope the two principles of this contract have a more workable proposition in mind on this occasion. Neither Roy or I fancy running the river through Dacoit territory with a boatload of guns, it would be like inviting World War III! I suggested that we would consider running between the islands into the river near Tenasserim and asked him to get back to us with the answer. He left to consult with his fellow conspirators with a smile on his face.

Kampong (Malay for village) Bahru Road is a narrow thoroughfare with a bitumen surface road that in the heat of the noonday sun bubbles at the edge alongside the deep monsoon drains. The roads twist its wash from the Shell filling station immediately opposite the *surau* at the foot of Mount Faber and the commencement of Kampong Radin Mas.

A *surau* is a privately owned mosque (compared to a mosque of general assembly). Suraus exist throughout certain regions of Sumatra and the Malay Peninsula. It is said that the *surau karimat* is the place where a miracle worker is buried. A *wali keramat* or *dato keramat* is the spot where the local Malays claim the original Malay dignitary of high rank on the island—or Temenggong—was buried. The Temenggong was responsible for maintaining law and order and for commanding the police and army.

The Radin Mas Malay School is just a little further along the road, opposite the bungalows of those people employed by the Singapore Harbour Board. This area is rather appropriately called Bushy Park.

This is also the home of 1047 Port Operating Company of the Corps of Royal Engineers from October 1945 to April 1946, when the company disbanded at the Keppel Road end of the Kampong Bahru Road. Just below Bushy Park, at the junction of Keppel Road and Nelson Road, we have a former Australian prisoner of war camp which, ironically, is full of Japanese surrender prisoners. The Coolie Lines are where Chinese and Indian labourers for the wharf are housed, just below the wharfinger bungalows on Bushy Park hill. The *wharfinger* is the individual in charge of all goods delivered to the wharf, who usually works out of an office on the dock. He is responsible for day-to-day activities, including slipways, keeping tide tables, and resolving disputes.

There is an early morning street market around the junction of Kampong Bahru Road and Nelson Road, immediately opposite Kampong Bahru Police Station. Fresh fish, meat, and vegetables are on sale. There are also a number of street-food hawkers who frequent this place, so eating is never a problem if you are comfortable with their level of food hygiene. In fairness to the trade, I have never gotten sick eating from the street-food vendors here.

Gloria is teaching me to speak Tagalog; some of its linguistic semantics can be identified with both the Malay and Spanish languages. There are approximately eighty-seven different native languages and dialects spoken in the Philippine Islands, all of which are closely related to one another. Ilocano is the language of the Northern Philippine provinces. Tagalog is the language used by the people of the central portion of Luzon. Visayan languages are spoken in the central or Visayan islands. But the national language is Tagalog, though both English and Spanish are taught in the schools of the Philippines.

Filipinos are predominantly Roman Catholic due to the influence of the Spanish missionaries. Ferdinand Magellan was a heroic Portuguese nobleman and staunch Catholic with an anti-Islamic agenda. He discovered the Philippine Islands and landed at the island of Cebu on 16 March 1521. Only after a few weeks of trade and press-gang conversions to Catholicism with a local chief there did Magellan end up losing his life after being hit by a poison arrow, while fighting the chief of a rival tribe. In due course, the conversions of many Filipinos to Catholicism took a firm hold.

Before that, Filipinos had worshiped their native gods or had no religion at all. The Augustine friars who came with the Spanish conquistador Miguel López de Legazpi some forty years later continued the work of conversion. The Franciscans arrived later, in 1577, the Jesuits and the Dominicans in 1581, the Recollects in 1606, and the Benedictines in 1895.

Gloria is rather superstitious, and I tend to humour her in this respect by not starting any of my business trips on a Friday. Filipinos tend to entertain a large number of quite interesting superstitions, which the better-read will often honour. Superstitions persist in almost every country and amongst so many diverse classes of peoples. Thus I will always heed Gloria's counsel when it comes to matters of local folklore practices. This is the heritage of days long ago, when primitive man lived in fear of the long, dark nights where phantoms lurked or the mysterious unknown. Strange though it may seem, quite a number of superstitions are well known in Europe. Some believe that when Friday falls on the thirteenth of the month, for instance, accidents are more likely to happen, so people avoid going out at all if they can help it. When a cat wipes its face with its paws, it is said, a visitor will be coming to the house.

Friday, 7 March 1947
St Francis Xavier's crab

The Filipinos, like most island people, are rather partial to seafood. I had brought a basket of live crab with me, freshly caught from the Johore Straits. Gloria took one look at them and said quite definitely that I would have to put them back into the sea. "The Chinese and Malays eat them, but we Filipinos don't!" I was informed.

Father Francis (John Raposa, 1506–1552), a Jesuit missionary priest, was sailing in a *carracca*, a rather small boat, from one of the islands off the coast of Malacca early one morning. A tempest broke out that was so strong all on board thought they would perish.

St Francis called out to God for help to calm the sea. Taking off the crucifix which he always wore suspended at his breast, he dipped it into the sea. But as he did so, somehow the crucifix slipped from his hand and was lost into the undercurrents. The storm then calmed down. Faustus Rodriguez, a Portuguese, as well as seven other eyewitnesses all swore an oath that this was true. A day later, while walking along the beach after disembarking from the small ship, St Francis saw a small crab coming towards him—carrying in its pincers the exact same crucifix that he had thought lost at sea!

St Francis blessed the crab, making the sign of the cross on its back. He recovered his crucifix and then gave thanks to God.

218

As legends do, this story got passed through the many Catholic generations of Filipinos, many of whom were devout Catholics who attended mass regularly, saying rosary-bead prayers. With each generation a little more was added or a few details changed. The story I heard was that St Francis put his rosary into the sea, not a crucifix.

The shell of the crab is a dirty blue, almost green, with a distinct sign of the cross in the centre of its back. Eight legs extend from a short, broad carapace, four on each side, extending from a small abdomen which curls forward beneath the body of the crab. A short antennae and a pair of limbs modified as pincers are also in evidence. This particular crab is a member of the *Brachyura* tribe and a living legend in these parts.

I returned the crabs to the sea and, funny though it may seem, never made that mistake again.

We have our moments, both with the authorities and our principles, to say nothing of adventures with the numerous pirate boats which also operate in these waters. To date we have been rather lucky, as we've always managed somehow to come through it all. Our worst problem is that we are often mistaken for Dutchmen, for when on this turbulent anti-colonial Indonesian terrain, this in itself can be quite dangerous. Some of the Indonesians are fanatical in their hatred of the Dutch and even worse in their dealings with those they consider Dutch collaborators.

Teris and her friend Ah-Leng are busy with their bicycles again, up and down the lane at the back of the house. They have both had a good meal of *pancit luglog*, which they topped off with a few heart-shaped mangos, the golden-yellow kind.

I don't know where they find the room in their stomachs to put all this food, but they are both growing girls, or should I say tomboys? The Mestiza dress or *traje de mestiza* is quite similar to a formal dress and is most distinctive because of the large butterfly sleeves, made from stiff netting. *Traje* is the Spanish word for dress and *mestizo* came from the Latin word *mixticius*, meaning mixed.

Roughly translated, *traje de mestiza* means mixed dress. The "Maria Clara", forerunner of the butterfly sleeves part of the dress, consisted of a blouse having full, embroidered sleeves and a skirt with wide black-and-white stripes. The dress was worn by all the up-and-coming Spanish ladies during the early days. The mestiza dress has since become the national costume of the Philippines and has kept pace with the times, evolving under various foreign European gowns, except for its distinctive sleeves and neckpiece.

The unique butterfly sleeves, with their native charm and feminine appeal, are practically all that remain of the original model, with the neckpiece, or *panuelo*, fast disappearing. The dress can be traced back to the sixteenth century and the days of Magellan. It has a direct line, its forerunner being a Malayan style of costume consisting of a long piece of plaid wrap-around skirt topped by a long-sleeved jacket. Teris, Gloria's daughter, looks more woman than I thought. She is fourteen and will be fifteen on the 11 September next. She still has that impish tomboy in her smile and is rather a real imp in many of her ways. Most of her leisure is spent on her bicycle or climbing tress with her friends. Gloria is rather strict with her rules of behaviour and a little quick with the cane when she thinks it's necessary. But before I came into their lives, they were living a rather harsh life, making ends meet on a day-to-day basis with black-market food, as the Japanese had deprived them of their diver husband and father during the war.

Chapter 12

Kasim the Fortunate
Saturday, 8 March 1947

The Kasim Bahagia

The G.H. Café in Battery Road is a gold mine of essential information and a place for wheeling and dealing if you are astute enough to sort out the sharks from the genuine. The secret is to listen, only paying close attention to detail, but especially not to let your left hand know what your right hand is about to do. That way your enemies can never guess your next move or read you. It's a fact that both Roy and I have no political opinions or agendas, as we do what we do clearly and naturally with a view to making hard cash and earning a living. We both have scruples, but we always keep them under wraps. We do not run hard drugs, recreational controlled substances, or white slaves, although we have both been approached on many occasions concerning these.

Bill Elwell and I concluded our business and had a drink together in celebration. I had just paid cash for some surplus jungle-green uniforms that would bring me a respectable profit on Karimata Island, and Bill wanted to know what other requirements I had.

There are those people who consider that money is power and can buy you anything your heart desires, so as long as the price is right. But everybody in this life has a price, although not necessarily a fixed monetary one. It could also be an exchange of some sort. It was at the G.H. café that I first met Emile Czaja, a 38-year-old charismatic individual in the ring, better known by his professional wrestling champion name, King Kong. He was an Indian wrestling champion, born in Hungary in 1909.

Emile Czaja

Emile, despite his stature, was a friendly character, and his presence filled any hall or stadium. Emile was in the G.H. Café when I was there that day, and by heck, he certainly knew how to kill a Tiger beer.

Sadly, there are also those people with money who place their nearest and dearest in harm's way by the foolhardiness of their greedy desire for more cash at the expense of the consequences to their personal lives.

Wee Fook was a go-between with a contract offer, if I wanted it. The contract was marginally difficult, which meant, by his accepted standards, damn bloody well dangerous, as no one else out there save yours truly would touch it with a barge pole!

It appeared that the daughter of a wealthy Chinese family had been kidnapped while on holiday. Apparently the father had already negotiated a deal for the girl's safe return but she'd failed to reappear. I had done one or two little jobs for Wee Fook in the past, and the payoff had been fast and prompt, minus any haggling at all from him once I had completed my end of the deal. There was no point in being speculative without all the necessary modus operandi, which would have to be straight from the horse's mouth. Wee Fook promised me he would set up another meeting with his principal that evening.

Roy appeared to be keeping a low profile in the afternoons these days. I had an idea that my partner was busy shagging the arse of someone he shouldn't be! But wasn't up to me to catch him at it—or was it? I decided on the latter action and dropped in just in time to hear the concluding notes of a Bridge over Troubled Waters played out on tortured bedsprings. I gave Roy a loud coitus interruptus shout, calling him downstairs. The sound of musical bedsprings stopped abruptly. A moment later, after some cheerful grumbling of expletives, Roy came trundling down the stairs.

"This had better be good!" he said gruffly. He looked for all the world like a man who thought he was coming when he was going and wasn't sure which. Perhaps he had gone off half-cocked?

Anyway, I cut out the sarcasm for the moment and came to the point. "Chinese tauke had his daughter kidnapped!" I said.

Roy's eyes brightened, and he laughed. "Anybody we know?" he asked, his interest suddenly stirring.

"Wee Fook is setting up the meeting with the principle involved," I told him

"Ah so! Little Dick," Roy said with a smile on his face. "Isn't he the guy who saw us so well paid on the last job we did for him?"

"That's the guy," I said. "See you at the GH Café at 1500 hours sharp. And don't be late—its business!

Roy nodded without saying a word and went back upstairs, most likely to take up where he'd left off with those fatigued bedsprings.

I headed for home and a spot of lunch without further ado, after which I spent the next hour exercising the dog on the hill behind my bungalow, far, far away from the madding crowd. I acknowledge that neither Roy nor I are not saints, and I suppose that the business we get up to may be considered morally wrong by some, because we deal in war surplus. But as mentioned previously, we do have a line we won't cross.

It's a question of morality and nothing to do with money or politics. The people-trafficking and hard-drugs trade are degrading to humanity, and we will never be a party to those. Here is the difference: The people whom the traffickers move around can be used over and over again until there is nothing left whole inside them. Some are driven to suicide rather than remain drugged up and used as sex slaves. The hard drugs can be sold and used only once, but both destroy people and their families.

I do not share Roy's view that all women are fair game and there is quite a lot of reactionary arse being passed around by men about women. I strongly believe that a man's wife is sacrosanct. I never work my games on them. A woman is like a good watch; each has a different and separate movement, of which the end result is never quite the same. Play it again, Sam! It makes me smile when I reflect on the wartime love story line of that 1942 black-and-white Bogart movie starring the curvaceous Ingrid Bergman. The original line by Casablanca bar owner Rick, played by Humphrey Bogart, was of course, "You played it for her; you can play it for me!" The song, "As Time Goes By' is a true classic, despite the Hollywood inaccuracies in depicting the war.

The lunchtime crowd had gone when I arrived at the G.H. Café. Wee Fook was seated at the same table as before, and when he had got the drinks in, he handed me a card with the name and address of the principal. The appointment was for 1630 hours at Pasir Ris. Roy was late and arrived instead at 1800 hours, one and a half hours later. Having completed his unfinished symphony, he was bent on giving me a synopsis of the event. He looked rather knackered, but then it would make one tired after a while.

The bungalow at Pasir Ris was large and impressive, set in spacious grounds, complete with groundsman and guard dogs. The latter were obviously the immediate result of the recent kidnapping.

We were shown into the study, where walls of shelves were well stocked with books, each shelf methodically catalogued and labelled. A Chinese gentleman in his middle forties, wearing a well-cut tropical business suit, sat behind a large teak desk surrounded by four easy chairs. Each of the easy chairs had an ornamented carved-teal side table suitably spaced.

The man rose to greet us. "Take a seat each, gentlemen," he said. His handshake was firm and his voice well-modulated. Once Roy and I had settled in our respective easy chairs, a maid dressed in the traditional garments of the amah cult, with her hair in a long braid hanging down the length of her back to her waist, served us refreshments. Out host wasted no time in coming directly to the point. His daughter had mysteriously disappeared from his brother's villa at Ayutthaya on the twenty-sixth of January last. (Ayutthaya was the second Siamese capital, after Sukhothai.) A massive search, involving both the military and police, had turned up nothing, not even the slightest trace of his daughter.

On the twenty-eight of that month, his brother's gardener had found a cloth sack which had been thrown over the wall surrounding the villa during the night. It contained the decapitated heads of both his daughter's personal bodyguards plus a ransom note demanding seven million dollars for her safe return—or she would be sold to slavers. The money was to be paid in three instalments in Malayan Straits currency. The first instalment had been paid at Sing Biri on the thirtieth of January, and the recipient had sent a letter, which had been posted in Bangkok the day following the payment. It contained a small lock of his daughter's hair.

The note said that she would be returned safely once payment had been made in full. But any further police or military intervention would result in his daughter being sold immediately. The second payment was made at Phra Phutthabat on the second of February. Army trackers traced the courier to a house in the suburbs of Phanom Dong Rak, which they immediately surrounded. Fifteen people were killed in the ensuing gun battle. But there was no trace of his daughter there, either. Then, on the sixth March, two top private investigators found that she was being held near Chanthaburi on the coast. But when they raided and searched the place, they discovered that she had been taken on board an Arab dhow that afternoon, together with a number of other girls.

They traced the dhow to the island of Kas Kong, where they found it had already put to sea, homeward bound for Ras al Hadd in the Arabian Sea.

"It's a job for the Navy!" Roy interjected.

"No!" our host shouted, holding up his hands in protest. "Do you know what will happen to all those girls if a naval vessel suddenly appears on the scene?" he said. "The dhow is a slaver. The girls are all shackled together to a length of chain, which is attached to a heavy weight. At the first sign of interception by the law enforcement authorities or the Navy, the weight will be dropped overboard, taking all the girls with it. These slave traders are ruthless and will have no problem disposing of their human traffic rather than face prosecution."

"The gulf of Siam is full of dhows; we don't know which will be carrying the girls," Roy pointed out.

"The *Kasim Bahagia*," our host replied. "She put out to sea yesterday."

"What's in it for us?" Roy said

"Name your own price," our host replied.

"We will give it a go," Roy said, "but we will have to move fast."

Roy and I spent the rest of the evening studying all the

meteorological and navigational charts of the area that we could put our hands on. Those Arab sailors knew the sea in this area like the backs of their hands. They knew every cross-current and every wind and, like us, would navigate a course well clear of the shipping lanes to avoid detection. But there was an insurrection going on in Java at the moment. Perhaps this was a small but significant point in our favour. Dutch naval vessels on the lookout for gunrunners in the Java Sea were a good enough deterrent, and an Arab dhow in the area would draw the Dutch gunboat like flies to a jam pot. The other deterrent would be the British naval base at Seletar in Singapore.

The British send out regular anti-piracy patrols to operate in the Straits of Malacca. The route the dhow would follow from Kas Kong would be along the coast of Cambodia and Vietnam, into the South China Sea, between the Anambas Islands, and into the Karimata Straits. This would take them along three main shipping lanes: Singapore to Cocong and Saigon-Cholon, Singapore to Hong Kong, and Singapore to Manila. The dhow would have to cross at night and obviously at the place where these three shipping lanes converged, thus killing three birds with one stone at minimum risk. The obvious place to wait for the dhow was on a bearing east of Johore Bahru in Malaya and west of the Anambus Islands.

Due to the Dutch Java problem, it was more than logical to assume that the Arab dhow with our kidnap victim on board would be going around Singapore in darkness and then proceeding up the Straits of Malacca, hugging the coast of Sumatra to Kutaradja, with a heading after that for the Indian Ocean. In that case, their journey from Kas Kong to Ras al Hadd would take approximately five to six weeks. Roy and I got the crew together, taking stock of all the provisions and fuel necessary for this journey, including our weapons stash for the task at hand. We put both our motor patrol boats to sea at 2200 hours, setting a course for the Anambus Islands.

That was not bad time to mobilize for a rescue mission, all things considered. The idea was to sight the dhow during the hours of daylight so that we could identify the shadow of her silhouette and follow her at a safe distance until an opportune moment presented itself when we could move in on her quickly. We toyed with a few ideas, including disabling the dhow's rudder with explosives. Only I didn't fancy a dip in the ocean during the hours of darkness, as in all probability the sharks would be in favour of a night-time snack.

Maybe we could use a crossbow and set fire to her rigging and sails. That would create the necessary diversion and an excuse for boarding her. But the women were supposedly being held chained on deck. I had visions in my mind of returning the girl's body to her father, nicely fried on both sides. We were here to pull off her rescue, not to do a reprise with "the girl stood on the burning deck"! I could not help but wonder if the knights of old had had this problem with their maidens in distress. In the end Roy and I decided to play it by ear. We didn't know exactly what we were going to do, but as always, when the time came we would just do it. It was a gamble on probability, based on what we considered was the dhow's most likely course, heading, speed, and route.

We did our best guessing, based on our personal smuggling experiences in these waters and consideration of alternatives the slavers might take. Our slavers might be good at their human trafficking trade, but then we were much better at this game of cat and mouse on the open seas, where the hunter often became the hunted. Roy and I realized that our rescue plan, for want of a better word, was skewed. It had holes in it; it was a long shot without any real-time intelligence, and it was laced with a lot of *What if?* suppositions. But it had a chance of success, albeit a slender one, as its best outcome.

Strange though it may seem, the old established route between the Spice Islands and Arabia, where the trade winds blow, is littered with stories of fast dhows and the abduction of young maidens through the sordid trafficking trade, which became very active again at the end of the Second World War in this area. The women of Chiangmai in the North of Siam were the most sought after by Arab traders at the moment, so we had been told. These girls were taken by the local syndicate and brought down to Chanthaburi on the coast, where they were sold and moved on to Ko Chang for shipment to Arabia.

Sunday, 9 March 1947

It was nearly dawn around 0530 hours when we reached the fringe of the Anambas Islands, a little way beyond the main shipping lanes. We ate an early breakfast of egg banjos for a change, my ship's cook having managed to scrounge a few dozen fresh eggs from one of the local market traders before boarding late the day before. Egg banjos refer to a military style makeshift sandwich made from half-stale bread, spread on both sides with oily fat of any description, usually lard, with at least one greasy fried egg slotted in, preferably soft yolk.

We then proceeded to fill all our fuel tanks to the maximum level from some of the drums of diesel we each carried in our holds. Next we established that the chafing fenders on both boats were secure and adequate for the coming task of boarding an enemy ship. We also prepared the grappling hook and ropes required on deck of my boat for boarding our princely price. After all, our principle had said, "Name your price" for this rescue mission to recover his daughter from the slavers.

Pirating was, of course, armed robbery, only you robbed someone at sea, in international waters, taking his possessions with armed force. The only difference at sea is that you were most likely to get your arse wet in the process. Our intention was always to minimize the risk to all my crew as far as is possible. We paid careful attention to every detail and were never deliberately careless. Sometimes we did make mistakes.

The plan was to steer clear of Terempa on the main Anambus Island. We planned to systematically go around each atoll and island in the group until one of us sighted the delinquent Arab dhow. I was working on the logical thinking that a slaver, having a criminal bent, would stay well clear of Terempa to avoid drawing attention to the human trafficking activities.

Roy took his boat and headed off for one of the smaller atolls to search, whilst I directed my boat to another of the smaller islands. Whoever first sighted the dhow with our objective on board was to ignore her and keep well clear. Then he would lose headway and fake a breakdown at sea. The other boat would come to assist, thus allaying any suspicion on the part of the Arab crew of the dhow. But first we had to locate and identify the dhow, learn her disposition, and watch her leave the islands before we could work out her course and trajectory.

It was 1500 hours when Roy found her in a sheltered bay close to one of the small islands and some twenty more minutes before I arrived on the scene. Roy had heaved to ahead of her in a cloud of smoke, a well-authenticated sudden breakdown, and I pulled in alongside him. Roy had found her, the *Kasim Bahagia* or *Kasim the Fortunate*! The dhow was sheltered from both prying eyes and the wind. Fortunately for us, she was smaller than we had anticipated, which was rather an anticlimax, as there appeared to be only one Arab on watch. But her trim was good, and she'd be fast with a steady wind.

We watched her or a while longer, and there was no activity except for that single sentinel on board. We took it as read that the single lookout on board had a beady eye on our activities from the bow of his dhow. Certainly, there was no outward sign of any slave girls, but then, on closer inspection with my night binoculars, I noted that the flimsy attap palm-leaf thatch at the after end of the dhow appeared to be that little bit larger than that required to accommodate just the crew of the vessel. Roy and I were all for taking her over immediately, but the bloody island was also inhabited, and gunfire would draw undue attention. The next few hours seemed like a lifetime as we tinkered about on Roy's boat, just killing time.

The dhow had a lateen rigged, with a large triangular sail on a long yard at an angle of forty-five degrees. The stern was high and decorated with carvings. She was fast and compact. We could tell from the cut of the jib that the dhow was Omani. The Omani had a great seafaring tradition. Vasco da Gama's discovery of the sea route to India in 1498 was made under the guidance of an Arab pilot from Oman, who had been supplied by the sultan of Mozambique.

At 1600 hours I decided to take Roy's boat in tow and put to sea, slowly heading in the direction of the Karimata Straits. This caused a sudden flurry of activity on board the dhow, with her crew hard at work hoisting sail. We counted five Arabs in all, and then she was underway, passing us well to port. We watched her go, making good her headway as she went full on sails. We would shorten the distance between us and our quarry during the hours of darkness, but for the moment we were content keeping track of her on our radar.

Monday, 10 March 1947

The slaver dhow was running on a course for the coast of Sumatra that, in my estimation, would take her between the Riau Islands and Singapore around 0400 hours. That is where we intended to board her and take over. At the moment there was a slight swell running around us, with moonlight and cloud cover. Our only foreseeable problem was the noise we would make at high speed on our run in.

At 0350 hours it was time to make our move. Together with our boarding party, we crouched on the deck as we brought our Packard aviation engines to full capacity—and it was all systems go! We sped in quickly on either side of the dhow and grabbed her with the grappling hooks, quickly reversing engines while our crew secured her and boarded. Our bow waves, together with the tumult of the backwater we had created by reversing engines at full power, rocked the dhow, and for a moment I thought she would capsize.

The Arab tiller man fired his rifle at us and fell backwards into the sea as we boarded her. The others gave up quickly, and we bound them amidst quite of lot of cursing and swearing. Our boarding party quickly cut the slaver dhow's rigging, which brought her sails crashing down upon her deck.

We found the girls in a rather sorry state under cover of the thatched amidships. They were huddled together in two groups of ten, with both legs shacked by their ankles to a long length of chain that ran along the deck. They were all in a state of semi-consciousness, drugged up to their eyebrows. The next twenty minutes we spent removing all the girls to our boat and chaining up the Arab crew in their place.

We also fished the tiller man who'd shot at us but missed out of the drink, and he was rather cooperative. The girls had been heavily drugged by the Siamese human trafficking dealer at Chanthaburi, but the effects were wearing off now. Generally the Omani slave dealers discouraged the use of drugs on their prospective victims simply because an addict was worthless on the slave market back in Omani. On the other hand, drugs made the girls easier for the dealers to handle on the journey between Chiangmai and the island of Ko Kut in the Gulf of Siam. Most of the girls seemed to be between the ages of 12 and 17 years. The Chinese girl we'd set out to rescue was the oldest of the lot at 23. We had rescued her, but both Roy and I were convinced that her captors had put her on drugs early during her captivity.

At 0600 hours Singapore time we cast the Arab dhow adrift so that the force of the incoming tide would carry her through the main shipping lines. I rigged a small but powerfully hot incendiary thermite charge with a delayed timer to allow us time to get off the dhow. This would set her sails and rigging afire. I set it to go off at 0630 hours, fully aware that the local port authorities would act rather quickly. A ship fire close to port would be a great danger to other shipping in their port area. It was time for us now to head for home.

The slave dhow in flames off Raffles Quay at 0630 hours

Our first call the next morning was to return the girl, our primary rescue mission objective, safely back to her father, who had his daughter immediately admitted to hospital for treatment. She remained there for quite some time due to her enforced drug addiction and a few other problems. The thought *Poor little rich girl* entered my mind at the time. Being wealthy does not always bring with it much happiness, for other human beings of a lesser nature will want to take that wealth from you, it seems.

The notion of making a living by selling young girls as sex slaves to the Arabian brothels or private harems sickened both Roy and myself. Those traffickers cause so much human misery. The other nineteen Siamese girls we'd rescued, still under the influence of drugs, suddenly mysteriously appeared in the compound of the Siamese consulate in Singapore, where they are probably trying to figure out how in the hell they got there! I think they all said "*Sa-wa-dee*" rather nicely. Like the "Aloha" of Hawaii, it can mean greetings or just goodbye! Anyway, it sounds rather melodious.

What followed next was that the local papers were sporting stories concerning the Arab dhow on fire in the harbour that morning, with the Arab crew making a vain attempt to bring the fire under control. Roy and I agreed that our slavers must have eventually got the keys we had left just a little bit out of their reach and quickly released the others. We are not murderers, after all. Did they attempt to put the fire out? I doubt that very much. It was more likely that they all jumped overboard as soon as my silent but effective incendiary thermite grenade fired off, starting a huge, unstoppable, very intense flame on the dhow's sails and rigging. This throwback to my Force 136 Special Operations Executive South East Asia sabotage kit days had done its job well.

Roy and I, together with the rest of our crew who'd taken part in this successful rescue operation, are never smug; that feeling of being too pleased with ourselves is not for us. When somebody is taken, the more time that passes after you learn where the hostage is being held, how many criminals there are, and what means of firepower they can wield, the more risky and prone to failure the game becomes. There are often several deaths, including some of your own men and the people you are trying to rescue.

The first to die in any failed rescue attempt are always the hostages or prisoners. We never take for granted that our enemies are amateurs; all our opponents in the game I consider professionals and very dangerous. That is why we hit them fast and very hard, with overwhelming odds, using two-boat boarding crews, fully armed, in the assault. But we do not condone the mindless murder of prisoners under any circumstances. We have both seen enough of this kind of summary execution of captured prisoners under the pretext of "I was only following orders" when perpetrators are called to account by war criminal tribunals.

What came out of this was a rather unique sense of a job well done, which we could not speak about in public! We could neither claim credit nor mention that we had ever been there. That was what we had promised to our employer regarding this sensitive matter. But because of our timely rescue mission, twenty bound and humiliated girls headed for the Arab slave market in Omani were now, despite their terrible ordeal, free to live out their lives once again. The feel-good factor in saving those twenty young female lives was priceless. Any fool could take life, which was why we did not terminate those Arab human traffickers as much as they may have deserved it.

This was one of those few occasions when Roy and I were well pleased with both the rewards and the outcome of our rescue mission. Had it gone the other way, our reputation would have been tainted with that remembered failure. Nobody wants to employ a boat crew that fails in its allotted task. Granted, this was somewhat outside of what anyone else would class as a normal trading job mission! If I'd had to rely on trading merchant goods alone, I would have gone bankrupt shortly after starting up our free enterprise on the high seas. It was these extraordinarily high-risk contracts that made our boat deals profitable while remaining inside our moral compass of good and bad.

Me and my dog, Rex

We paid both our boat crews off this afternoon for a job more than well done. Together, Roy and I laughed all the way to the bank, where I presented yet another generous cheque for a princely rescue from a grateful father. Then we killed off a few Tigers at the GH Café while Roy, true to his nature, went off to get himself laid downtown. I went home afterwards to a good meal and later took my dog, Rex, out for a walk. It was not that I had anything against getting laid, mind you. I had a very strange feeling that my next long-distance journey over water would be between the parallels of five and twenty-one degrees north latitude and ninety-seven degrees east longitude— perhaps Major Langley's cargo? There remained also a number of other commitments to take care of in the near future.

Who can really say that they know just what tomorrow will bring?

Chapter 13

The Berstanding
Tuesday, 11 March 1947

Fame Alvares

The Malay word *bukit* refers to a hill, *anak bukit* is a hillock, *kaki bukit* the foot of a hill, *penara bukit* the level ridge at the crest of a mountain range, *bukit berapit* hills connected by a low col or ridge connecting two mountain peaks, often comprising a pass.

The Malay term *orang bukit* refers to aboriginal tribes dwelling in the mountains. The word *permai* means fair, pretty, lovely, and beautiful. There was an anti-aircraft battery on Bukit Permai during that last war, with a few of the guns there still in position as a reminder. These were spiked of course—the colonial British back then blew up the gun barrels rather than let the Japanese capture them. But I suppose the Army will get around to removing them one day. Bukit Permai is a nice hill. The wild dwarf *Alexis* trees fan out along a ridge at the crest, and there are lianas, mosses, and ferns.

There is a sweet scent of lemon grass and old mango trees. The beauty of nature is slowly overcoming the grotesqueness of man's war machines and returning the landscape to normality.

Those two tiger fighters Kow Ong and Kow Sai (Big Dog and Dog Shit) were still hanging around the wharf this morning when I did my routine check on our boats. I wondered why those two hired gangsters were lurking around my business premises. They gave me an uncomfortable feeling. Perhaps I should have a little talk with them both, I thought, and use my charms of persuasion by banging their bloody heads together. They were fast becoming a habit I would rather be without.

I would need to have a little talk soon with Bah Sam Seng, who happened to be the headman of a 303 Chinese gang in this area. He should be able to throw some light on the question. My housekeeper, Gloria, thinks I should just set the dog on them. Or perhaps I should take them both out on a long, invitation-only, one-way boat trip into the South Pacific Ocean. Maybe not today, though, as I have far more important fish to fry.

Business is business, and to date I have never found it difficult finding work out there for my boats and crews. The trick is balancing that work with my integrity.

You may be wondering what I eat in this part of the world, with a lifestyle so far removed from my United Kingdom home back in Ebbw Vale in South Wales. My cuisine out here is curry mostly, but not the way the Indians make a curry. I eat chicken curry, goat curry, and fish curry, all at once and cut into small pieces and served with a variety of spiced dishes, along with Siamese number-one rice, which is the flakiest rice you can get here. Barbequed chicken is served in small bites on a coconut palm stick, which I then dip in a sauce of mashed peanuts, curry, and coconut milk. You have never tasted anything quite like it; it is very good. Appearance, or rather food presentation, is everything. This is just a typical main meal of the day in my life out here in the colonies.

The fish in my curry is *ikan merak*, the red snapper

On its immediate right is a small dish of salad next to a dish of vegetable curry, and below that is a dish of curry chicken. In the centre is a dish of curry sauce made with coconut milk and mashed peanuts, a dip for the satay pieces of skewered kebabs, and on the right are meatballs made from fresh goat meat.

Sambal, of course, is the generic term in Malay for the condiments which are served with curries in Malaya. To create a Malay curry paste with authentic flavours, you may use the following ingredients:

2 tablespoons of ground coriander
1 tablespoon of ground fennel
1 tablespoon of ground cumin
1 tablespoon of ground cinnamon
1 tablespoon of ground chili
1 tablespoon of black pepper
1 inch piece of fresh ginger root
the yellow zest of one lemon
1 small onion
4 cloves of garlic

6 macadamia nuts
1 teaspoon of salt
1 teaspoon of ground turmeric
1 tablespoon of white vinegar

Blend everything to a fine paste, using as much water, little by little, as you need to make a fine paste. *Belachan* is a paste of prawns and *ikan bilis*, which are anchovies or whitebait. The popular local name of this concoction is Malacca cheese; it is used as a relish in most Malay curries. *Budu*, on the other hand, is ikan bilis preserved in brine with their scales and entrails. *Achar* means pickles, and no meal out here with curry is complete without them. *Chendul* is a kind of thin broth with cakes of dough floating in it—not to be confused with the Malay word *chenduai*!

Minyak chenduai is an oil made from a flower; it is used for enticing women by the magic art. *Chendana* is better known as *Santalum album* or sandalwood.

The *sireh* box is a small casket, *laksana chembul dengan tutup-nya*, the casket and its cover exactly suited one to the other. The leaves of the vine *Piper longum* are chewed after a good meal. Sireh is sent to typify a formal proposal of marriage and also used for *sireh meninang*, typifying the formal acceptance. *Sireh-lelat, sireh-genggam*, the best man at the wedding. I have a rendezvous with a *pedewakan* at sea on the fifteenth. That's a Bugis trading ship. It will give me an opportunity to drop a few things off in the Berhala Straits, an area of water separating the island of Sumatra and Singkep in the South China Sea. That will allow me to carry out two of my objectives at the same time.

Wednesday, 12 March 1947
Muka in Malay refers to face or countenance. In the East there is always the question of face or saving face.

Ayer muka refers to an expression or look.

Chahaya muka refers to the charm of the countenance.

Muka refers to feigned feelings or hypocritical airs, which we can well do without!

Mukarram is the Arabic word for honourable or distinguished.
Mukah refers to fornication and adultery.
Kemukakan means to bring forward as a proposal.
Nikah is a marriage ceremony.

Becoming a mistress in the East leaves the woman concerned open to the feigned feelings and hypocritical airs of other people, the kind of rather bad behaviour we call gossip in the West. This situation could lead to much unhappiness if not dealt with immediately in the proper way. Nikkah is the obvious answer, and so it is done.

The ceremony commences with the male guests coming up, one by one, to the *pelamin*, taking first a little of the yellow rice and throwing some to the right and some to the left of the couple. Then the same is done with the *berteb*, the parched rice. Next the guest takes the sprinkler of leaves, dips it lightly in the mixture of *setawar* leaves, and touches the backs of the couple's hands with it. This is the *bersanding*, the sitting together of the bridegroom and bride on the bridal couch. The feast and the *zapin*, a mixture of Arab and Malay music and dancing, will go on well into the night. This is the night of consummation, and in the morning will come the bathing, after the Nikah tradition.

Kamisah, flanked by her two daughters

The wife of Idris, Kamisah, leads the way to the pelamin flanked by her two daughters, each bearing gifts. She walks proud and upright. Kamisah is noted for her no-nonsense outspoken manner and is reputed to have silenced wagging tongues with a single glance of disapproval.

In front of the dais and on the topmost tier of the pelamin is placed an *astakona*, an octagonal pedestalled tray containing a well-moulded mound of cooked yellow rice. It is studded all over with *bunga-telor merah*, or eggs painted with red dye and impaled on sticks of bamboo, topped with artificial flowers. At the summit of the mound of yellow rice is placed a big *tajok*, a bouquet of artificial flowers made from *kertas perada*, tinsel or gold or silver foil. The bersanding ceremony is an affair of womenfolk, who enjoy themselves feasting their eyes during the *adat bersuapsuapan*, the ritual ceremonial of yellow rice between the bridal pair.

Listening to the colourful comments of the womenfolk was an edifying experience in itself, provoking the theory that gossip between womenfolk seems to be universal. Because I only kept to Arabic in the course of this ceremony, they naturally assumed that I did not understand their native Malay, completely ignoring the fact that all Islamic peoples throughout the world speak Arabic, which is the language of the Muslim religion.

Of Bathsheba and King Solomon, the Bat means "daughter of" and sheba suggests "abundance." The story goes that Bathsheba was a beautiful, manipulative, and unscrupulous woman.

Bathsheba was secretly observed by King David, possibly by her own design, to lure him as she bathed. He thereafter desired her sexually and then subsequently became pregnant to him, even though married to the soldier Uriah. It is a timeless biblical love story, with tragic consequences for the child born of their illicit union, who soon died thereafter. Bathsheba's second child, born to Kind David, was of course Solomon, said to be the wisest of all the men in Israel. The Arabic name for Solomon is Sulayman. Beth-Sheba or Bath-Sheba, the Queen of Sheba's name was Bialiks, Belkiss Rainha de Saba, or Balkis, or also Bath-Sheba Jeroboam.

Fame had taken the Arabic name *Belkiss Rainha de Saba*, at my insistence, without further argument. I had long since decided to throw in my lot with the Malay community for obvious reasons, and the taking of a wife rather than a mistress would in their eyes legalize the situation according to their own customs and points of view.

Dowries and expenses are rather interesting. For an ordinary *anak-anak raja*, or maiden of royal blood, the dowry is four hundred dollars, mentioned in the register as one *kati* of gold, and the *babtaran*, articles sent with the dowry, is agreed upon by the two parties concerned.

A *kati* is one and a half imperial pounds in weight. For the widow of a sultan the kati is one hundred dollars and a ring, usually diamond, along with a sarong. For women of the sultan's palace, it's forty-four dollars, a ring, and one sarong. For the daughters of a *dato*, which is an honourary title one hundred dollars, a ring and one sarong. For Bugis maidens of gentle birth, it was sixty dollars, a ring, and one sarong. Other maidens associated with the sultan's palace, forty-one dollars, a ring and one sarong. There is a connection between the sultans of Selangor, Johore, and Pahang, along with the Bugis of the Rhio Archipelago. Sultan Almarum, Sulaiman Badrul Alam Shah is also the Yang Di-pertuan besar of Rhio Lingga.

The Lingga Archipelago is better known as the Dutch East Indies. Alam Shah is the current Sultan of Selangor. It's strange perhaps that both Fame and I were born on a Sunday during a leap year (even though there is twenty-one year's difference in our age). There is another woman I know who is also born on a Sunday during a leap year, but in her case there is eight years and one month between us. Perhaps I attract a kind of fatalism where my women are concerned, though I am not convinced that all the events in life are marked by fatalism or decided by fate alone. We shall see what we shall see. Women are women, and they all need to be loved. I have found that human love is rarely unconditional.

The world is too full of meaningless emptiness without any sense of purpose, or belonging, for that matter. Well, there is nothing unreal about this berstanding or the political significance it will have where they Malays are concerned. A journey is commenced with just a single step forward—and likewise a relationship! *Kadar asmara, laillat la kadar asmara.* Perhaps this was how Scheherazade appeared when first she distinguished herself in her dance of the seven veils. The pleasant scent of jasmine and roses, together with meaningful conversation long into the early hours of the morning, commenced this relationship which was to successfully flourish for the next twenty-five years. My best friend, Roy, and I did not see eye to eye on the question of Fame Alvares. It was all right to take a mistress, in his view, but why go all to the bother and inconvenience of a marriage ceremony?

Roy's philosophy was plain undecorated simplicity. He was also rather drunk at that point. "Find them, fuck them, and forget them," is what he said. But in fairness to my friend, it was the drink talking. He always apologized in the morning when he sobered up. I cut Roy a lot of slack, knowing all the mental anguish and trauma he'd experienced as a POW in Singapore during the Japanese occupation. The Japanese had made secret plans to execute all the British and Allied prisoners of war if the British attempted to recapture Malaya and Singapore with military force.

I never expected Roy to fully grasp or understand the politics of these islands which our very living and well-being depended on. The islands were accessible by boat; thus by aligning ourselves with the Malays, we had a good advantage where trade with the islands and the Bugis was concerned. We could come and go as we pleased, unmolested by the many Bugis pirates who operated frequently in these waters. Making a boat run carrying a whole load of contraband required a cool head and a manageable crew.

There are fifty things that can go wrong on a run, so if you can only think of twenty-five of those possibilities, you should consider taking up another profession. Life perhaps is nothing more than a cunning complex of errors, both dangerous and yet rather ludicrous.

It's a sort of comedy but not always light and amusing. Life is full of satirical characters who seem rather humorous at times and on other occasions quite, quite deadly. But we are old enough to use our own discretion.

Roy and I both decide what is most suitable and do the necessary when the situation demands it. We are quite open with each other and have few disagreements. Neither of us is impressed with money or the want of it but rather by people, and people can be a little precipitous at times. We are both reasonable judges of character, and we both enjoy a good challenge. Most of the chances we take are well thought out, calculated risks that have nothing to do with luck or good fortune. We have a reputation for honesty—a deal, after all, is a deal—but we are as different as chalk and cheese. There is an old Malay saying, *bangsa menunjokkan bangsa*, or "a man's manners show his descent". Ask a Malay what his race is, and nine out of ten will answer "Islam." The tenth will say "Melayu".

I expected the news of this berstanding would reach the islands quickly; this was the object of the exercise and the best way of getting close to the Bugis. They would feel free to talk on equal terms, so it was a political marriage as well as a personal one. This would give me the opportunity to build the necessary trading facilities for the future. I sat on the bridal couch beside Fame, who was perfectly still, her eyes downcast in womanly modesty. My mind was focused on everything except the night to come. Momentary thoughts went through my head, and I caught the chance remarks of some of our guests. A few witticisms were voiced during the witnessing ceremony, in an attempt to force us to laugh, but nothing was uncomplimentary.

Strangely enough, the faintest whisper was audible above the background noise of the *keronchong* orchestra. But then we were both captive listeners, there on the *singgabsana*. Keronchong, or rather *kroncong*, is the name of a ukulele-like instrument played in an Indonesian musical style that typically makes use of the kroncong to produces the sounds *chrong-chrong-chrong*, so the music is called keronchong. At the appointed moment, I linked the little finger of my left hand to that of Fame's right hand, and we stood upright together before our guests. Slowly we proceeded to the beautifully prepared and decorated bridal chamber. We sat on the *tikar-sila*, the ceremonial mats before the decorated bridal bed.

Kamisah, who the *emak pengantin*, then guided Fame's hand in the ceremonial hand clasp. This represented our first introduction to each other, and we were left alone so that we might get to know each other. Fame was led away to be dressed in the costume of white, which is customarily worn during the first night, and the bed sheets and pillowcases were changed from the ceremonial ones to new white ones.

Thursday, 13 March 1947

I seemed to have more on the go than I usually did at that time of the morning. Indeed, I was quite energetic despite the humidity, now that the sun had well and truly risen after a rather wet dawn. I spent most of the morning studying my charts of the Karimundjawa area, where we had a little business transaction off the coast of Java shortly.

Karimunjawa consists of a large group of small islands, the two main ones of these being Karimunjawa Island and Kemujan Island, with yet smaller ones, namely Menjangan Besar Island and Menjangan Kecil Island, along with other even smaller and, to my knowledge, still uninhabited islands. These islands are an excellent refuge spot for pirates and secret rendezvous.

We saw the *SS Orontes*, a passenger ship owned by the Orient Line, arrive at 0700 hours PST. This ship was built in 1929 by Vickers Armstrong Limited, at Barrow-in-Furness in England and served during the war as a troop ship doing her rounds on the Tilbury Docks in London England-to-Sydney Australia run. The *SS Orontes* is a 20,186 ton vessel with two steam turbines and twin screws. In peacetime she could carry approximately 1,600 passengers, some 500 of which would be first-class passengers. Her top speed was about twenty knots.

On this occasion, the *SS Orontes* was engaged in the assisted-passage scheme, carrying English and other emigrants to Australia. She was one of the few pre-war liners still engaged on the route she was originally built for. She came up from Sydney almost empty but will leave Singapore crammed with a full load of British troops returning home to England.

Roy arrived just after lunch, looking rather bleary-eyed and a little worse for wear. I said nothing at the time but thought quite a lot. A hair of the dog seemed to put matters right, and we got down to the business at hand. (The expression "the hair of the dog" refers to an alcoholic drink taken to cure a hangover. This comes from a shortening of "a hair of the dog that bit you", regarding an old belief that someone bitten by a rabid dog could be cured of rabies by taking a potion containing some of the dog's hair.) Roy and I agreed to leave for Karimunjawa late the next night. We both knew the score and the dangers of those waters, so we wanted to be in and out of that area quickly. On this occasion, we intended to change our route and come out of that area the long way around. Our immediate business concluded, Roy took a long drink from his glass, settled back comfortably in his chair, and gave me one of his uncomfortable, half-inquisitive looks. I anticipated the question he was about to ask even before he opened his mouth. I suppose it was the boyish expression on his face.

"How was it?" he said.

"It?" I asked, pretending not to understand his question, which made him go rather red with embarrassment.

"Fame!" he said. "You know what I mean!"

"Graciously gratifying," I said. "I was quite enriched by the experience, which I fully endorse. Perhaps you should look for an older woman to have an affair with. Someone with a bit of notoriety would do you a world of good."

"It's nourishment I want," he said, "not punishment."

Those two Chinese rowdies, Big Dog and Dog Shit, were still around, apparently watching two young Chinese girls who ran a small business collecting shellfish and selling it. The two thugs in question were probably running some sort of protection racket. It's a rather dishonest way of making money, cheating and threatening people who are attempting to make an honest dollar. Roy seemed to think that if we let them get away with it they would attempt their extortion racket on us. It would be quite unfortunate and unforgettable for those two pieces of walking dog turd removed from the sewers should they try it on us.

I think the word for it is *shanghai*, an old naval piece of terminology. Now you see them, now you don't anymore—and better still, nobody will see them ever again! Roy and I had no scruples when it came to dealing out rough justice to murdering thugs or hired assassins. It was a very long swim in shark-infested waters from some of the remote islands we tended to leave them on. Enough said on the matter.

Well, the Highland Division is finally leaving Singapore for home, and soon the British Military Administration will be handing over its authority to the Colonial Office. The garrison here will be replaced by British National Servicemen, complemented with local Singapore troops.

Most of their current National Service officers are men returned to service from the Indian Army. That is to say, they are British officers who have served in action with the Indian Army. The farewell party at Gillman Barracks was quite a wild affair and well underway when Roy and I arrived on the scene—better late than never. However, we soon got into the swing of things and had a rather good time of it all amid the skirl of bagpipes and the sound of beating drums, not to mention the steady slurping of Tiger beer. Strange though it may seem, where the jock regiment was concerned there was little or no fighting on this occasion. There was rather quite a lot of elation and, of course, one or two sad faces.

I was there to see all the soldiers return home. Contrary to all the nationalist politics about independence from the British for Malaya or Singapore, the post-war local population considered themselves still very much a part of the British Empire. On Friday, September 7, 1945, the British Military Administration in Singapore declared that all the pre-war Malayan and Straits Settlements currency notes and coins would be legal tender again, making the Japanese military currency known as "banana" money become worthless overnight.

Now this was the regiment that had suddenly lost all the play money in every Monopoly set in the barracks back in 1945, together with three or four large bottles of number nines from the clinic, which rather bewildered the medical officer at the time. I understand that he had visions of a group of men with a bad case of constipation. It seems that another group of Highlanders had partaken of the offerings at a Chinese brothel in Desker Road but paid the girls there with Monopoly play money, informing them that this was now the new British currency. They had also thrown in the bottles of number nines which they had liberated from the base pharmacy, telling them they were vitamin tablets.

Vitamin tablets at that time, post-Second World War, were in demand on the black market. No doubt most of the good-time girls were too busy running to the toilet for the next few days to lodge any kind of formal complaint. But those were the men who had taken Rangoon away from the Japanese towards the end of the war, during the Burma campaign. Every man jack of them was a soldier tried and tested at the gates of hell! I suspect that the population of occupied Singapore knew full well that the British were coming back and coming soon. There were eleven air raids carried out on the island of Singapore between November 1944 and March 1945, conducted by the United States Army Air Forces (USAAF) long-range bomber groups. They targeting the island's naval base and dockyard facilities, as well as conducting mine-laying missions in nearby waters.

Leaflets were also dropped from the air onto the islands, informing the population to avoid the Japanese troops, as the Allies were coming back to retake the islands. First Earl Louis Mountbatten of Burma was the supreme Allied Commander in South East Asia from 1943 to 1946, after which he became the very last Viceroy of India. Mountbatten remains one of the very few gentlemen officers I knew back then who would always speak to you man to man as an equal; he would never talk down to you as if you were a lesser being, as did so many other officers I knew.

British officers from the lower echelons of rank and file tended to do be pompous arseholes, especially so within the House Guards regiments. Mountbatten's plans for the re-conquest of Malaya were, of course, forestalled by the sudden surrender of all the Imperial Japanese Forces in South East Asia following the dropping of atomic bombs at Hiroshima and Nagasaki. This was done by the United States Army Air Force 509th Composite Bomber Group, using one single Super-fortress B29 known as *Enola Gay*.

Operation Tiderace was the codename for the British plan to retake Singapore from the Japanese Occupation Forces with the use of minimal military force following Emperor Hirohito's surrender in 1945. To retake Singapore, Mountbatten had ordered British troops to set sail from Trincomalee and Rangoon (which the Japanese had renamed Yangon) on August 21, 1945, for Singapore. The hope was that the Japanese in Malaya would hand over Singapore without a fight.

By dawn on September 4, 1945, British troops had reached Singapore. Lord Louis Mountbatten, Supreme Allied Commander of South East Asia had instigated Operation Tiderace instead of Operation Zipper, the yard-by-yard liberation of Malaya. Operation Tiderace was a huge gamble by Mountbatten, who hoped that the Japanese forces in Singapore would abide by their emperor's call for the end of all hostilities in South East Asia. This paid off, as the Japanese surrendered aboard the *HMS Sussex*, in the sea off Keppel Harbour, Singapore, without any arguments—although a tense atmosphere ensued when the two war foes met.

Lieutenant-General Alexander Christison was Mountbatten's representative at the initial surrender talks. Christison refused to afford General Seishiro Itagaki, commander of the Japanese Seventh Area Army, any option but immediate unconditional surrender, even though he had a capable land army of over 70,000 fighting troops in Singapore and many thousands more scattered at bases across Malaya. What followed next were the mass suicides of many Japanese NCOs and officers on the island who had previously sworn oaths to fight to the death no matter what the outcome of the war. These were possibly motivated also by fear of having to account for their heinous war crimes during the island's early occupation. That was the mass summary execution of tens of thousands of innocent civilians early during the Japanese occupation. With the prospect of facing an impending war crimes tribunal or losing face, some 300 of these Japanese officers, after drinking sake and saying a final farewell, all fell on their short samurai swords (*tantō*) choosing seppuku (cutting the belly) ritual suicide rather that capitulating to British rule as prisoners of war or being hanged for their crimes by the British Military Authority.

The local Chinese during wartime in Singapore hated the Japanese with a vengeance, and perhaps this also added to their inclination to commit suicide.

Officially denied today, Japanese officer suicides also took place in other parts of the island, not just at a rather famous Singapore landmark hotel. The Syonan Ryokan Hotel was a favourite watering hole with Imperial Japanese officers back then, but most people know this place as the famous Raffles Hotel in Singapore. During the war, the Japanese had renamed it Hotel Syonan Ryokan, meaning "Light of the South Hotel" and its main entrance was moved to the east side to catch the morning sun.

My best-guess theory remains that the bloody place must be haunted by some three hundred Japanese ghosts. The Singapore Sling cocktail was concocted before the war, in 1915, by a Hainanese bartender named Ngiam Tong Boon. Primarily a gin-based cocktail, the Singapore Sling also contains pineapple juice as a main ingredient, along with grenadine, lime juice and, most importantly, Dom Benedictine. Giving it the pretty pink hue are cherry brandy and Cointreau.

The retaking of British Malaya and Singapore back from the Japanese the British felt at the time were paramount for maintaining British regional presence. More importantly British prestige as well as boosting the confidence of her former colony, which had been decimated by the fall of Malaya three years previous to the Japanese. This plan was after we had forcibly recaptured Burma from the Japanese, with the loss of many brave Allied and Colonial soldiers from all points of the British Empire. I will always remember the pride on the faces of the Gurkha POWs at the camp just outside the barracks at Port Dickson. They had defiantly refused to bend to Japanese pressure, and that of some of the renegade Indians, to join the Indian National Army (INA) and fight against the British.

For their stubbornness, the Japanese made the Gurkha POWs pay dearly. The INA was mainly Tamils and Sikhs, with very few Indians of any cast. Cannon fodder comes to mind. The Japanese would place the INA out in front during all their attacks on British well-defended positions.

At this point during the war, the British troops in the |Far East were seasoned, battle-hardened troops. Most of those troops having experienced the Nazis on beaches of Normandy and then jungle warfare with Wingate's Chindit Long Range Penetration Groups in Burma. We had stopped using tactical withdrawal as a means to an end. Instead, we held our ground firmly and paid the price for our refusal to surrender or lose any more battles against the Japanese forces.

Having paid in blood, the British and Colonial regiments defending India repelled nearly all Japanese Imperial Army attacks by using hundreds of flame throwers on their elite Japanese Imperial Guards, backed with many light machine guns well zeroed during their many banzai assaults to capture India, the jewel in the crown, via the city of Imphal. If the Indian National Army soldiers held weapons at us, we shot them dead. If the INA threw their weapons away or put their hands up, their newfound Japanese "friends" shot them dead.

It is important that you realize the Indian National Army was a fringe group and not representative of India's loyalty to the British crown. Most of all, the Colonial Indian Regiments during WWII fought bravely and admirably against the Japanese—the Raj Pathans and the Bengalis to name but a few.

The Raj Pathans landing

The picture shows the Raj Pathans being landed upriver in an American built Royal Navy Landing Craft Infantry, or LCI 120 after the battle of Rangoon. This sort of operation in the river was only possible at high tide. This American-made Landing Craft Infantry, or LCI, included several classes of seagoing amphibious ocean-going assault ships. These were designed specifically to land large numbers of infantry directly onto beaches in a second wave. The LCIs were developed by United States shipyards as a response to British request for a vessel capable of carrying large numbers of troops rather than several smaller Landing Craft Assault, or LCA.

The result was a small steel ship that could land up to 200 fully equipped troops, traveling from rear bases as an independent entity, at speeds of up to sixteen knots and a range of around 4,000 nautical miles.

Friday, 14 March 1947

I watched the Orient liner *SS Orontes* at Gate 5 and 6 loading up with the last of the old Burma troops. The *SS Orontes* was a passenger ship owned by the Orient Line and served as a troop ship during WWII, from 1940 to 1947. She left on the tide with the sound of bagpipes and the cheers of the soldiers crowded on her deck rail. There was not a dry eye on the quay as we all watched her go, taking with her the men of the forgotten British Army. Yes, they had it hard in Europe! But these men had held fast and fought their way across Burma against otherwise overwhelming odds, at Myingyan, Maymo, Mandalay, Kayah, Rangoon, and Moulmein.

We who were there remembered also all those lives lost who would rest beneath the soft soil until Gabriel finally sounded reveille and awakened them once more. The campaign in Burma lasted from January 1942 till July 1945 and remains a contentious one from my viewpoint. It fared poorly in the history books which covered many other campaigns but seemed to ignore the significance and sacrifice made by the British and Colonial troops towards the outcome of the entire war against the Empire of Japan. War historians arguing about how little an impact this made against the Japanese tends to be upsetting to those who were there. To the contrary, it was a long and very bloody land war campaign that resulted in the total military defeat of the Japanese forces in that region.

***SS Orontes* at Gate 5 and 6 in 1947**

The entire military might of the Japanese, which a few years prior had seen the British continuously run and withdraw, was halted and their own expertise and experience in jungle warfare used against them. A great many lives, estimated at a million or more including civilians, were lost in that conflict long since forgotten about. The Burma campaign to push the Japanese out of that region remained historically the longest and bloodiest little-remembered campaign of the Second World War.

The British, Commonwealth, and Allied soldiers came from many other nations, including the United States and China. They spoke at least a hundred different tongues to take on the Japanese empire. The Flying Tigers, or more precisely the American Volunteer Group, were a band of American mercenary fighter pilots who flew for China during the early part of 1942, led by Major Claire Chennault. The Flying Tigers achieved great success in their aerial battles against the Japanese. Their mercenary air force consisted of around a hundred Curtiss Warhawk P-40s distinctly decorated with the famous red shark mouth. They successful led aerial and ground attack sorties against the Japanese, both in China and Burma inflicting heavy casualties on the Japanese air and ground forces.

A small note goes out also to the battalions of "comfort women" the Japanese managed to sexually exploit and bring along with them to service their troops in Burma and elsewhere in South East Asia and the Pacific. Comfort women were innocent young female civilians who were taken away from their homes, raped, and then forced into prostitution by the Japs in countries they occupied, such as Korea, China, and Indonesia. It is a sickening legacy of mass-scale organized human female misery these inhumane land-of-the-rising-sun savages allowed to happen during the war.

Do I hate the Japanese? you may well ask. No, I do not hate them. It was an all-out war of survival, and they were the enemy. It was different than the Nazis, who brutalized and raped most of Europe, created concentration camps to exterminate political enemies, and deprived Northern Europe of her treasures by looting. The Nazis reshaped the history of Northern Europe while killing off many of her indigenous tribal peoples. The Japanese, on the other hand, were barbaric and brutal, but they treated their own soldiers brutally and with equal contempt.

As for wartime atrocities, hell, even we committed atrocities in Germany and the Pacific that are best left out of the history books. The British fought back hard and with a determined ferocity, enduring monsoons, mud-entrenched unpassable jungle tracks, mosquitos riddled with malaria, and dysentery, along with many other exotic tropical diseases that plagued the campaign. They became known as "the forgotten army". They carried out heroically many holding actions, never giving ground. A "hold at all costs" action meant that you were to hold that position until relieved or dead fighting to the last man, a suicide order if you like. Many of those who were there and fought in it would never forget, particularly their fallen comrades or the men left behind as rear guard to slow down pursuers whilst others evaded capture during deep penetration behind enemy lines.

We must remember also the survivors among those tens of thousands of British prisoners of war taken from Malaya and Singapore, whom the Japanese brutalized with savage beatings, starved to death, murdered, and forced to work until they dropped dead on their notorious Burma death railroad. Members of Force 136 who came across British POWs working on the Burma railroad during their close-observations secret reconnaissance patrols were unable to assist or intervene due to their strict orders of observation and intelligence gathering only.

Below is a Singapore Traction Company trolley bus with a first- and second-class compartment, along with the necessary insignia, STC, which should really mean Slow, Terribly Crowded. The tyres were thick solid rubber, full of bounce, and the journey was subject to the odd flash of electricity from the worn overhead pantograph heads. The journey from Tanjong Pagar to Geylang in one of these buses would leave you with a feeling that you had just experienced a bad attack of St Vitus' dance. The chief engineer of their company was Sandy Cameron.

It appeared that Sandy had an up-to-date, sophisticated design on his drawing board that would soon replace the outdated solid-tyre trolley bus with its two-class system.

Singapore Traction Company trolley bus

Geylang was where the Malay settlement was situated on the island of Singapore, with a number of my boat's Malay crew living there. On the other hand, Idris, one of my scuba divers, lived in Radin Mas at Kampong Bahru. That was not very far away from Haji Hasan, who happened to be an old Malay diver who worked with Gloria's late husband, Anthony, on occasion. Haji Hassan spent most of his time at the *surau* (private mosque) in Kampong Radin Mas these days, but he was handy for advice whenever I required a second opinion.

In his prime, Andy had been a master diver in the trade; those divers were few and far between. Anthony had died during the war as a consequence of the Japanese forcing him to dive for them at Keppel Harbour with minimal to zero safety diving gear or the necessary armoured boots and gloves. Wartime Singapore during the Japanese occupation was harsh for the local population and even harsher for anyone who the Japanese considered an enemy of Japan. If a civilian complained to the authorities about unfair treatment, lack of medical attention, or anything else, it was likely that he or she would be punished. For that reason the locals under occupation both feared and hated the Japanese with a vengeance.

Sadly, Anthony sustained a diving injury, causing his foot to gangrene. With penicillin being virtually non-existent and no trained hospital surgeons alive in Japanese-occupied Singapore, he lost his life. This was not helped, of course, by the murderous Japanese, who executed many doctors and nurses along with hundreds of patients at the Alexandra British Military Hospital. Many, if not all the British nurses were also repeatedly gang-raped before being summarily executed at the Alexandra Hospital massacre on the island, which took place between 14 and 15 February 1942. In short, they Japs butchered all the medical staff who might have been able to save Anthony's life, even with basic medicines. It has always been a sticking point with Gloria, that is to say, the Japanese brutality.

I have little love for any nation that brutalizes its innocent civilian population and even less care for those who justify their crimes against humanity by claiming they belong to some imaginary master race. It find it strange how such a cultured country can do that. The *bushido* of feudal Japan did not extend to purges of innocent civilians, but that feudal Japan died out a long time ago!

Chapter 14

The Bugis Rendezvous
Saturday, 15 March 1947

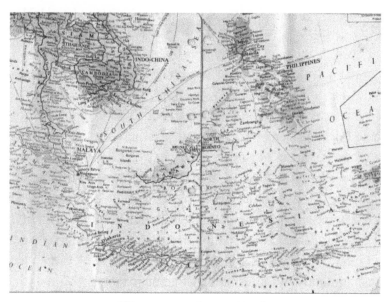

The sea routes we took

We put to sea at 1940 hours, along with the Malay fishing boats from Kampong Tanjong Penuru. There was a swell running; otherwise things were pretty routine. Once clear of the fishing boats, I set course for Berhala and handed the wheel over to Zainal. We were running without navigation lights, and there was nothing of any consequence on the boat's radar to give us cause for concern. "*Siti juga di-angan-angan*"—my lady is ever in my thoughts—Zainal said with a wide grin on his face.

"That's not what I was thinking!" I said with a laugh. "The glass has dropped," I noted. There was rather heavy cloud cover, and the wind had picked up a little during the last fifteen minutes.

"*Angin puting beliong*"—Wildcat whirlwind!—Zainal shouted.

I could see a tall, black pipe-shaped body of air moving rapidly in a circle towards us. Zainal had the good sense to turn the boat quickly into it, and we both hung onto the wheel, keeping her as steady as possible while she pitched and tossed around in the stormy sea. All of a sudden the whirlwind was gone as quickly as it had come, but it was raining heavily. We had lost nothing, and no one had been injured, though a rather indignant voice from the engine room wanted to know what was going on topside!

I gave Roy the signal and got back the necessary reply; he was half a mile astern of us. We had lost a little headway, making it necessary to re-establish our course. Perhaps this was fated to be, though I am not convinced that all events are decided by fate. The movement of the sea itself is all envelopment at various degrees of force, natural and unaffected by man's abilities to muck things up.

We sighted the *pedewaken* at 1100 hours, and Roy circled her while I made the dead-slow approach. The Bugis boat was larger than we had anticipated. I cautiously scanned her closely from stem to stern for any possible signs of hostility. But she had a number of women on board, which ensured her friendship. The Bugis do not carry their women into danger, so at this point I knew it would be safe to make my final approach. I then shouted the customary greeting, and after receiving the required recognition to come aboard, I went alongside the pedewakan. I reversed my engines to bring the boat to a halt, while my men threw the necessary lines to the crew of the pedewakan, who made them secure. This was a dangerous time; the first few minutes has to go well for all concerned when one is trading with pirates.

On board the Bugis boat

We have what in Bugis terms is a *perjanjian tiad membuat pelang-garan*, a kind of non-aggression pact which is observed by both sides. We had lunch on board the pedewakan with our Bugis hosts, the men eating separately from the women in accordance with the *adat*, their customary laws and behaviour when at sea. But once the meal and formalities were over, it was time for us, as their guests, to put on a little light entertainment. My host chose the weapons at random from amongst those I had brought along, all of which were, of course, for sale at the right price. Now, a marksman can shoot well with just about any gun, provided that the weapon and ammunition are both in good condition.

All ammunition has a shelf life. This depends in part on careful storage out of direct sunlight or damp, or the primer and propellant start to break down and hence become unreliable, with many misfires. It is also a question of allowing the weapon to become a part of you for a few moments each time you are required to fire it. You must take careful aim, allowing for the iron sight picture to settle at the correct estimated range, but with great gentleness, and after taking up the first trigger pressure, slowly increase pressure until the firearm discharges on the surprise.

That is to say, do not snatch the damn trigger! Watch closely where your first shots land or strike, as the case may be, and then almost instinctively adjust your aim, compensating for variables such as distance, elevation, or wind direction. To an experienced, well-trained rifleman of the marksman level, all this is done instinctively because of prolonged training, without even having to think about it. No two weapons will ever fire exactly in the same way. Remember to always take your time over it, for your very life may depend on neutralizing an enemy shooter intent on killing you. Shooting skill is rather like riding a bicycle; once you have mastered the technique, you never forget it.

I shot dead my first enemy soldier on the battlefields of Normandy in Northern France at Gold Beach, Arromanches, on June 6, 1944. As with all things that transpire to endanger your life in war, it happened rather quickly and suddenly. A Jerry clad in feldgrau stood up as if from nowhere and opened fire at me from about a hundred yards with his K98k carbine from his entrenched position. I instinctively returned fire with my SMLE No. 1 Mark III Lee Enfield rifle, placing two quickly repeated, well-aimed .303 rounds into his centre torso. He dropped down like a stone. My German enemy missed. I did not.

After what seemed a long pause, I decided to move in and inspect his body, to make sure of the kill. But as I turned him carefully over to view his face, I saw just another young kid, about the same age as me, lying dead, not one of the supermen fanatical Nazis who'd beat the British into the sea and that our instructors in England had warned us we would be facing here. Killing armed, dangerous men is an unnaturally nasty business, no two ways about that and certainly nothing to boast about. It was his life or mine. No real soldier I know likes to talk about war and glory, whom they killed or how they killed them as we fought for our very survival and the survival of those who stood next to us. Many of my brothers in arms did not make it back home from that war.

The deal was closed at fifty rifles and two thousand rounds of .303 tracer ammunition, paid for in bolts of Chinese brocade with raised patterns of silver and gold threads. The arung (prince) was rather pleased with himself, and so was I where the brocade was concerned. The Bugis were against Ahmed Sukarno, and I would supply the guns they required to fight him. The Bugis dialect is related to the Mandarese and the Makassarese, as well as the Toradja. While most of the Bugis and Mandarese are Moslem, the Toradja have resisted conversion to Islam, remaining animists or embracing Christianity.

The old arung would never bend to Sukarno and his Javanese cut-throats. He would rather serve the Dutch who had established control of the region at the beginning of the twentieth century, when South Sulawesi consisted of a multitude of petty kingdoms, each ruled by a prince of the highest "white" blood. The Arung was considered to be the descendant of a heavenly being sent down to earth to bring order to a chaotic world. The Dutch recognized the authority of the most powerful rulers and gave them additional power under a system of indirect rule, in which all who were of royal descent constituted a noble class, unless they had sullied the purity of their bloodline through frequent marriage with women of lower status.

South Sulawesi, by the way, is the Bugis name for the Celebes. But this arung had his kingdom in Sumatra, near Tempe. There was another arung at Teluk Betung. Both these arungs had a reputation for piracy, and their crews were the most skilled sailors in these parts. But the Bugis were not the only people in this area of Sumatra. There were the Batak and the Toba, the largest group of these Proto-Malay people, who were reputedly cannibalistic, said to have eaten one or two missionaries. The Toba–Batak lived around Lake Toba in the Bukit Barisan area of Sumatra.

The Bugis village was called *wanuwa*, and the arung's people are his *desa*. This arung was rather wealthy, with a large desa and a vast household. The chief occupation of the women was weaving sarongs of silk. Bugis sarongs are famous with their hand-painted or intricately woven designs. I knew I had to keep a close, watchful eye on both our boats crews and Roy especially. The arung would consider any amorousness towards his women a great disgrace, even though some of the girls were willing and able. I didn't want to see any of my crew, especially Roy, swinging by his cutlass of love from the yardarm of a Bugis pedewakan!

Feeling an urgency to depart after making the deal, I got underway again at nightfall and headed down the Berhala Straits on a heading towards Cape Mendjangan. I needed to pass between the island of Bangka and Pelambang in Sumatra during the hours of darkness and well into the Sunda Straits before dawn. But I was also aware of the possibility of running into Dutch gunboats that frequented these waters with persistent regularity. Our boats went along the Sunda Straits, running between the island of Sumatra and Java. A great naval battle had taken place here against the Japanese navy with the Australian light cruiser *HMAS Perth* and the American heavy cruiser *USS Houston*. It became known as the Battle of Sunda Strait. This occurred during the Second World War, between the islands of Java and Sumatra. The battle raged from 28 February until 1 March 1942, ending up with the disastrous sinking of both go-it-alone Allied cruisers and a victory for the Japanese naval forces. Over a thousand Allied souls were lost.

Sunday, 16 March 1947

The dawn found us west of Krakatoa, and we changed course again, heading up the west coast of Sumatra in comparatively calm seas. The Indian Ocean was being kind for once, and we made the most of its benevolence. There had been one or two difficult moments during the night when we had picked up on the radar what we first thought might be a Dutch gunboat, always a likelihood in these waters. But we had made it without any incident and were accordingly most thankful. Strange though it may seem, from my perspective guns don't kill people. It requires the human touch to turn a gun into a tool of murder. I strongly believe that guns have only two enemies: politicians and, of course, iron oxide or red rust.

What damn hypocrites those politicians are who sanction bloody conflicts in remotest parts of the planet by supplying legally arms yet with the next breath politicize "gun control" as a means to prevent gun crimes by legislating against civilian ownership of firearms. We are not the only gun-runners in this field of operations, but I suppose that we will not be the last. In the first place, gun-running is against the law and considered morally wrong. Yet certain powerful nations openly supply guns to both sides of countries in conflict, fuelling wars and destroying or destabilizing regimes no longer in favour with their own self-interests. All of this is fuelled, of course, by the want of money and power by the corrupt ones in high places.

It remains a very dirty business all round. I suppose it's a question of endurance. The Bugis arung prefers tracer bullets, claiming they have a demoralizing effect on their Javanese adversaries. At this juncture, I believe that the Dutch are already onto us. They must be! But if the Bugis can keep Ahmed Sukarno busy around the islands and along the coast of Sumatra for them, they are obviously prepared to turn a blind eye to our activities, at least for the moment.

We sighted the island of Enggano at 1000 hours. The weather is fine, with a calm sea at the moment. We are making good headway, and there appears to be no other shipping traffic for miles.

The ship cook got a few fishing lines out, so chances are it was going to be fish for dinner. Everything being well, we expected to sight the island of South Pagai around 1300 hours.

Penicillin was our next drop. The drug is an expensive item, and what our customers would offer us in trade for the drug would not even cover my cost. But the deal we had made with the Bugis had more than paid for this little venture, which I felt was a kind of atonement for our gun-running. A matter of conscience, perhaps? All serious daring comes within one's self! Our customer would give us a list of requirements, a good meal, and his blessing.

Once you have had anything to do with these medical missionaries, there is nothing you could ever refuse them. The next time you are in a church, take a good look at the crucifix with the figure of Christ. What does it say to you? "Down on your knees, sinful, wicked one.

You did this to me"? I think not. If you look closely at the crucifix, its message is clear—forgiveness for all your wrongdoings.

It was 1500 hours when we passed Siberut, well to the east, and at 1800 hours we were off Batu Island and on a set course for Gunung Sitoli, on the island of Nias, and the missionary station.

Monday, 17 March 1947

I reduced the boat's speed so that we would arrive at the island in daylight. Nias had been occupied by the Japanese during the war and raided by Force Z a number of times. No, not the Force Z Royal Navy battleship and heavy cruiser which was sunk by the Japanese Air but rather the Special Operations Executive Australia, an Aussie Z Special Commando Unit. They were essentially a specialist reconnaissance and sabotage unit, which included British, Dutch, New Zealand, Timorese, and Indonesian members. This elite military unit predominantly operated on Borneo and the islands of the former Netherlands East Indies.

Subsequently the Japanese laid hundreds of beach mines just below the waterline at high tide back in 1944. It is not that I am timorous, but I didn't want to be blown to kingdom come in the middle of the night just yet! I had my men, boat, kith and extended kin to think about also.

I don't suppose you have ever seen a rice water stool. This looks like water in which rice has been boiled, due to the presence of fragments of epithelium from the lining of the intestine, which is a typical symptom of cholera. We have with us a cholera vaccine for preventive inoculation and some sulphaguanidine, which is used for the treatment of enteric infections, sterilization of colon, and other conditions, together with some Vitamin D tablets for the medical missionaries on this trip.

We understand that rickets is rather a problem with some of the children. There is an old man with Romberg's sign, the inability to stand erect on his own two feet without swaying when his eyes are closed, a sign of locomotor ataxia. They may have their failures, these missionaries, but they don't give up easily. It takes a lot of guts to pick up a ragged bundle of humanity and nurse it back to health. The missionaries here are not alone in their struggle against poverty and disease.

Most of the sickness and diseases you will find on these islands is the immediate result of privation. There are nuns who run a leper colony in Singapore and the Little Sisters of the Poor, who beg for food in the marketplace and feed the poor before they themselves eat whatever is left over. We reached Pulau Nias at 0530 hours but it was 0700 hours before I decided to make our run to the beach, with great caution because of the leftover unexploded ordinance.

We beached without incident, and the welcome we received was overwhelming. The islanders soon got to work offloading our cargo under the supervision of the boat's crew. I have brought a load of rice provisions with us on this trip, together with some surplus British Army rations in the form of tins of meat and vegetables. This was one of those occasions I wished I commanded a much larger ship instead of a small PT boat. The intelligence the missionaries here provided us was priceless. It appeared that things were not going well, for the Dutch have been losing ground. The Dutch were faring badly against the insurgents around Semarang, Magelango, and Jogjakarta in Java, where the insurgents of Ahmed Sukarno had them under siege.

There were reports of a serious lack of food and many deaths, either from the fighting or starvation. A large number of Magelango please
survivors it seemed were living by eating cats and dogs and rats. There was no way we could run food into Java without becoming involved with the Dutch or the insurgents fighting against them. And neither could the small quantity of food that my boat could carry make any impact on thousands of hungry mouths there. It would be an insignificant drop in the ocean of this self-inflicted human misery, which was based on one man's selfish anti-Western idealism about Indonesian Nationalism.

Japanese beach mines at Pulau Nias, March 1947

But I could make a difference here, however small, by removing this dangerous hazard on the beach left behind by the Japanese. At low tide several huge clusters of unexploded Japanese sea mines could be seen honeycombed all along the beachfront. These remained a constant threat to the islanders, particularly adventurous young children who saw no danger in life. It was, in my opinion, death waiting to happen. We spent the next half an hour or so cutting lengths of bamboo poles and carrying them down to the beach.

These beach mines were just below the surface during high tide and left to bake in the tropical sun while the tide was out, which would likely make them unstable. I had thought of exploding them by rifle fire in the old naval tradition. But these mines had been set out in clusters so that in theory they would all explode simultaneously in a kind of chain reaction, and I didn't know the full extent of the minefield. There could also be other land mines hidden from sight under the sand, another potential hazard. I set up my high-explosive (HE) charges after establishing my safe distance parameters.

I then began to systematically fill the hollow jointed bamboo with high explosives, constructing three good Bangalore torpedoes, Royal Engineers' fashion. It was my intention to destroy the whole minefield cluster on this beach via sympathetic detonation. In plain speaking, a small explosion causes a chain reaction and sets off all the much heavier ordinance. So I slowly made my way, tip-toeing all the way, until I reached the outer edge of the minefield, at what I conceived as a reasonably safe distance from the mines, carrying my three improvised bamboo Bangalore torpedoes.

There was no point in risking any of my crew's lives. This was what I had been trained for and my area of expertise during the war, though I did feel like a prat on tip-toes. I placed one improvised Bangalore torpedo at each end of the mine cluster and one in the middle for luck. We were all set, and I waited for the pre-arranged ringing of church bells to inform me that all of the islanders had been safely accounted for and were away from the threat area. On hearing those church bells ringing, I lit all three safety fuses. I then proceeded to walk calmly away, like the good sapper I was, to the safety point, where I took cover.

There was one hell of an explosion, and the island had its first inshore deep-water berth as a consequence—but no more damn bloody mines! Scared? Of course I was bloody scared! Huge explosions might alert my enemies, especially the Dutch gunboats, to my presence here, so I prepared to leave those islands forthwith. This was another one of those times in my life when I felt my actions would save lives and that I had actually made a difference out there. I couldn't leave those unstable Japanese beach mines to be set off by some curious child, now could I? Besides, the beach was safe for me to use in the dark now.

It is remarkable how nature will always reclaim her own, and the threat that once was will be no more. The sea would clean up the huge holes caused by the mines exploding, and it would all be calm and safe here once more.

Tuesday, 18 March 1947

At this juncture there was an urgency for me and my boats to get away, so we headed off immediately, until we got well clear of Pulau Simeulue, heading for the Great Channel between Kutaradja on the tip of Sumatra and the Nicobar Islands. We should make our right turn into the Straits of Malacca around 0300 hours.

All societies recognize that some acts should be discouraged for social reasons, but not all regard these as sins or moral offences. The idea that all men are born in a state of sin because of acts committed (according to biblical accounts) by the very first man and woman derives from Judaic tradition, but it is important to realize that this concept is not universal. Perhaps because of the last war, the concept of sin has become unfashionable in what is now a permissive society. It would be pertinent to ask, therefore, whether a sense of sin should be regarded as an inherent trait of human nature or whether it is a phenomenon peculiar to only certain periods of history or types of civilization.

Throughout two millennia of the Christian era, the problem of sin has played a crucial role in Western philosophical thinking. Heaven and hell have symbolized the division of the world into contrasting realms, and few Christians doubt that man's ultimate destiny is determined by his virtuous or sinful actions on earth. The doctrine of original sin has also attempted to explain the existence of evil and suffering in a world believed to be the creation of a benevolent God. The paradisiacal state destined for humanity was supposedly ruined by the first transgression.

This was according to biblical accounts of the first parents, Adam and Eve. Moreover, the original sin idea was believed to have caused an "evil inclination", inherited by all of Adam's descendants. Recent discoveries regarding the early stages of man's development have suggested to many theologians that the myth of paradise requires reconsideration, abandoning the doctrine of the fall of man as an actual historical event. Yet the debate on the nature of original sin could not have continued for close to two thousand years if the awareness of sin as a blemish on human nature had not been deeply ingrained in the human psyche.

There is no European language which does not contain a word for *sin*; obviously Western people have long been convinced that sin was common to all of mankind. Christian missionaries discovered languages which did not contain the word sin; the people who spoke these languages had no concept of a form of conduct which would bring men into conflict with the supernatural powers believed to be the guardians of morality. An investigation of a cross section of societies on different levels of economic and social development demonstrates a great variety of attitudes about behaviour which do not conform to accepted Western moral ideas and, indeed, to the whole problem of the origin and nature of evil.

At that time, men and women did not indulge in sexual intercourse. Therefore, no children were born. When a man became very old, he was placed in a lake and he arose from the waters fully rejuvenated. In this way no one died, and there was no need to replenish the population by sexual procreation. This idyllic existence ended, however, when the creator's adversary persuaded men that a life in which they had nothing to do but eat and sleep was dull and unsatisfactory. The adversary advocated a world in which men and women would experience the joys of love and a woman would bear children, but at the end of their lifespan people would die and be replaced by their sons and daughters.

People were tempted by this prospect, so by abandoning the life laid down by the creator, they gained the pleasures of sex but also brought upon themselves the evils of pain, illness, and death. The idea that sinful actions on the part of men can bring about disaster prevails among many peoples. The Semang, a pygmy tribe of Malaya, believe that thunder and lightning are caused by the transgression of certain moral rules and that the danger inherent in these phenomena can be averted by the act of expiation. This is executed by the offering of a person's own blood. The blood is drawn from a small incision in the leg, mixed with water, and thrown into the air.

This is an irksome duty, not necessarily a sign of contrition, but it does indicate that the Semang have a sense of sin, the consequences of which must be counteracted by shedding blood. The most serious sin is incest. If not expiated this attracts the punishment of death by lightning. The taboo applies not only to the act but even to conduct which may potentially lead to it.

A lack of reserve for example, between son-in-law and mother-in-law is condemned and subject to supernatural punishment. More surprisingly, equally stringent rules cover behaviour towards animals; it is taboo to tease dogs, cats, and monkeys. Nothing suggests that the Semang believe in retribution in the world beyond, however. Punishments incurred by men on account of their sinful actions relate only to their fate on earth. All men, good and bad, are thought to enter the same Land of the Dead, where they live a carefree existence. The concept of sin clearly depends on man's ability to choose between "right" and "wrong" behaviour.

Wrong behaviour is often linked with a sinister force antagonistic to human welfare, which in turn leads men to choose wrong conduct and thus become enmeshed in sin. In the Judeo-Christian tradition, the "fall from grace" of Adam and Eve in the Garden of Eden is responsible for the evil inclinations inherited by their descendants and is the source of suffering. The Buddhists, on the other hands ascribe to the system of karma, in which sins are but natural events in the chain of cause and effect, which can be atoned for by acts of virtue. But then in Buddhist ideology, the whole universe, men as well as gods, is subject to a reign of law.

Every action, good or bad, has an inevitable and automatic effect in a long chain of cause and effect that is independent of the will of any deity. This may, though, leave no room for the concept of sin as an act of defiance against the authority of a personal god. Buddhists speak of sin when referring to transgression against the universal moral code. Central to Buddhist thinking is the principal of the balance between merit and demerit. My own view of original sin is that Eve committed adultery with Satan. The seduction of a wife is described as the surest means of breaking an opponent's power, for a man's power depends not only on his virtue but also upon his wife's chastity.

This notion that the evil consequences of a wife's unfaithfulness affects her husband rather than herself is certainly different from the Christian concept of the wages of sin. Women are seen as the cause of many sins, and they appear in numerous myths as temptresses of sagas or ascetics.

At 0745 hours we sighted the Royal Mail Ship *Corfu*, which was the sister ship of the *RMS Carthage*; both vessels had been on the China run. But in September 1939, the *Corfu* was requisitioned by the Royal Navy and armed with eight 6-inch guns as part of her conversion to an armed merchant cruiser.

HMS Corfu served as an armed merchant cruiser in this role until February 1944 and as a troop transport from then until the end of the Second World War. In 1944 the *TSS Corfu* was a troop ship on the route between England and Bombay. While the ship was alongside at Bombay, the gunnery officer commenced to put his gun crews through the load-and-unload sequence, unaware that the crew of one of the naval guns had loaded it up with a live shell. On the command "Fire!" the shell shot out to the centre of Bombay's offshore islands. Fortunately, no one was killed or injured and little damage was done.

At the end of the war, the ship was returned to the Peninsular and Oriental Steam Navigation Company and put into service on the Hong Kong-to-London route.

Roy and I parted company at that point. He was heading into Malacca with a full cargo of sarongs, while I was en route to Singapore for a few days of well-deserved laughter. I would pay off my crew and do the rounds again before planning my next job. It was not so much the excitement of these little excursions into the back of beyond, or even the challenges we faced with each trip we made but rather the need to well and truly wind down slowly and relax for a while.

The forays we made were like living on the edge of a knife, relatively dangerous. I told Roy to pay the duty due on the sarongs when he arrived in Malacca and to keep his nose clean with the port authorities. But Roy's idea of winding down was to jump the bones of the first willing female that happened along. I preferred to weigh my women up first, so that when I did decide to make my move on them and get down to the nitty-gritty, they would stay in harness, like a well-trained horse. Roy had more of a river ferryboat mentality—roll on, bang-bang, roll off. You had to love him for this, as he never changed, always staying true to his womanizing nature and looking for chance opportunity.

Wednesday, 19 March 1947

The port engine is doing a little spluttering at the moment, and it has become necessary to investigate further to find the fault. I spent the early hours of this morning with Ali, checking our fuel lines. It appears that dirt and gunk has collected in one fuel tank, and this seems to be the cause of the problem. At the moment we are running on one engine, which makes the tiller rather heavy. I will need to clean out the fuel tanks and lines and then re-bleed the engines. I set to the task of getting this done, and by 0200 hours, after some simple diagnostics at sea, we had cleared the fuel line in question and switched over to the other fuel tank.

We are running normally once again, but this has set me back and made us late. It was not until 0600 hours that we finally reached the marker buoy at Tanjong Piai and commenced our final run into Singapore. I make the run into Singapore, with our navigation lights on, at a steady twelve knots until we reach our anchorage. You can almost smell the sea air that is home to me and my boat crew. I will have to get a marine engineer to overhaul my engines sometime in the near future. But for the moment, and once we dock at the pier, an intermediate engine service is in order.

The poor are not conscious of their poverty
Nor the rich conscious of their own prosperity.
Not a pin to choose between them,
For in their own poetry it goes beyond
Into subject and object,
A priori to the existence of transcendental man.
I am here, seen and not seen,
Heard and yet not heard.
Where are you if not with me?

Achievement: There is one fixed rule!

Formulate and stamp indelibly on your mind a mental picture of yourself succeeding. Hold this picture tenaciously, and never permit it to fade. Never think of yourself as failing nor doubt the reality of the mental image. That is most dangerous, for the mind always tries to complete what it pictures. Thus you must always picture success, no matter how badly things seem to be going. Whenever a negative thought concerning your personal powers comes to mind, deliberately voice a positive thought to cancel out the negative. Say it out loud and clear so you can hear it. Why do you think I say "bollocks!" out loud so often?

Do not build up obstacles in your imagination. You must depreciate every so-called obstacle. Minimize each one quickly. Difficulties must be studied and efficiently dealt with in order to be eliminated, but they must be properly analysed and seen for only what they are. Remember that fear is just a state of mind, not a reality. Do not be awestruck by other people or try to emulate them. Nobody can be you as efficiently as you can. Remember also that most people, despite their confidant appearance and demeanour, are often as scared as you are and just as doubtful of themselves.

There are many pathways through life, some which require a little more patience than others. Patience is more often than not the key to successful hunting. Everything comes to he or she who is willing to play the long game, with a well-thought-out and planned strategy. Patience remains the key to success. It's far better to try and fail than to fail to try. Success does not come to people who give up after their first failures, only to the daring of heart with a will of iron. The man who never makes a mistake is the man who never does anything. Lastly, money alone and the acquisation of wealth does not necessarily make you sucessful in life. Always ask for what you need, not what you want. Think about this.

My cabin on the *Wilful Lady*

It was 0830 hours by the time we finally berthed, and the next half hour was spent paying off my crew. I made the necessary arrangements concerning the strip-down of the fuel lines and the cleaning out of the fuel tanks. We would have to take first things first and empty the tanks, filter the remaining fuel, and then get the steam jenny going under pressure on the empty tanks. We needed to check, clean, or replace the filters on the fuel pumps and get everything shipshape again. Once all that was done, I returned to my bridge to relax a little and make plans in my mind for the next job.

Thursday, 20 March 1947

I had a good breakfast and felt full of pep and ready for work. I had filtered off the remaining fuel and dismantled most of the fuel lines when Idris and Ali arrived on the scene at 1000 hours.

"Had difficulty leaving it?" I asked. They both grinned at me rather sheepishly.

"I was waiting for Ali," Idris said in his defence.

"It's the homecoming, not the getting away from it," Ali expressed.

Ali was my marine engineer who happened to have three wives, along with a string of children. I had to admit he didn't look any the worse for wear. Certainly, there is nothing like a good roll in the hay to tone up one's muscles.

It was 1500 hours when we'd completed reassembling, fuelling up, and test-starting all engines. Sludge in the bottom of one fuel tank had been the cause of the problem. I hated to think what the consequences would have been had I been making a getaway and my engines had suddenly packed up! Well, she was running like a bird now, and we would make sure sludge was never a problem again.

Roy would be back on the twenty-seventh, with any luck. I wanted to make a run up the East Coast of Malaya to Bangkok for that load of Siamese silk required by Bill Langley of the West Traders in Malacca Street. Ali fed his pet squirrel and the ship's cat, which of course was his excuse for the daily visits to the boat when we were tied up in Singapore. He was quite a good engineer, and I had no objections. But between the lines, my crew said it was only an excuse for him to keep out of the way of his three demanding wives! Can you blame him? Believe me, on my boat we never had a dull moment.

I dropped Ali and Idris off in town and made my way once again to the G.H. Café for a few Tigers and the most recent news on the bamboo grapevine. It seemed Hock was in the market for four or five Gray marine engines, and I was informed that Low Sack Chuan was looking for me. It's nice to be wanted.

Tommy Clark was having a few jars with Joe Wright and wanted to know if I was still in the market for a load of "panacea"—something that would cure any illness. I assumed he meant penicillin. He had perhaps killed too many Tigers himself?

Fame and I liked to take a quiet walk in the cool of the evening, as often as not around the church of St Teresa on the hill in Kampong Bahru. It was said that a stone had fallen from the scaffolding, killing the parish priest while the church was under construction some years ago, and as a consequence, most of the local non-Christian community actually believed now that the church was haunted. People claimed to have seen the ghostly form of a black-robed priest walking the grounds on late moonlit nights. So had I, for that matter! We said Good evening to each other! It was Father Lee, doing his rounds before bed. The early mass in this church was at dawn, subsequently the "ghostly" priest could be seen again just before dawn each and every morning.

There was a Chinese Taoist temple in Bukit Permai Road, behind St Teresa's school, just a short distance from the church. The steady toc-toc beat of the fish-head gong there mingled with the low chant of Taoist nuns, leading to an uncanny, austere atmosphere to the church grounds at night. It remained a forbidding place to be.

A little further along Bukit Permai Road stood the Temple of Hanoman, the Hindu monkey god. The Malays believed Hanoman was an evil, dog-faced spirit. The temple was run by a Chinese medium who claimed his body was possessed by the monkey god. It was a convincing show of sorts, as the medium painted his face with theatrical grease paint and went into a trance to the sound of drums and clashing cymbals. His head rose and fell in time with the drumming, gathering moment to the point of frenzy, at the peak of which he cut his tongue and spit the blood over joss papers on the temple floor. The joss papers were then sold as a cure-all to his followers, which was convenient.

People believe what they want or need to believe, and I have caught and uncovered several charlatans in my time who were profiting from the gullible. It was not strange to find a Catholic Church in the immediate proximity of pagan temples; after all, that was what missionary work was all about. St Teresa of Avila was dedicated to converting of all humanity to the Christian faith. The Catholic communion at St Teresa's Church was quite large. It was run by French missionaries in that part of Singapore. St Teresa sought and found a new relationship with God. The Church of St Teresa at Kampong Bahru Road remains the only Catholic Church in Singapore to feature Romano-Byzantine architecture.

The label commonly attached to St Teresa was that of mystic, denoting a person who by ways that reason cannot fathom enters into direct communion with divinity. Teresa's mystical visions were apt to cause raised eyebrows in an age when reason ruled supreme rather than intuition or the supernatural. But her written accounts of these experiences achieved unusual weight through her self-analysis. Even the sceptic respected Teresa's honesty and her expansive, cheerful personality.

Her influence remains persuasive, for she is a living memory in her beloved Spain, where her statue graces some thousand churches or more! Her writings have gone through more than a thousand printings, and today she is read worldwide in many languages. Moreover, her life's work, the religious order of the barefoot Carmelites, still shows extraordinary vigour. Despite the severity of its rules, the order now encompasses well over a thousand religious houses and convents. During her twenty-seven years at the convent, she became deeply spiritual. In her prayers she sensed a divine presence. It seemed to her that she was *being addressed by inner voices and seeing certain visions.* The most dramatic of these was an encounter with an angel holding a golden spear tipped with a point of fire.

St Teresa of Avila Church in Kampong Bahru, 1947

St Teresa wrote this:

> I saw an angel very near me, towards my left side, in bodily form, which is not usual with me; for though angels are often represented to me, it is only in my mental vision. This angel appeared rather small than large, and very beautiful. His face was so shining that he seemed to be one of those highest angels called seraphs, who look as if all on fire with divine love. He had in his hands a long golden dart; at the end of the point methought there was a little fire. And I felt him thrust it several times through my heart in such a way that it passed through my very bowels. And when he drew it out, methought it pulled them out with it and left me wholly on fire with a great love of God.

If anyone thinks I am lying, I pray to God in his goodness to grant this person some experience of it. Those watching Teresa during her more and more frequent trances said that her face shone with an inner light while her body became limp. Some witnesses swore that they had seen her being lifted off the ground to remain suspended for long moments in the air. Describing her experiences, Teresa wrote, "He appears to be the soul by a knowledge brighter than the sun is seen, or any brightness. But there is an unseen light that illuminates the understanding, a soft whiteness and infused radiance causing great delight." Such visions made Teresa conscious that her abode, from which she could come and go at will, seemed more like a fashionable boarding house than a convent. So she planned to set up her own sanctuary where a few dedicated souls could live a life of poverty, contemplation, and prayer, far from the hubbub of the world. It was at San Jose, in Avila, where the flame lit by Teresa was kept alive by twenty Carmelite nuns. Thus the reformed order was born. Teresa took the religious name Teresa de Jesus and called her followers the Discalced Carmelites or Barefooted Carmelites. Their habits were dark sackcloth covered for choral services by white mantles.

Her outstanding work is *The Interior Castle,* a book on how to get close to God through prayer. Unrivalled as a guide to mystical theology, it takes its theme from one of Teresa's visions, in which God showed her a large crystal globe. The globe turned out to be a castle, and in the castle there were seven mansions. In the innermost of them there dwelt the King of Glory, whose light pervaded the whole translucent structure. A young priest, Juan de Yepes, later became known as John of the Cross. A mystic like St Teresa, Juan de Yepes became her disciple and was later canonized by the Church. On October 14, 1582 Teresa uttered her last words: "My Lord, it is time to move on. Well then, may your will be done. O my Lord and my Spouse, the hour that I have longed for has come. It is time for us to meet one another."

The Barefoot Carmelites in Singapore were a teaching order, and they ran a school next to Kampong Bahru. Their convent was on Bukit Teresa. I had never heard of St Teresa before my arrival in Singapore, and it was at first hard for me to believe all they told me concerning her. Many years passed before I considered embracing the Catholic faith but not necessarily accepting all her creed or doctrines. But then, have I not always been a rebel?

Friday, 21 March 1947

I spent an hour or so looking around the flea market in Rochore Canal Road this morning. The Malays have a name for this place where everything you can possibly think of is for sale at the right price—Robinson Petang. *Petang* means evening/afternoon; *petang hari* means late in the day. I wanted to see one of the dealers, and catching him while he was busy setting up his stall had its desired result pricewise. It was just a case of the early bird catching the reluctant worm. Had the man in question been a *Banian*—a Hindu trader—the ploy would not have worked. However, he was a *Keck*, and a Keck trader must make his first sale of the day, even if it is below his costs!

I had purchased his entire stock of ex-army jungle parangs at 6 per cent above his original cost. The parang is a type of machete or cleaver used across the Malay Archipelago; it is quite a lethal blade. Of course I knew from my sources on the grapevine what he'd paid for that job lot in the first place, but one must leave a Keck trader a little dignity on such occasions.

Tommy Clarke was his usual self when I dropped into his place in Henderson Road an hour or so later. His woman had in all probability given him a hard time.

In contrast, there was nothing that she wouldn't or couldn't do for Tommy. But she had this rather bad habit of nagging him. It was little wonder that Tommy was keeping a low profile around his sheep pens. He had the Army contract for importing sheep from Australia via the Blue Funnel shipping line. The sheep were held in pens at Henderson Road before being sent to the abattoir in Jalan Besar. Tommy had a number of Gray marine engines he was rather anxious to get rid of, and we did a little deal. Hock would take all the engines off his hands in return for a fair price on the penicillin he had offered me in the G.H. Café. Tommy haggled over the price for a while, but his heart was not in it. In the end he dropped his price, seeing as I wanted the healing drug for the missionaries.

Now it was a question of lunch. I had lunch with Balkis, which ended up as a rather luxurious affair lasting until evening and making tea quite unnecessary. There are many stories and legends about the Queen of Sheba, or rather Balkis, also known as Queen Balqis in the Arab World. These stories are both intriguing and conflicting. Not only is she mentioned in the Holy Quran, the Bible, and the Ethiopian Orthodox Kebra Nagast but also in legendary tales that extend from Ethiopia to India, Persia, and Arabia. It is not every day that one has lunch with the Queen of Sheba! Balkis was also Fame's Arabic name. We had so much to talk about, matters apart from ourselves that required our attention.

It is rather interesting to observe the way some men look at women. Very few men, it seems, look at women straight in the eye. (The same can be said when men first meet or greet other men, for that matter.) They always seem to focus on the crotch, that point of the female anatomy between the top of her thighs and torso. But this generally is a fleeting glimpse, supposedly unobserved by the lady in question.

There are your leg or pin-loving men, your arse or buttocks men, and of course, breast or titty men. But I am not inclined that way, and when I look at a woman, she knows I am looking at her. I first observe the way she wears her hair, then the colour of her eyes—are they blue, green, or brown? Next I look at her nose, mouth, breasts, hips, legs, and lastly, her feet. Then it's back up to her face and, of course, her smile. Well, nearly always, if not necessarily in that order on every occasion. I suppose it is when they don't smile back at me that I need to worry about losing my mojo! Uniquely different in so many splendid ways, women are to me the guardians of our species and so very special.

Perhaps where Fame and I are concerned, we were destined to be together. Call it fate if you like, for want of a better word—that which had to happen and was intended by fate. There is much to be said concerning the wisdom and experience of an older woman. It is an experience every young man should attempt at one time or another during his escapades through life, providing he does not disobey all the rules and cause trouble. Escapism? I think it's more like a mutual desire on the part of both of us, a kind of dignified desire, which we work at together diligently in every dimension. It's rather nice to know that there is always good steak waiting at home and I don't have to waste time catching young chickens to eat. There is twenty years' difference in our ages, which in no way inhibits the sensuality of our togetherness. This can't be compared with some of the much younger women I have known; they have rather a lot to catch up with.

I have made the necessary arrangements for a trip over to Telok Mawar, in north-eastern Johore tomorrow. There I hope to collect the cash outstanding on a load of Javanese sarongs I sold on credit in one of the kampongs. I trust the Malay involved in the deal, but sadly, they have defaulted on the payment that was due last week. I dislike deals that have gone south. If you don't call, I don't get paid! This, of course, is my own fault for misplaced trust. That is the difficulty where the small Malay retailer is concerned. But we would see.

Roy returned early this morning. He is having trouble with the screw of his port engine. We took his boat out on a test run first thing after breakfast. The continuous vibration was rather profound and could only mean that either the screw had lost one of its blades or the blade was badly bent; possibly the propeller shaft itself was bent out of true windings. That would mean a rather expensive dry-dock repair job for us. We both returned to the dock and tied up, making the necessary preparations for a preliminary inspection.

Me diving off the dock

Chapter 15

The Double Cross
Saturday, 22 March 1947

Kim Soo, shellfish girl and businesswoman

Roy started the compressor while I kitted out ready to make the dive. But when I got down to it, I discovered that an old length of ship's mooring rope had somehow become tightly tangled around the screw and the propeller guard. I then spent the next hour cutting away slowly, piece by piece, that rope tangled around the boat's screw. On completion, I found that there was no other apparent damage to the screw, and once I had satisfactorily finalized my visible inspection of the propeller shaft and screws for any other noticeable damage, it was time to surface. Roy was leaning over the rail, busy talking to Kim Soo, when I surfaced and climbed the ladder onto the deck of the boat.

He immediately started the engine, bringing her up to maximum revolutions. There were no apparent vibrations; he had been lucky on this occasion. He decided to take her out on a test run while I got out of my diving kit and re-stowed my diving gear. I told Roy that I was heading over to Mawar, and this seemed to have a rather magnetic effect on Kim Soo. Apparently she had been trying to induce Roy into taking her to one of the Malay fishing villages on the Johore coast. She was intent on buying a load of fish that she could resell at a reasonable profit in Singapore.

Kim Soo and her elder sister ran a little business of their own, collecting shellfish from the sea, which they then sold to Chinese restaurants. Shellfish moved around in the sea, and the beds were almost depleted in this area of the coast. Kim Soo had been thinking the problem over and arrived at a sudden desire to become a fresh fish wholesaler in a big way. She had a thousand dollars of capital of her own to make her first deal with, along with the necessary determination to see it through.

If I had been aware of the true circumstances of her situation at the time, I would have booted her arse off my boat, and that would have been the end of our association. But women are divisive at times. Who can truly fathom the depth of a scheming woman? It was not that Kim Soo was in any way dishonest with me. My trip over to Telok Mawar took over an hour and was rather uneventful. I managed to collect the cash outstanding on the sarongs I'd loaned out on credit and was four thousand dollars the better of for it, with an order for another load of Javanese sarongs in a month's time.

I took Kim Soo along to meet the headman of the local Malay fishing village. He told us the catch had been quite good of late, mostly ikan merak, red snapper, a fish which brings in a good price on the Singapore retail market. Kim Soo was over the moon about it, but I should have scuttled her there and then. However, she had purchased the catch unseen after quite a bit of haggling and had spent all the cash she had with her. This posed the problem of her waiting for the return of the small fishing fleet with the high tide around 0300 hours before she could take delivery of the fish. It would be an hour's run back to Singapore to meet up with the 0500 hours delivery and sale of the fish on the wholesale market.

"You trade by bartering?" she said all of a sudden.

The question was quite unexpected, taking me by surprise. We had shared the evening meal together on board my boat—well, I couldn't leave her around the beach at night on her own, waiting for the fishing boats to arrive.

"Yes, of course," I replied. "I use the barter system in the islands where the currency is unstable. The commodities must be viable and not perishable," I hastily added.

"The commodities I have in mind are unique and much sought after in Chinese circles. They have the power of rejuvenation if in mint condition," she said.

"Jeng Seng," I said. "It must be Korean—any other kind is no good."

The laughter bubbled up within her and brought tears to her eyes. "*Chee!* You stupid red devil," she suddenly exclaimed.

We were speaking her language, a dialect in which pitch and tone, together with the particular quality of the voice and the manner of expression determined the meaning of the word.

"*Chou shou?*" I asked, meaning to sell, bargain, or dispose of.

Kim Soo blushed and nodded her head, her eyes watching my every expression."

"Two thousand dollars?" she said, watching my face as she spoke. "I need cash for my business," she went on, "and the price will give you immediate access for the next five years."

"What's the commodity?" I asked, feeling rather stupid.

"*Chieh!*" she said, lowering her eyes in modesty for the first time since the commencement of the conversation.

We left the bridge of the *Wilful Lady* together and adjourned to my cabin. Kim Soo was rather businesslike where the hard cash part of the deal was concerned, but there her bravado ended. I had not believed her story for one moment, with those Jap soldiers all over the place during the war. It was doubtful that there was one intact Chinese hymen in all of Singapore. But the apprehension in her eyes was real enough once we got down to the nitty-gritty, and I found myself where no man had been before. It brought tears to her eyes, but then it was quite a hymen, and of course most women cry the first time. I have never been able to make up my mind whether it's because it hurts or they are tears of joy. Had she been the last wartime Chinese virgin?

I accept that I was party to the deal Kim Soo had made with me, and about which I had no qualms. Indeed, the very first principle of Rex's law was opportunism. But I could not help but wonder why she had been in such a hurry to divest herself of the one thing that would ensure her future marriage. For women here in the East, shame is centred more simply on sexual modesty. This emphasis demands chastity for unmarried girls and total fidelity by married women. Sexual shame is the keystone of a woman's social personality and standing, while all other qualities tend to be judged by its absence or presence. Shame is seen as the expression of an inner purity and restraint, and this alone makes a woman sensitive to the demands of society and thus able to conquer the evil elements which conditioned her nature.

For this reason, marriages in Chinese village society are still arranged, for "falling in love" allows the weak sensual elements of a woman to endanger the family interest and commitments on which their society is based. Virginity is treasured as an absolute. Young Kim Soo was rather astute and businesslike for her age, though I had detected a kind of a kind of deviousness in her thinking. She was not direct and probably not completely honest.

I had the distinct impression she thought in terms of "the world against Kim Soo." She had arrived in Singapore four months after the Japanese, back in 1942, to join her mother and sister, who were already on the island. Her family had been living in the village of Tenang in Johore when the Japanese army swept through the place early one morning. Her mother and elder sister had been taken captive and later brought to Singapore by Mura Saki, a Japanese officer who had made them both his mistresses and placed them under his protection. The women had little choice in the matter; either submit or be sent to a Japanese Army Comfort Women house in Singapore.

This had tainted both women as Japanese collaborators in the eyes

287

of the local Chinese population. It's strange times during war, when whatever action you take to survive occupation by a barbaric foreign power can be viewed by others as treasonous or dishonourable. It may be easy for some people to say or judge, but we do what we must do to survive during wartime. Kim Soo's sister later gave birth to a son, half Japanese and half Chinese. The child would remain a constant reminder of their perceived collaboration with the enemy. Through no fault of their own, the war had made them outcasts to their own families.

The British had come back, and the Japanese had left; the war was over. Returning to their village at Tenang in Johore was now out of the question because of their alleged collaboration and her sister's child. They sisters had found a living collecting shellfish along the coast, but now the shellfish bed was almost depleted. It was time to seek another means of supporting her family and to open up a new chapter to their life. Kim Soo's story answered a number of questions I had in mind, one of which concerned her reluctance to have any dealings with the Chinese fishing villages in Johore.

Sunday, 23 March 1947

The fishing fleet arrived shortly after 0300 hours and brought in a rather good catch, most of which was red snapper. The *pawang pukat*, or witch-doctor—and there is one with almost every village fishing fleet—said that the catch was the best they had had so far that year. The first of the catch was the property of the pawang, a man who exercised the skill of his profession, practising magic in connection with various kinds of fishing. This pawang witch doctor in particular was rather renowned for his skill.

We had completed the loading of the red snapper by 0400 hours and put out to sea immediately, heading for Singapore. Customs were rather strict when I finally arrived at the fish port off Beech Road—as if I would do anything as stupid as run a consignment of contraband into port, when I knew every small cove and narrow inlet Singapore had to offer! I suppose the port custom authorities had to work off their frustrations when the opportunity arose, but some of them enjoyed playing at being bastards too much for my liking!

The market price in Singapore for red snapper was good, with the result that Kim Soo made a rather good return on her investment. Roy was in his cabin when I came alongside his boat and tied up. He had a black eye and several minor abrasions which looked rather sore, with a foul temper to boot. He looked like he had just been run over by a tank.

"Go and pulverize those two Chinese bastards in the hold!" he said in no uncertain terms. I took a look to find Big Dog and Dog Shit, the two Triad gang *samsings*, hog-tied on the floor of the hold, with every appearance of having been run over by a steam roller. The sudden surprised gasp from Kim Soo standing immediately behind me and staring white-faced at the two captives in the bottom of the hold said it all.

I got the distinct impression that she was somehow involved in the fracas, if not directly responsible for it. These two thugs had been keeping a watch on her and her sister for quite some time now, and of course Roy and I had naturally thought that their surveillance had something to do with the protection racket run by the local *Tiong* in the area. Obviously we had both been wrong. However, we could hardly let these two Chinese gangster thugs go; the risk of starting a full-scale gang war was too great. So the immediate question was what we were going to do with them. Roy and I argued that the two tiger fighters should be kept out of harm's way for the moment.

The Tiong that Kim Soo had approached with her original proposition was one of several splinter organizations operating at the street end on crime and prostitution in Singapore. These splinter groups paid a tribute to the larger Triad organization, and it was now a question of which Triad society. Kim Soo's proposition had been taken without exception and the community inspected and certified intact by one of their dragon women. Finally the money had been paid and the two tiger fighters instructed to safeguard the Tiong's investment, pending its disposal to a suitable rich client. In all probability this was an old Chinaman intent on restoring his body self, a harmonious relationship between yin and yang. A little juicy *chieh, The Yellow Emperor's Classic of Internal Medicine.*

Kim Soo had been rather naïve or perhaps foolish in her belief that she could obtain hard cash from the Tiong by selling herself as a "contract virgin" to them. Many affluent elderly Chinese businessmen saw this as big medicine and would pay well to own the contract; then afterwards they would pull off a deal that would set her up in the fish business and repay the money owed to the Tiong without further obligation.

"It's a question of practical profit," Low said. "The group concerned is one of ours.

She will have to honour the deal she made with them. Low stared at me for a moment, his right eyebrow raised in anticipation.

"I popped her cork," I informed him.

He appreciated that and burst into boisterous laughter. "Carry a gun or leave Singapore," he advised me, still laughing.

"That means the Burma job is still on?" I said quietly.

"The hell it is!" Low replied. "It means the leader of that group has lost face, and he will be gunning for you. He'll first pick up the girl and her sister, put them both into one of the Tiong whorehouses to work off their debt, and go gunning for you."

Low was thoughtful for a few moments, and finally he came to a decision. "Leave the problem with me," he said. "Take the two women with you on one of your trips around the islands. Leave now, and do not come back for one week."

I felt rather relieved by what he'd said, this Chinese Mister Fix-It. "Do Englishwomen have corks?" Low shouted after me.

I could still hear Low's laughter as I ran down the corridor towards my waiting car. I left Kim Soo seated in the car in front of the temple. Indeed, it was one of the safest places in Singapore for her at the moment. She was not too happy at the prospect of having to leave the island with her sister but quickly saw the logic of the argument. Roy had a trip down to Singkawang in Dutch Borneo and I would do the Langley run up to Bankok and back. Kim Soo and I collected her sister and her young child from their house in Kim Keat. I kept quiet during the drive back to the boats while Kim Soo explained the rudiments of the problem to her sister.

Roy was elated with the idea of female company on the round trip and suggested that he take them both with him. Kim Soo, on the other hand, wanted her sister to come with us on my boat. We spent the next hour fuelling up, and at 2100 hours commenced our run out towards the Anambus Islands and the South China Sea. Kim Soo, her sister, and the little boy had the use of my cabin on the run out. I could hardly expect a woman and child to travel with Roy and those two villainous thugs he had (although well and tightly secured) in the hold of his boat.

The run out through the shipping lanes around Singapore always required diligence for the first hour or so due to the large number of small boots scurrying around between the ships at anchor in the inner and outer roads of the port. It was not until 2230 hours that we had outdistanced the last ship at anchor. The inexperienced would have taken much longer, but this was one of our good nights, with everything quietly going our way.

The ups and downs in life are such, and we have learned the hard way to make the best of those bad periods but the most of the good. I set course and gradually brought the boat to cruise speed. It was good to feel the steady vibrations of the boat making headway through the waves. It made me feel vibrantly alive, powerful, and excited. All this was because of two women and a small boy, two Chinese tiger fighters, and a gang leader who had lost face! Roy was all for bumping off the two thugs. But then, Roy was the injured party, so to speak. I doubt that if it came down to it he would actually perform the necessary act. Killing in a kill-or-be-killed situation is rather different than cold-blooded murder.

People under stress act out more of their emotion, like hatred and grief, under those circumstances, being in an excited, adrenalin-charged state of mind. But Roy had seen the logic of my argument. Casting them away on some strange and lonely island in the South China Sea would be a kind of servitude for the two thugs. No doubt their leader would assume the worst but would have no proof for the moment. Low remained the only fly in the ointment. The Tiong required us to do the Burma job, so much so that they were prepared to protect us both against one of their minor officials. Perhaps we were playing into Low's hands.

No doubt the Burma run was of some paramount importance to the Tiong. I was not very good at subterfuge. Did one moralize the ideal, or did one remember those atrocities committed against people in the name of idealism? Perhaps we were wise to live out our lives according to our nature, without the dogma we were expected to accept without reasoning. There is no morality in politics, none whatsoever.

It was 1486 miles from Singapore to Manila and 885 miles between Singapore and Bangkok. At the moment we were on a course for Terempa in the Anambas Islands. One of the advantages of the sea in this part of the world is the lack of the small flying insects that prick your skin and suck your blood. The mosquito knows that it is a predator, takes its fill, and is on its way. It does not rob you of all your possessions and leave you helpless!

Monday, 24 March 1947

It was one of those bright, sunny mornings with a calm sea and an atmosphere of everything being right in the world. That was one of the reasons that I loved these boats so much. The 5-year-old child was the first to appear on the bridge, and I spent the next ten minutes or so fitting him up with a safety harness that would prevent him from falling over the side of the boat. One can never be too careful where children of his age are concerned. He was a sturdy little lad, strong and firm of limb, with typical Japanese features. His mother had named him Shang Chi, a merchant of ability and cleverness. The Japanese officer, Mura Saki, had planted his seed well, and here was the fruit of his endeavour, of which he could be proud.

But things concerning our well-being and safety would not be back to normal until we had rid ourselves of those two Chinese thugs. Kim Soo was rather apprehensive where Roy was concerned, even thought I had pointed out that it was a case of mistaken identity on the part of those two thugs who had attempted to beat the daylights out of him. I think she was afraid he would dump her on some island alone with those two thugs in question. I couldn't see Roy being so adverse, at least not until I had finished what we had started back in Telok Mawar, if then. One thing for sure, it would not be before I had finished running her in to my complete satisfaction. At the moment she was a novice, although she was learning fast the rudiments of natural movement required of her. *Yes,* I thought. *I'll keep her involvement under cover for the moment.*

Zainal took over the watch while I went for breakfast and a spot of shuteye. It would be at least another six hours before we got to the islands, and well, we all have to sleep! Kim Soo could wait; there would be time enough on the run up the Gulf of Siam to continue her education. I thought of Fame. She had once said she saw the little boy in me. George Apple had laughed at the comment at the time. Kim Soo had also said she could see the little boy in me! Strange how the boy in me had by chance found his way into both of them and for posterity planted his seed deep within each living furrow.

Idris was on the bridge when I awoke from a deep, dreamless sleep, refreshed and hungry. I poured myself a vodka orange and went on deck en route to the galley. We were amongst the islands now, and Roy signalled that he was coming alongside to pick me up. A few moments later I was on the bridge of Roy's boat, heading for the island where we had first run across the Arab slaver *Kasim Bahagia* back in early March of the year. Roy reversed his engines short of the tideline, while the crew offloaded and manhandled the two captive thugs. We left them high and dry on the beach with a case of tinned food. Neither man moved when I finally cut them free, which was probably due to the fact that they had been hog-tied in the hold since Saturday. They remained passive while the crew and I re-embarked. Then Big Dog was on his feet, shaking his hand angrily, his voice shouting expletives at us barely audible above the din of the boat's engines as we backed off into the deep water and turned before putting back to sea.

"Do you think the islanders are cannibalistic?" Roy asked.

"Well, look at it this way," I answered. "Would you fancy eating either of those bastards?"

For a moment I saw the glint of a mischievous smile on Roy's face. He seemed about to say something, but then he shook his head and went about his business on his boat, still looking at our castaways on the beach.

Roy brought his craft alongside my boat, while both crews made fast in quick time. During the next hour, we topped up our fuel and had a meal together. Roy got along well with Poo Choo and her son, and I made up my mind to transfer them both to Roy's boat, once he had made up his mind and decided to make the trip with me up the Gulf of Siam and into Bangkok. Now, Kim Soo had a liking for orange juice, and I made sure each glass she drank was three parts Russian vodka. The transfer of Poo Choo and her boy onto Roy's boat was carried out efficiently without question. We both cast off and set a course for Thailand.

"I'd rather have the other one?" Roy shouted at me from the bridge of his boat. He was pushing his luck! This reminded me that Kim Soo had a habit of sleeping in a *samfoo*, a style of casual dress worn by Chinese women consisting of a waisted blouse and trousers. I hated fumbling, so I gave her one of my sarongs. It was not my intention to get her drunk but rather to allow the vodka to induce sleep.

At 2100 hours we were in the jaws of the Gulf of Siam, central between the Condore Island off the coast of Vietnam and Tanah Merah in Malaya. But we were well clear of the established shipping routes, the last one we crossed being the 648 miles from Singapore to Saigon and Cholon.

This was a rather dangerous place because of the number of reefs. Constant careful scanning was the obvious requirement at such times, but we were experienced in these matters and had an aptitude for picking our way through at low speed. We had the occasional close shave but fortunately were spared the anguish of those moments when the boat shudders under the scrapes of the reef. By 0400 hours we were running in deep water again. I signalled Roy and received the answer that he was clear without incident—which was not surprising really, since he had followed closely in the wake of my boat.

Tuesday, 25 March 1947

I had a cup of coffee, reset my course, and brought my engines up to cruising speed. I then handed the watch over to Zainal and went below deck, where I found Kim Soo fast asleep on my bed when I entered my cabin. It was one of those hot, airless tropical mornings, and the vodka had had the desired effect. By now, some several hours later, the alcohol in her system had worn off, and she was in a deep sleep. The sarong I had loaned her was around her midriff, that part of her body between her chest and her waist. Who wanted to see her naval anyway? The rest of her was much more interesting. She lay on her back with her head to one side on the pillow.

Her breasts were small and pointy, with rather large areolas. Her right leg was bent at the knee, with her right foot flat on the surface of the bed. Her left leg, however, was out at an angle, giving me an uninterrupted view of her apple of delight, which looked none the worse for the couple of batterings I'd given it. She'd cried on the first but cried and fought on the second. This was going to be the third. Was it perhaps a little premature? You were supposed to give a virgin time to heal. She had three long hairs on the mound of her vagina, which I had been too busy to notice before. For otherwise it was bald. I blew on it gently, breathing onto its gate for several moments and observed her vulva swell and moisten, opening out like a flower to reveal an erect clitoris proud and pink. The Chinese are right about it being the valley that never dies. Self-lubricating, dripping wet, and ready for the plunge. Kim Soo awoke with a start, sunk her teeth into my right shoulder, and commenced to ride like she had never ridden before, enjoying every moment of it without weeping. The expression on her face when she finally reached orgasm was well worth the bite she gave me. I was rather pleased with myself because my little Arab experiment had appeared to work. Kim Soo was running in just the way I wanted her sex-wise. She would always be an exceptionally good ride from now on.

The rest of the day was routine, and we were making rather good headway in deep water. I left the running of the boat to my crew with strict instructions to call me immediately if anything untoward appeared on the horizon. This was standard operating procedure when the situation around the sea was quiet—skipper's privilege, if you like. I noticed Roy on the bridge of his boat on each occasion I checked our course and heading. He had that peevish look on his face. It was obvious that Poo Choo had not indulged him with any sexual favours; I had expected Roy to hoist her petard from the yardarm of his boat.

He'd be rather touchy now, have a row with me, and storm off on some spree just to keep his own conscience intact. I later commented on this to Kim Soo, who in her matter-of-fact way of speaking said, "Poo Choo will talk to him, but she won't do anything else." The sea has a remarkable effect on some women, and there was always the possibility she would come good for Roy before we arrived in Bangkok. Sex was, of course, the best pastime on rainy days and long, slow sea voyages. *T'ung* is the Chinese word for virgin. To be and not to be arise mutually. Difficult and easy are mutually realized; long and short are mutually contrasted; high and low mutually posited; before and after are in mutual sequence.

Yang moves, yin is still. The *Tao of Qian*, perfecting the male. The *Tao of Kun*, perfecting the female. The ten thousand things transforming and growing. The two *chi* of maleness and femaleness reacting within the influence of each other. *Chiao kan*, change, and bring the myriad things into being. Plan your own personal design for achievement! The next three days were routine with quite a difference. Gone were her initial emotional energies, for she was no longer afraid. She thrust caution aside to take the bite firmly between her legs at every available opportunity.

Like the old Chinese sage once said, "Chiao kan can bring the myriad things into being." It can also give you both the backache! There is another old Chinese superstition: "A young man should never have sex with an older woman. She will sap his strength to replenish her own youth."

Wednesday, 26 March 1947

At 0130 hours Zainal shouted down into my cabin that I was required urgently topside. At this point I had only just drifted into a dream about troopships and the crossing over from the Far East of the Empire towards Britain via India and home, with my wife Pam in mind. There is nothing worse than the smell of unwashed men crammed together in the confines of a troopship homeward bound, and I simply had to get on deck to stop me going mad from all that snoring and sweaty feet, or so the dream was telling me. Again, the call came from on deck by Zainal, and I snapped out of my dream state. I awakened Kim Soo and instructed her to lie low on the deck of my cabin; then I then headed up on deck to find three fast-approaching bleeps on my radar, on a heading towards our boats.

These waters were notorious for Siamese pirates who used small, fast, well-armed boats to sneak up on their prey. I was nobody's plunder! I sounded the alarm, signalling all hands to stand to, and as I looked across at Roy, who was my ghost, he had long since switched off his navigation lights, so it would appear for all intents and purposes that there was only one craft on the water. Preparing the twin-mounted .303 light machine guns on his boat also, Roy was my back-up when we were headed towards the mainland. At this point, all my crew were at the ready and well-armed but with strict instructions not to shoot randomly. They were to mark well their targets and only if the pirates attempted to board us.

I, on the other hand, was with my helmsman Zainal, who was the ammo mag loader on my twin-mounted Bren guns. These were fully loaded, both cocked and ready to go. The adrenalin built up with my anticipation, but we had rehearsed the stand to drill many times; that was how we survived in these waters. I got my naval infrared binoculars out but could not see anything yet on the horizon in this darkness. We were ready for them, establishing clear arcs of automatic fire whilst my boat took point and Roy's boat acted as rear guard. Keeping our boats back to back but close in was probably the safest way to prevent us from shooting each other in the dark.

We had tracer .303 rounds and knew the pirates coming up fast on our position did not like them; they seemed to have a demoralizing effect when fired effectively from two boats; hopefully we would catch them all in our lethal crossfire as they ran past us. Both our boats carried radar, with someone on watch around the clock in these pirate-infested waters. I heard the loud noise of powerful outboard motors and then saw the first dark shape of a fast boat coming up on my port side at speed, outboard motors roaring, followed by a second boat and then a third.

Zainal fired the flare from his ex-military Verey pistol into the air over the Siamese pirates for illumination, thus signalling the order to open fire. I opened up immediately, fully automatic effective Bren gunfire, using the .303 tracers to hone in on the pirates' high-speed cruise past, raking all their crafts with many strikes and reloading some twenty-plus magazines of .303 tracer rounds at the lead, second, and third fast-attack boats. These then headed off away from my position, suddenly disappearing mysteriously from both our radar screens. What seemed like an eternity of machine-gun tracer bullets firing suddenly ceased as the last of the pirate boats high-tailed it away from our location. It had all felt like slow motion, the adrenalin rush of the moment between life and death.

Between Roy's twin-mounted machine guns and mine we must have placed close to 1500 point 303 tracer rounds into those three boats, and we could only assume, as they'd suddenly disappeared off our radars, that we had sunk them all. There was no second pass at us, and boats did not suddenly disappear off radar unless they took in water and sank. The lucky thing was that no one on those small Siamese pirate boats had managed to get a shot off at us, probably due to the fact that they had been expecting only one unarmed civilian merchant vessel as easy pickings—certainly not two well-armed former motor torpedo boats with an ex-Malayan Royal Navy-trained veteran crew!

Roy and I were used to being hunted. Both of us would do what we had to do without hesitation to survive out there. The same was true for our crewmen. I guessed those Siamese pirates were now shark bait, because we were still on the high seas and in very deep water. Roy and I decided to throw caution to the wind and set a new course using red light only, altering our original headway in the hope that we would not encounter anymore threats on our journey to Bangkok. We left it for another two hours on our new course, maintaining a blackout through the darkness just in case those pirates had managed to get a radio signal out before they sank.

We could not risk those pirates calling for more support or rescue. After ensuring none of my crew or Roy's had been injured in the fracas, we took stock of all the ammunition we had actually expended, approximately 1300 rounds. We cleared up the mess of spent cartridges into empty ammo boxes on deck as best we could via red torchlight, to save anyone tripping over them and falling overboard. There were forty-two 30-round Bren gun magazines or twenty-one magazines per boat gun platform. That was about ten fast twin-gun reloads. Needless to say, both my Bren gun barrels were red-hot to touch. I carried spare barrels just in case.

After replenishing our main defensive armament, the light-machine-gun magazines, with more ammunition from the ammo boxes stored below decks, we carried out promptly a damage-control check on our boats, just in case we had missed any small-arms fire that had hit us in the dark. I didn't recall any small-arms fire coming from the fast boats; they had not gotten a chance to fire on us because we'd acted first and foremost, raking heavy fire on them to win that firefight. He who *gets* first wins—not he who *dares* wins! Now I know what you are thinking: maybe we should have only fired warning shots across their bows.

Screw that! There were three of those bastards against two of us, probably well-armed with light automatic rifles and hand grenades! Nobody comes up on a boat on the high seas in total darkness without navigation lights and at high speed with good intentions. I needed a stiff drink after that, as did most of the crew. I went below to reassure Kim Soo, who was shaking uncontrollably, that all was well again and advise her to try and get some sleep despite what had just happened. After taking a tot of rum, I went back on deck and took over the watch from Zainal, who had been on watch way too long.

Zainal, my veteran Royal Malayan Navy helmsman, always came through for me. He had established himself as quite a warrior and brave to boot, no matter how desperate the situation. What had just happened could have gone the other way had we not been sharp and on our toes. I told him to get some shut-eye; I would steer the boat until my relief came in the morning. It was now about 0540 hours, with the brandy ball appearing at first light. We spent the rest of the day making good headway after thoroughly checking over our boats again for small-arms-fire damage, this time in daylight, but found none. Before long, as night follows day and vice versa, it was dark again.

A spot of light rain was falling from the heavens, and there was a slight swell on the sea. Our main meal for the day was flavoured curried rice with spicy chicken. Thanks to the ship's cook, this was a luxury and a treat for all of the crew. It made a damn change from fish, I supposed. It was at times of high anxiety that |I longed for some semblance of civilized eating and fine cuisine.

Thursday, 27 March 1947

Way back in 1702, the British East India Company set up a settlement on Paulo Condor, or Condor Island as it is better known today, just off the coast of Vietnam. To the Vietnamese it was known as Con Son. But sometime during 1705, it seems, all the Europeans there were massacred by Bugis pirates, every last one of them. It appeared that the Bugis had mutinied and murdered all Europeans as well as the local employees of the British East India Company on the island. Condor Island was renowned as a French penal colony or "Devil's Island". French colonists established it in 1861 to house political prisoners. So the island had a morbid history and reputation for cruelty and violent deaths, although you would not have thought so had you landed on it and visited her white beach sands under any other circumstances. These would have appealed to many island-hopping, beachcombing adventurers imagining the place as some sort of tropical paradise. We humans, and particularly nations, have this habit of screwing everything up wherever we go, turning nature's wonders into tropical hell mouths.

At 0930 hours, we stopped off at one of the smaller inlet islands in the Gulf of Siam to refuel our boat in the relative calm of the lagoon via our spare fuel drums in the hold. As well, we wanted some well-deserved shore time to stretch our legs and look for fresh water and possibly catch a few local game animals or find some fresh fruit. Roy and I took the two women and the child ashore, and they seemed the better for it.

I would, of course, need to fill up my spare fuel drums and take on fresh supplies of food and water once we reached Bangkok, but any little extra along the way helped to make our journey a little more comfortable, especially with our female passengers and the half-Japanese child on board and after that firefight in the dark the day before.

I find it simply amazing how children are so much more resilient than adults. There is an innocence to them that is often disregarded. Even though their immediate surroundings and circumstances may remain hostile, they have no problem playing away at their boyish games without any real concern as to what has happened or the danger around them.

Before the heaven and earth existed, there was something nebulous, silent, isolated, standing alone, unchanging. It eternally revolved without fail, worthy to be mother of all things. I do not know its name. I address it as Tao. If forced to give it a name, I should call it Great Being, great implying reaching out in space. Reaching out in space implies far-reaching. Far-reaching implies reversion to the original point. She who in the beginning gave birth to the people. This was Eve. How did she give birth to the people?

Well, she sacrificed and prayed that she might no longer be childless. She trod on the big toe of God's footprint, was accepted, and got what she desired. First in reverence, then in awe, she gave birth; she nurtured. And this was Cain. Indeed, she had fulfilled her months, and her firstborn came like a lamb, with no bursting or rending. With no hurt or harm to manifest his great power. God on high gave her ease. So blessed were her sacrifices and prayers that easily she bore her child.

The rest of the day went by without incident, but I couldn't help contemplating the fragility of life, especially considering the lives we'd been forced to take in the dark last Wednesday morning along the Gulf of Siam. These pirates had all been bad men whom we could not reason with. When it came to them or us, I'm afraid it would always be them.

Saturday, 29 March 1947

The term *Tai* refers to a group of languages spoken in South East Asia which are as diverse as the romantic languages of Europe. In all there are approximately sixty-two million Tai speakers, some fifty million of whom live in Thailand, whilst the other ten million or so occupy parts of south and south-western China, north and north-eastern Burma, Laos, and northern Vietnam. Some 3000 years ago the Tai people and their cultures were based in what is now called south-central China, just south of the Yangtze River. With the other races who shared the area, they moved in a southerly direction as the culture of the Han people dominated the area.

Up to around the thirteenth century, the large multi-racial kingdom of Nanchao flourished in the lands which now surround the southern borders of China, the Tai people being the ruling class. Kublai Khan then arrived on the scene with his Mongol barbarians, his invasion pushing the Tai people further south so that the Tai chiefs formed an alliance with the waning Khmer Empire and slowly began to gain control. They settled amongst the numerous small rivers of the present Shan State of Burma, Yunan, Laos, the Irrawaddy and Salween rivers into Burma, the Mekong into Laos and Siam, with the black and red rivers into Vietnam. Historically the political system of the various traditional Tai states, all of which are called *muang*, have much in common. They are all characterized by forms of feudalism with a king.

There existed a ruling class of royal princes, aristocracy, nobility, and officials and an intermediate class of free-peasant cultivators who owed rent in kind and in compulsory economic, domestic, and military service to their political superiors—rather like the warlords of China.

It was 0500 hours when we finally arrived in the river estuary and commenced our run into Bangkok, heading for an anchorage where we could tie up together. Bangkok has been called the "Venice of the East" and rightly so because of its maze of canals, called *klongs*, intersecting the city and extending out into the countryside. These klongs are crowded with boats of just about every size and description. Boatmen chant in rhythm as they pole their heavy loads through the water en route to the marketplaces. The canals are fed by the Chao Phraya, Tha Chin, as well as the Mae Klong rivers and their tributaries. The Tai word *khlong*, better known as klong, is not limited to artificial canals; other regional small rivers are also referred to as Khlong followed by the name of the stream.

Small motor launches scurry about between the other craft in crazy fashion, with scant regard for their own safety, but this is the way it has always been here. We finally found a berth not far from the place where they kept the sleek fleet of beautifully carved decorated wooden boats formerly used by the kings of Siam when they visited the country areas via the river and klongs. The keeper and watchman of these royal sheds breeds Siamese fighting fish as a kind of paying hobby. *Betta splendens*, or the Siamese fighting fish, is best known for the propensity of two males put together to fight like two cocks in the same pit. Officials from Thai Customs arrived on the scene rather quickly—almost, it seemed, as if they had been tipped off, which was rather unusual in this part of the world. The boat's weapons were checked and sealed for the duration of our stay in port.

Roy and I were issued the necessary police permit to carry sidearms, once our international health certificates had been authenticated and our bona fide letters of credit verified. The unit of currency here was the *baht* or *tical*, twenty baht to the US dollar or fifty-nine baht to one pound sterling. Of course we had no prohibited items, no narcotics (hemp, opium, cocaine, heroin) or obscene literation, no pictures or articles at all, for that matter. At 0830 hours, Thai Customs gave us a clean bill, and we were free to go about our business. Roy and I decided to hire a water taxi rather than risk leaving our own dinghy unattended in one of the klongs while we went in search of the silk merchant.

The two women had had a rather angry argument when they met up again on our arrival in port; the atmosphere between them was hardly reasonable. But they remained cordial when I showed up, and it seemed very much as if the elder sister was exhorting her authority over Kim Soo. The water taxi arrived, and Roy and I left to cross the river, heading for *Wat Arun*, the Temple of Dawn, which is strikingly and unusually decorated with shells and pieces of broken pottery and porcelain. Roy and I climbed the steps of the *prang*, the spire, and took our bearings from the skyline view of this strange city. We saw the pair of demon gatekeepers, huge and fierce-looking fellows whose business it was to keep evil spirits at bay.

Roy and I could see Rajdamnoen Avenue in the distance, and once we had returned to the water taxi, we set off in that direction; we were off again. Healthy looking brown-skinned youngsters tumbled in and out of the water while grown-ups took their morning dips in the night-cooled klongs. Housewives busy doing the family laundry on their just-washed steps giggled at each other's banter in a light-hearted way. Small boats filled with chattering children paddled along on the way to school. The postman, on his route in a small craft, dodged in and out of the long convoy of barges.

There was so much of life there, along the waterway canals loaded with water jugs, sand, and lumber. Water-borne coffee shops stopped to sell a bite of breakfast. This was Siam, the place they called the Land of Angels. The klongs were busy places at the best of times, full of happenings, each with its own special difference. This was a place of the people and for the people! It was quite a long journey, though never the laborious one that some much shorter journeys tended to be. There was far too much of interest going on all around us and not one single unhappy face in sight. The klongs were nothing like the Singapore River, full of every disgusting disease known to man.

Here the Thai kept their waterways clean, with only the exceptional outbreak of cholera or yellow fever. We saw a number of Lisu traders on the klong. These people were from the Chiang Mai area of Thailand. The Lisu were torn between their desire to be far from strangers who might trouble them and to be near a lowland market where they could purchase cloth and so forth. The Lisu were a delightful, timid people from the hill country, where a number of them had been enslaved by the Lahu, Akha, and Meo of that mountainous region, all of which fell inside the opium-producing area known as the Golden Triangle.

Lisu derives from *li*, meaning customs or laws and *i-su*, "one who runs away from", hence together the names mean outlaws or rebels. The Lisu use chopsticks to eat from a bowl, rather like the Chinese. Lisu women sew their own colourful clothing from purchased material. Narrow strips of coloured cloth decorate a long, loose dress that is worn with an elaborately tasselled waistband over baggy trousers. Both men and women wear the traditional turban. The women of more wealthy households display elaborate silver jewellery.

Now, this may surprise you, but we did not see one single Siamese cat anywhere on our travels there. It seemed that all these elite domesticated felines had emigrated.

There were quite a number of snakes there, many of them deadly. Amongst the better-known snakes were the cobra and the krait. Unless you go looking for them or accidently step on one, they won't look for you! The jungles of Thailand are populated with bears, wild boar, wild buffalo, leopards, wild elephants, black panthers, and of course tigers. As I said, unless you go looking for them, you should be all right.

Thailand is the place of the coup d'état, a swift stroke of policy (also referred to simply as a coup). This usually takes the form of a sudden violent overthrowing of an existing government by a small group of people, often high-ranking officers of some standing within the existing military forces. On 24 June 1932, a number of Army officers, together with some members of the civil service, forced then-King Prajadhipok to grant them a constitution.

Up until that moment, Thailand had been an absolute monarchy. The newly established constitution provided for the first time a national assembly, half of which were elected and the other half specially appointed. The next coup d'état was on 9 June 1946, when King Anandha Mahidol was found shot dead in his bed. Again it was elements inside the Thai Army that were suspect in this matter, although nothing was ever conclusively proven. The founder of the present Chakri dynasty was Phya Chakri, who as King Phra Buddha Yod Fah Chulaloke Rama I established his capital at Bangkok in 1782.

The old Thai capital was at a place called Ayudhya, which fell to the Burmese in 1767 and was almost totally destroyed. General Phya Tak Sin managed to escape with some 500 followers, and within a year he was crowned king and raised a force sufficient to drive out the Burmese. He established his capital at Dhonburi, across the river from the Bangkok of today.

Religion played an important in the daily lives of the Thai people. There were 300 or more Buddhist wats, or monasteries, in and around Bangkok.

Wat Benchamabophit, sometime called the Marble Temple, had a main building constructed of white marble, with orange-yellow glazed roof tiles which glittered in the sunlight. The gables were carved in the form of the celestial serpent Naga, the demigod of rain. In the galleries around the courtyard was a unique collection of fifty-three images of Buddha. Wat Po was the temple of the reclining Buddha, where the image was said to be 150.88 feet long. The Grand Palace and the adjacent Temple of the Emerald Buddha were marvels of Thai architectural skill and interesting mosaic work depicting the Ramayana, or Ramakien, the epic tale of events in the life of Buddha.

The famous Emerald Buddha is just twenty-two inches high and is actually made of green jasper, not emerald. Jasper is an opaque variety of quartz, which in this case appeared to be dark green.

A group of young men were busy playing the game of *takraw* with a ball woven from wicker. The object of this game is to keep the ball in motion high in the air, without allowing it to touch the ground. It can be hit with any part of the body, including the heel, knee, instep, shoulder, or forearm. It sounds simple but actually requires a lot of skill and stamina. It must be said, however, that takraw is not unique to Thailand.

In Malaya it is called *sepak raga* and in the Philippine Islands *sipa*. Since the ball used is made of small lengths of woven rattan, rather than being a solid ball, it is light and flexible and can bounce rather like a tennis ball.

Eventually we arrived on land, at the scene of a large ornamental spirit house, which became the focal point of our excursions into Bangkok. The many little houses perched on poles were not bird houses but spirit houses, complete with offered dishes of fruit, sweets, flowers, candles, and incense sticks.

Almost every Thai home had its spirit house, in which the *Chao*

Ti'or or "lord of the land" lived. They were built at the same time as the house was constructed and in a spot that faced the most important room in the house, either the master bedroom or the living room, and where they were not over shadowed by the house itself.

Thai spirit house, 1947

Where I am concerned, it is not just the adventure but rather the discovery! I want to discover what I know is right, yet still do what is wrong—an oxymoron, perhaps, but I want to discover myself.

Locating the firm of Thai Silk Traders was not difficult, and once we had made the necessary arrangements for the loading of Bill Langley's consignment, we took a good look at what they had on offer with a view to making a small purchase of our own. Thai silk is handwoven in a variety of weights and colours which range from brilliant peacock hues to subdued pastel shades. The silk is durable and does not crease or wrinkle easily.

Silk is a particularly fascinating and beautiful material; no true woman can resist such elegant material in its multicoloured hues and shades. I prefer some of the more traditional Thai silk designs, all of which appear to be colour-fast. Once our host discovered we were intending to purchase a second boatload for hard cash, we were generously plied with double brandies as part of their sales technique.

Roy became rather inebriated; it always made him feel randy! Any clichés about drinking booze seem to fit with Roy. Certainly "brandy makes him randy", especially when any willing women happens by.

Bill Langley had gone for the more conventional colours in silk, those he felt would be in keeping with the accepted customs and standards of the Singapore European woman. I was going for the local Chinese and Malay end of the market, which would not compete with Bill's project. We haggled over the price for quite some time before finally reaching an amicable agreement. Our host was not the only Thai silk manufacturer, even though he would have liked us to believe that was the case.

Thai silk is the product of village industry, which is why the weave of each piece of material is unique and cannot be easily copied elsewhere by other competition in the trade. Hence our host merely bought and sold the product; he was the middleman in this business!

Siamese number one rice is the flakiest rice I have ever eaten in this part of the world. I thought whilst I was out here that I try the rice grown and cultivated in Siam myself directly from the people who grow it with a view to import the rice more cheaply than the current traders in Malays or indeed the local Chinese shopkeepers in Malaya sell it for. We ate it together with a large number of spicy dishes, and it was quite a meal. The Tai eat with folk and spoon instead of the customary chopsticks of the Chinese. Small bites of barbequed chicken or pork are threaded onto a coconut palm stick for you to dip into a sauce made of curry, coconut milk, and mashed peanuts, all of which are very tasty.

The hand movements of the classical dancers in their elaborate traditional costumes and tall conical headdress was rather cultural. But then, these classical female dancers were from Chiang Mai, and Chiang Mai was famous for its beautiful women, lovely roses, Thai silk, cotton weaving, lacquerware, and silver crafts. Our business concluded, we made the necessary arrangements for the delivery and loading of the consignment. Each consignment would have to be checked and itemized into the boat's log, complete with bills of lading and Thai Customs documents.

Buddhist begging bowl, 1947

Our host and his wife made a point of filling the begging bowls of a number of Buddhist monks with food, a good omen where the Siamese are concerned. The monks were by tradition not permitted to touch money at all! All the food for them was prepared by the street food vendor, bought for cash by the benevolent, and placed into the monks' begging bowls for their meal of the day. Young men, regardless of their social status, were expected to spend a minimum period of three months as a monk, usually during the Buddhist Lent or the three months of the rainy season.

This moral and religious training was reflected in their soft-spoken, thoughtful demeanour, both in business and in the home. The saffron-robed monks on the streets had their bowls generously filled with food by people who gained merit through their generosity.

Our host, in contrast to what I have just said, also dabbled in the odd opium deal with American "black-operations" cohorts (quite possibly out of Langley, Virginia) who were running rather large quantities of the drug out of Thailand via their US Air Force bases. I ignored these matters out of a necessity not to get myself or my crew killed over foreign policy-induced drug wars.

Dhanarajata, my trader here, was taking every advantage, but like most businessmen, he was an opportunist with a few high-placed connections. Opium was part of the gravy train—Roy and I had nothing to do with! It was a question of morality. Yes, we ran guns, but guns themselves do not kill people. People are killed by other people, mostly out of greed or for opposing a particular brand of political beliefs. It is all part of man's inhumanity in the quest for gain and power, that willingness to be cruel and harm other human beings. One does not become addicted to guns; there is no crazed craving such as leads people to part with their most precious possessions for a few moments of the opium pipe.

Costume in the oriental dances is largely traditional, often exceedingly beautiful, and quite cumbersome to Western eyes. The way in which it is managed by the little dancing girls is in itself something of a miracle. These costumes are the property of the temples for which the girls dance. Often, as in the dancing of the extremely popular *Legong* legend, the chief garment is a golden tinsel sarong. This is wrapped tightly around the dancer from the breasts downwards, leaving a long trailing train which must be handled with the same skill and definite action as is accorded to every other movement in the dance.

In the more dramatic dances, headdresses and breastplates are often extremely heavy, for they are cut out of leather and richly gilded with studded gold. Some of these dances contain so little choreography that they rank as pure drama or pantomime; others are dances pure and simple. In some dances the men take part, as in the drum dance, or at least supplement the chorus, especially in the more dramatic performances. But as a rule, it is the little dancing girls—who may have begun dancing at the age of four and who retire from the stage when they reach puberty—that bear the onus of this great art.

In some of the ceremonial dances which form part of the temple ritual, the girls perform in a trance induced by prolonged inhalation of incense smoke over a brazier. Indeed, without some such influence it is inconceivable that they would be able to dance a whole night through with unfaltering action and expressionless, mask-like faces. The arms, wrists, and fingers provide most of the expression, and masks are very often worn by the male dancers. They have a kind of lifting movement, on one bent leg, so that the whole body seems to be raised into the air—perhaps the most impressive item of their entire performance.

A slight swaying of the body is the only movement we would associate with dancing in the West. But in the East dance is a representation, sometimes of a story, other times of a state of mind and the oriental watcher reads deep meaning into each movement, each sudden flick or sinuous wave of the hands and arms of the dancer. As expressive as those of the most skilful artists, the dancer's hands and fingers fascinate, almost mesmerize with their strange ritual movements. All over the East the dance of the hands plays an important part in religious festivals and secular entertainment alike, and the dancers of Siam are true artists.

The winds are now blowing from the south and a number of grown-ups are busy flying kites. The tradition of kite-flying in Thailand stretches back to the very birth of the nation. Throughout the country's history the sport has been engaged in by royalty and commoners alike. It is literally a battle of the sexes, in which there are two contestants, the *chula*, representing the male in the form of a rather burly six-foot kite, and the *pakpao*, the female, smaller and much more graceful. The chula is equipped with barbed string, with which to snag the daintier pakpao and haul her to the ground within his own territory.

Meanwhile, the more agile little pakpao attempts to throw its loop, which is a twelve-metre length of string slung below the flying line, or her tail, around the male and drag him down on her side. There are two objectives in this male-against-female sport: male kites competing for the most female kites snagged, and female kites competing for the greatest number of male kites brought down. It's something like the notion of stone-age cavemen dragging their captive women by the hair into their caves. Some very large bets are made on the outcome of these kite fights, with entire Thai families turning out to witness or take part in the fray during the months of March and April.

Sunday, 30 March 1947

The commotion in the next cabin was rather noisy, awaking me from a deep sleep at around 0200 hours. I could hear Roy's voice raised in anger, which was rather strange, because he should have been on his own boat at that time of the morning. Then I heard Kim Soo scream. All of this was a little or more bewildering, me being half-asleep at that time in the morning. Nevertheless, I leaped out of bed, intent on bringing an end to the noisy fracas.

I entered the second cabin and was immediately confronted with quite a spectacle. Roy was on the bed with Kim Soo under him, and he was well and truly seducing her. Her torn clothing was scattered around where he had ripped it from her. The restraining hand of Poo Choo, Kim Soo's elder sister, prevented my sudden intervention, thus circumventing what could have been a rather violent fight between two good friends. Poo Choo followed me into my cabin and closed the door behind her, just standing there in awkward silence, waiting for me to speak. Strange though it may seem, at the time I felt betrayed and responsible all at the same time. Perhaps it was because I knew myself to be a rogue alpha male and very possessive where my women were concerned. But hey, ho—nobody is perfect! Roy, on the other hand, had a tendency to get carried away and have trouble keeping it in his pants, especially where young women were concerned.

"I told your friend Roy!" Poo Choo suddenly blurted out the news, blushing with shame. My hand smacked her across the face before I realized it had happened, and she started to cry. The story came pouring out of her in a flood of words. It was not her fault! If Kim Soo had not dreamed up that screwy scheme to use the Tiong money, my friend Roy would not have been beaten up, and all this trouble she had brought upon us could have been avoided. She had told Roy her side of the story, and this had been his excuse. I saw the reality of the harrowing experience Poo Choo must have endured while at sea on Roy's boat and understood the reason for the frequent quarrelling between sisters later. I suppose Poo Choo had seen Roy's escapade as her way out and had been waiting for an opportunity to spring the trap where her sister Kim Soo was concerned. She had settled her child down in a hammock on the bridge, complaining that the amount of humidity in the cabin was unhealthy. It all seemed plausible and a little paranoid.

"Your friend took a beating because of Kim Soo, so she owes him," she said.

"I think it's time you saw to your child," I said quietly

The mirror over my bureau appeared to be slightly warped; there was too much silver in its reflection. I saw reflected annoyance; the fierce feeling of anger I had felt initially had gone like a bad dream. This was just another chapter in the scheme of things, and that was all. It was a single period of action, like the scene in a play. "In a pig's eye!" I mumbled to myself and settled down in my bed to catch up on some seriously required sleep. It was 0900 hours when I made my check on the loading and found that everything was going according to plan, which was no mean achievement.

Poo Choo was mooning around the deck with her child on her right hip like some heavy burden and a fantastic look of doom on her face. Domineering nature she might have, but where my boat was concerned, I was the dominant one. Of course, at some point soon I was going to thump my good friend Roy on the nose, not because of the girl but because of the conniving way he'd sneaked onto my boat to accomplish his revenge on Kim Soo. In a pig's eye he was going to get away with it! I guessed that for the moment I needed to control my wild emotions and put them to one side. There would always remain more fish out there in the sea to catch.

"Excellency," the water taxi man called, and I boarded his flimsy craft for the quick trip across the river. Bangkok was unusually noisy this morning, its smell just a little more pungent than customary. Perhaps this was due to the fact that I was alone and just a little more aware of my surroundings, or maybe it was the weather this morning. The very hot season from March to May brought extreme temperatures.

I found Dhanarajata at the counting house and concluded the terms of our mutual agreement, obtaining in return the bona fide certificates for the cargo we had purchased from him in good faith. I certainly didn't feel like returning to the boat straight away. For the moment I had had enough of my associates to last me a lifetime and was determined to let them all just get on with it. Instead I thought I'd use this opportunity to explore Bangkok all on my own! Anyway, I wanted to have a look at rings made with onyx, that semi-precious stone having bands of various colours in it. I had wanted an onyx ring for some time now, and this was my chance.

I spent the next hour or so I spent watching Thai boxing, also called *muay Thai*, but I knew this martial art as Siamese boxing. In it the feet seemed to have as much, if not more, prominence than the fists. A prayer opened the bout, followed by a preliminary display of each boxer's skill and fighting style, a kind of open showboating before the actual fight. Then the fight commenced, quite furiously I must add, accompanied by Thai music consisting of two drums and a pipe. It was a rough-and-tumble affair, with the two antagonists kicking, elbowing, and punching the shit out of each other with such speed and accurate targeting of those vital knock-out points on the body that it almost seemed instinct rather than considered thought.

This ended with a well-placed knockout kick to the head. I found the skilled handlers who were feeding hamadryads (or king cobras, *Ophiophagus hannah*), and kraits and extracting the venom for the preparation of antitoxins much more interesting.

The Thai were into homeopathy, the practice of treating a disease by giving small amounts of a drug which in larger amounts would produce illness or even kill. Homeopathy is based on the principle of "like cures like". In other words, a substance taken in small amounts will cure the same symptoms it causes if taken in large amounts.

Once again, I found myself preoccupied. Everything was in man's own hand! I must never let it slip through my fingers. But indeed, I was always trying out new notions and innovations in my quest for adventure; new experiences always increased both my knowledge and appreciation of life, that greatest adventure. I liked the old accepted ways of life, in particular those of indigenous tribes which until the advent of more advanced Western civilizations had never been a part of modern so-called morality standards artificially imposed on them by the Christian Church or other religions sects.

On the other hand, there was always that streak of adventure in my own character that made me go for the outside-of-the-box phenomenon in human nature or the unusual. At the moment the streets of Bangkok were full of tired faces, or so it seemed to me. I was annoyed and no longer interested. Perhaps it was me? I had been provoked by the events of the previous night, my sense of personal pride and ego a little battered. The indignation of betrayal was not aimed so much at Kim Soo, for women were plentiful, but at my good friend Roy, who simply had not been able to keep it in his pants, regardless of the fact that the woman was partnered at the time by his best friend.

When it comes to lust, sexual wantonness, and desire, mixed with copious amounts of alcohol, fooling around remains the true nature of the beast in human beings. A fully erect stallion from an alpha male has no conscience, does it? I so abhor betrayal from anyone, let alone a trusted friend. Perhaps man was never designed, nor women for that matter, to have only one sexual partner throughout his lifespan. I could be wrong, of course. As far as I was concerned, the affair with Kim Soo was over, judging from what I had seen in the second cabin of my boat.

As far as I was concerned now, she had not suffered a fate worse than death from Roy. When I'd opened the cabin door, she had been working well at it, with him on top, and seemed to be enjoying herself. But I took satisfaction in being her first and the knowledge that where she was concerned, it was over for good. But I had been where no man had been before me.

The pleasant aroma of hot *mee Siam* and black coffee drew me to one of the street stalls, and I spent the next ten or twenty minutes indulging myself, much to the amusement of some of the local Thai people. Mee Siam is basically Siamese noodles, consisting of spicy fried rice vermicelli with shrimp, chicken, fried firm tofu, and shredded omelette. Mee Siam is usually served with a dash of sambal on the side and a piece of *kalamansi* lime, the juice of which gives an extra tangy kick to the noodles.

I doubted they had ever seen a white man squat and enjoy a meal at one of their roadside stalls before. Somehow, I felt much better after the meal, more of my old rogue self, the one fond of playing tricks. Of course I overpaid the Mee Siam hawker and complimented her on her cooking, as all real gentlemen do.

It was rather late when I finally returned to my boat, which was by this time fully laden with cargo. All that was left to do was the necessary final checks before we battened down. I decided to leave it until the next morning, as Roy and Kim Soo had already put out to sea in the late afternoon, heading for the state of Trengganu on the East Coast of Malaya. Perhaps he thought I needed time to cool off. Poo Choo was not in the second cabin, and I questioned Zainal with regards to her whereabouts and that of her child. Yes, he had seen them onshore shortly after Roy had made his departure but had not seen them since.

"Do you think we have enough draught under us to clear port without waiting for the full tide?" I asked.

"Yes, Tuan," he answered.

"Batten down and prepare to get under way," I instructed.

"Yes, Tuan," he replied.

I found Poo Choo feeding her child at one of the coffee stalls on the wharf, paid the hawker, and picked the child up in my arms before she could stop me, heading straight back to the boat. Poo Choo hurried along behind me, and I could hear the rapid clatter of her wooden sandals as she strove to keep pace.

Monday, 31 March 1947

Shortly after midnight, at 0030 hours, we were underway, having cleared shipping, and were heading out to the open sea once again. There was rather a strong groundswell running, and it was good to feel the boat alive under us with every familiar creak and groan. I set course for Kota Bharu in Kelantan, a little further north but also on the East Coast of Malaya, gradually bringing the old girl up to full cruising speed. Then I relaxed. It was 0230 hours now, and my boat, the *Wilful Lady*, was rolling due to the strong cross-currents in this part of the sea. This was caused by the tide and continued for the next hour or so.

I saw a shooting star streak across the heavens and disappear almost immediately. I made a silent wish, which I a moment later thought was rather silly of me. The night sky was a star-studded, deep indigo-blue canopy, beyond which lay the sunrise. It was still necessary to keep a watchful eye out for Siamese pirates in this part of the gulf, as proven by our earlier encounter. But once we reached the Isthmus of Kra and Malayan waters, we were comparatively safe from those thugs who appeared to infest these waters with murderous intent. Honey and salt, land smell and sea smell, as in long ago, as in forever. The salt of absence, the honey of memory. I was not always so poetic around this time of the morning!

I did another routine radar scan and was careful to examine the reading closely. There was nothing in this area that I should feel concerned about, and that in itself was rather a relief. At 0400 hours I handed the watch over to Zainal, with strict instructions to rouse me immediately if any threat appeared in these dangerous waters. But perhaps I spoke in haste and fate had another play going for us. "I've got two bleeps," Zainal shouted just as I was about to leave the bridge. I looked, and sure enough he had. A few moments later we could hear the sound once again of high-powered outboard engines running at full throttle. I cut my navigation lights immediately. I had switched them on because I was supposed to be in friendly coastal waters, but it seemed those bastards wanted another go at us.

This time round only two craft came for us, appearing as black shadow-like devil shapes silhouetted against the night sky, small and fast. We waited for the right moment and opened fire with two separate Bren guns, raking both targets with heavy fire once again, but this time around using my stock of 500 armour-piercing .303 HV (high velocity) rounds instead of tracer bullets. Both pirate crafts turned quickly and sped away. A few moments later, they had both disappeared from our radar as if they'd never been there. More Thai pirates, or perhaps local opportunists?

We would never know for sure, but my money was on it being the same bunch of cut-throat pirates as in the earlier attack on our boats. Perhaps they had lain in wait for our journey back home after being tipped off during our stay in Bangkok. Revenge was always a strong motivator. I decided at that point to remain on high alert and to black out from then on. You had to love these waters—there was never a dull moment. But then, I was also a war veteran and had seen far worse than what had happened to us early that morning. I went below to my cabin and was not surprised to find Poo Choo asleep on my bunk. I was just too tired to do anything other than fall asleep cuddled up to her.

Perhaps that is rather difficult to understand. I knew that Roy would never believe it. Poo Choo had wanted nothing to do with Roy and fought him off like a tiger. Roy, despite all of his faults, would never take a woman against her will. At least not intentionally— honour amongst thieves and all that. There was nothing like the soft, delicate touch of a woman to help you unwind after the tensions of the day, and I was sure Poo Choo was aware of this fact of life. I awoke at 0700 hours, alone in my bunk, and wondered for a moment if it had all been just a dream. But she had left some of her apparel behind, and my clothes had been neatly folded. There was also that womanly aroma about the bedclothes.

On the bridge I found that we were running true to course. The groundswell had eased a little, and the movement of the boat was more a steady pitch and less a sideways roll. At 1200 hours we were off the Isthmus of Kra, at a steady speed, and making good headway. Ali, my boat engineer, informed me the engines were running in top form, as together we checked the fuel. We also checked for any small-arms-fire damage to my boat. It had been nearly impossible to check for damage in heavy seas during the night without natural light, and as we had not been taking in any water and the boat engines had been running smoothly, I had not seen an urgency to do a red torchlight-only damage-control check in the darkness. All in all, we found no apparent damage whatsoever to my boat from the fracas with those two intruder crafts.

Considering our firepower and the speed at which they'd pulled away from us, I had to conclude that both craft had sunk. Perhaps they had thought we were unarmed? In that case the *Wilful Lady*, as well as defending her honour by repelling borders, would have given the pirates quite a shock. The question that remained unanswered was rather obvious. Had it been just another chance encounter with hostile craft? As we were running a rather valuable cargo, it was unlikely. But on the other hand, pirates were known to drift into the currents along the main shipping lanes at night, listen for the sound of approaching boats, and then suddenly pounce.

I placed Poo Choo's child, Shang Chi, into the safety harness and spent the rest of the afternoon with him playing around my feet on the bridge. The boy seemed to quite enjoy himself, chatting away with me until he finally climbed onto my lap, where he sat contentedly and eventually fell asleep. Poo Choo gently took the child in her arms, cradling his head, and carried him below to his bed. There was a tenderness in her eyes I had not seen before.

We saw the light of Kuala Tongkang at 2300 hours, and I changed course on a heading for the Kelantan River in Malaya. We would make Tumpat around dawn, and from there it was upriver to Kampong Gong Ketereh. Another thought had occurred to me. How much of this was down to the Thai Dhannrajata, back in Bangkok? Had the pirates been lying in wait for us?

There was no way to tell for sure, but where money and honour were concerned, those two entities certainly made for total opposites. I never trust anybody in this game unless I had known them personally for a long time. I trusted people even less when large sums of hard cash were involved. Reputation was everything and keeping true to one's word. A man could always attempt to make some more money when a deal went bad. But once he lost credibility—and more importantly out here, face—that could not be undone.

I have always held the view that making money should carry with it a level of honesty that does not involve inflicting misery on other people. If you cannot do it that way, then you should not bother doing it at all. All actions (or in some cases inactions) carry consequences. You should always ask yourself, What will be the consequences if I do this? Can I live with the outcome of my actions?

That is the way I've live my life, with integrity always in my business dealings, and I sleep well at night.

Chapter 16

A New Day

Tuesday, 1 April 1947

It was April Fool's Day, and I could smell the land even though we were far out at sea. Kelantan in Malaya is the land of magic and medicine men, though these magic people are locally known as *bomohs,* or Malayan tribal witch doctors. It would be incorrect to call them shamans as this is a generic term referring to the Tungus tribes in Siberia, where gods, spirits, and demons play a major role for such indigenous tribes in their religious worship. In Malay culture, these entities are said to be responsive to the will of the bomoh witch doctors who also act as mediators for unseen spirits both helpful and malevolent.

At 0300 hours I made my final check, handed over the watch, and went below for a spot of well-earned shut-eye. I was not surprised to find Poo Choo asleep in my bunk. I heard her murmur a soft, low sound, using her breath rather than her voice in the normal way of speaking. Here was a Chinese woman whispering sweet nothings in the Japanese language. Dreaming she certainly was. I sat on the edge of the bunk, fascinated, waiting watchfully for any sign of activity that would provide a clue to the nature of her dreams. Occasionally I would see a smile flicker around her lips and fade into her closed eyes.

Lying down beside her, I cradled her gently in my arms. She snuggled close to me and settled warm and comfortable without waking. I suppose we each have our own special ghosts, intangible though they may appear in our own more rational sensible moments. Spectres from the past, they haunt the quiet tranquillity of sleep and sometimes creep silently into our wakefulness when we least expect them. *"Mura Saki-san,"* she whispered with tenderness, and I saw the smile flicker around her lips again. She was in the arms of her Japanese samurai. Perhaps they met again in their dreams. I felt a twinge of that strange emotion jealousy, sadly the weakness of many alpha males.

She was supposed to hate him! Mura Saki was the man who had ravaged her, the man whose child she had since borne, the man who had been hanged in Changi as a war criminal. I decided to extract myself from the predicament. The opportunity presented itself when she turned in her sleep, and I was able to slip away from the bunk without disturbing her. The incident left me with several unanswered questions, but then human behaviour is rather a complex subject.

Rice fields near Tumpat, Kelantan, at sundown, 1947

The meaning of the Malay word *tumpat* is "filled up", as in a hollow. We were well into the Kelantan River on our way up to Ketereh (which in Malay translates as visible or obvious). But this photograph was taken far downriver in the late afternoon. It was rather interesting to see the number of *kerbau*, or domestic water buffalo, at large in the rice fields. The buffalo were used during ploughing and were quite able to bear hard work.

We were running at reduced speed and frequently taking soundings; nevertheless we made good time, and I took the opportunity of calling Roy on the radio. Roy had put into Kota Bharu, where he would wait for my arrival. I was relieved to hear his voice over the radio; obviously he had not had a run-in with the pirates on his trip down from Bangkok.

Drying rice seeds near Ketereh, Kelantan, 1947

It was 1030 hours, and we had arrived at Ketereh only to find that the man I was looking for was at Pulau Chondong, at the home of his second wife. His first wife was busy supervising the sun drying of the rice seed. This would be planted into prepared seed beds from which the young seedlings would later be planted out in the rice fields. The house itself was meticulously well kept, with a place for everything and everything in its place, in the Malay general way of doing things. I drank the customary cup of sweet black coffee and made my apologies. Time was of the essence if I was to be at sea again before nightfall.

"*Itu anak Jipon, Tuan,*" Che Ummul said. I nodded. "Father and mother killed in the war." I lied to her to protect and save face for Poo Choo, as Japanese "collaborators" were very much frowned on, even years after the war. I had taken the boy, Shang Chi, along with me, thinking the exercise would do him good. Che Ummul had been astute to notice, and of course she was right, the child did look Japanese.

It was 1100 hours now, with time running away, and I set a course upriver, heading for Pulau Chondong. The meaning of the Malay word *chondong* is leaning to one side, out of perpendicular. *Pulai* in Malay means a large tree, which in this case was the *Alstonia scholaris*, a tropical evergreen tree more commonly called blackboard tree, devil tree, ditabark, milkwood-pine, or white cheesewood. Pulai Chondong was indeed a large tree leaning to one side.

The coastal plain near Pulai Chondong, Kelantan, 1947

Life is full of happenings, each one with its own special difference. I found Nik Ismail at home, and together we got down to business, with quite a lot of haggling over the price on both sides. The idea was for me to establish another outlet for the sarongs Roy and I had brought back with us from Java. Padi planters are seasonally rich, so there was little or no risk on my part. At 1510 hours we were underway again, heading downriver towards the sea. I wanted to reach the bend in the river near Pasir Mas before nightfall because of the numerous sand bars in that part of the river.

The Kelantan River at Pasir Mas, northern Kelantan, 1947

The Kelantan River was tidal but subject to strong currents around the turn of the tide. It always paid to take time and care where river navigation was concerned. We arrived at Pasir Mas at 1750 hours, in low tide, although we had sufficient draft under us to continue our journey downriver at a reasonable speed.

We saw the occasional crocodile and quite a number of snakes in the water from time to time but nothing to be unduly worried about. *Pasir* in Malay means sand and *mas* means gold, hence the name meant golden sand. Our next stop would be Kota Bharu, which we had bypassed on our way upriver early that morning. We had a meal of roast fish with herbs and yellow rice. For once the cook had carefully taken out all the large fish bones as well as the gummy parts under cold running water. He was not a bad cook, but we would never make the mistake of complimenting him on a fish meal. Otherwise we could be eating fish for the remainder of the voyage!

The Kelantan River at Kota Bharu

At 2050 hours Zainal shouted, *"Melaut!"* We were in deep water once again, travelling towards the estuary of the river. We arrived at Kota Bharu at 2130 hours, and I decided to anchor out in the river rather than to move in amongst the large number of *bajau*, sea gypsies, along the shoreline of the estuary. Many legends have grown up around these people and their migrations, not to mention their prowess as marauding outlaws.

Of course, I don't live a quiet life! But I respect all people and allow them to live in their own way and in peace. I like good wine, romantic music, and quiet, intelligent conversation. I do not like loud music or chilled, freezing-cold beer. I partake of the grape but never to excess.

Poo Choo was in my bunk again when I went below to my cabin. But what man would believe that I could sleep with a woman without the exchange of feelings that makes people know each other more closely—I know!

Wednesday, 2 April 1947

We passed the night without incident, and dawn found me back on the bridge, ready to face another day. The sun climbed quickly from beyond the South China Sea, and I could almost hear it sizzle; it was mesmerizing and so surreal. But the sudden clatter of pots and pans brought me back to reality. At least the cook was busy in the galley on time. I waited rather patiently, heard him give a grunt, and knew instinctively the morning coffee was ready. He made a good cup of coffee but was almost unapproachable at that time in the morning, certainly not before he'd had his first cup of coffee.

The man on watch laughed and a moment later headed off in the direction of the galley, returning with two large mugs of coffee. I suppose it's one of the unwritten rules of any seagoing boat to always keep on the good side of the cook! Me, I was at my best this time of the morning, roguish and playful. It was in such moments that my thoughts created the imagery necessary so that everything fell into perspective. Then again, the road of broken dreams was strewn with other people's good intentions. Curled in my favourite chair on the bridge of my boat, I drank the peace of early morn and let my mind regurgitate time's forelock.

Those snippets of sense were gleaned during quieter moments from the whirlpool of events long since passed but somehow—all of our yesterdays and tomorrows—all on a piece of fabric we call time. I had often pondered whether the concept of time from the here and now perspective was linear or whether time fell into a weave-loop of continuing, never-ending cycles. In plain-speak, either we start from A, move on to B, and finally end up at C, or we are in some sort of space-time continuum where yesterday, tomorrow and right here and now are just different points in this never-ending loop. Perhaps I am overanalysing, but it seems to me that space and time are relative, as in the spirit world; none of these concepts exists. It would explain how some gifted "mediums" could accurately forecast events yet to come into being.

"*Salam alaikum, Tuan,*" the cook said, breaking into my private thoughts at that moment. "Peace be with you," he had said.

I returned his cordial greeting with a smile on my face. *"Alaikum salam."* He needed to know whether I would be in for lunch and what time we would be setting sail. He wanted a little time in which to visit the town and purchase a few necessary culinary ingredients.

"Budu?" I asked, as I knew he was rather fond of budu, the fish that was preserved in brine along with its scales and entrails, rather like a soused herring.

Kota Bahru was rather small in comparison with some of the other Malay state capitals, a kind of Sleepy Hollow like Malacca but on a smaller scale. I quickly found the office of the *shar-bandar*, a Malay kind of harbour master who controlled the river and shipping. He told me where I could refuel at the best price and where I could locate Roy. When I'd seen the *mega*—white, fleecy *mega berangkat* clouds chasing each other across the early morning sky, I'd known in my heart of hearts that this would be a good day for me.

Two Malays training in bersilat

Sarkawi bin Rafman ran the martial arts school of *bersilat* in Kota Bahru. Bersilat is the art or, if you like, mimicry of sword fencing. Bersilat in some ways is rather like sabre fencing; the cut-and-thrust weapon has a flattened flat blade and a round guard. Hits made with the whole of the front edge nearest the point on the trunk, arms, and head above of the waist are valid. There is quite a lot of trompement, the action of hitting an opponent at the end of a feint, after a successful deception or offensive blade movement; this deceives the opponents' parries. Sentiment du fer or feeling the opponent's reaction through contact of the blade. This is akin to a martial gut instinct becoming one with the spirit of the blade, hence being in harmony with the magic of the blade by pre-empting your opponent's next move to kill you. Malay superstition abound that every kriss blade has a spirit that dwells within the blade. The fighting is done with a sword in each hand.

Roy was rather apprehensive, and who could blame him? But this was not the case with the two sisters, Poo Cho and Kim Soo, who were much too interested in their own affairs to take much notice of Roy and me. Roy apologized for his unusual encroachment on my boat, but in a way I knew he was not to blame. Kim Soo appeared a little broader in the hips and darker around the eyes but none the worse for wear.

Together Roy and I sorted through the papers necessary for our return to Singapore. Our next port of call was to be Kuala Besut in the Malayan state of Trengganu, though I had a number of calls to make during our run down the East Coast, which would not take up a lot of my time.

We decided to take the next tide and head once again for the open sea. Even though we were legitimate according to the law, it was sensible that we arrived back in Singapore together. We now carried a reputation for running guns on the underground grapevine, although as yet we had never been caught in the act. Roy had come through the area between Bang Nara lighthouse and Kuala Golok in the early evening but had seen nothing out of the ordinary. I was convinced the Thai pirates were waiting for us and that Dhanarajata had something to do with it.

We spent some time watching a young group of Malays gambling against the bank held by an older Malay, who appeared to be quite skilful. They were playing the game of *hai weh* or *poh*. This game was played with a die placed in a square brass box, which it fit into accurately and which in turn slid into a brass cover. The lower end of the box was bevelled, and the die having been inserted, the box was spun on a board with a diagonal cross. The faces of the die were coloured red and white, and the stakes having been placed on the board, those opposite the red portion of the die when it ceased spinning were the winners. Roy, who was no gambler, was rather annoyed because, whenever the stakes were high, the banker would always be the winner.

"Look at the man's forehead, Tuan," Zainal pointed out. I saw that the banker had a faint trace of oily ashes over his eyebrows. The man was using a gambling charm; it would be coconut oil mixed with the ashes. I had heard of these charms before. The banker appeared to be having a rather good run of luck. Smearing the ashes over his eyebrows was supposed to enable the owner to see what was inside the brass box. The banker made no attempt to hide the fact that he was using magic, and I suppose he presented a challenge to those young Malays who were gambling against him. The charm was made by saturating seven pieces of thread in the blood of a dead man and that of a pink water buffalo, adding the eyes of a tiger along with those of a black cat, and burning the whole concoction to ashes.

I knew a woman who made love philtres from bruised dhatura mixed with human blood; this was apparently a potent love charm when smeared between the eyes. When a woman was thus decorated, men who saw her would become her slaves, it was said. But I thought that she was endowed with physical strength, much cunning, courage, and a power of imagination so developed that she could persuade men to believe in the quaint infallibility of her ideas.

"I knew a woman like that years ago," Roy said.

She reminded me of Em! Em was Roy's former girlfriend, who

had been killed in the bombing during the war. They had been going steady at the time, and then Roy had gone upcountry with his regiment. He had not even had the time to attend her funeral. I had always been aware of the fantasies of lonely soldiers, who would take the occasional prostitute and later swear that for a very few precious moments of desire they had been making love with a sweetheart or wife.

We got underway again at 1500 hours and headed out for the open sea once more. We turned at the mouth of the estuary and set course, heading along the Kelantan coast. It was good to be in deep waters again. I brought the *Wilful Lady* (in Malay *Wanita Bangsawan Sengaja*) up to her full cruising speed with no apparent difficulty.

I checked with Ali, to find that the engines were purring away like a couple of well-satisfied cats. I watched the sunset, which was almost as quick as the sunrise had been that morning, and observed the old brandy ball disappearing into the sea. For dinner we had *sate kambing*, pieces of goat's flesh cooked on skewers like kebabs, with all the necessary condiments and served with a variety of imaginative curry sauces. I consumed my first brandy of the day and sipped it slowly whilst I watched the canopy of stars clearly visible in the night sky above. It was strange the things that would come to mind during such moments.

I thought of brier brambles, those rough, prickly blackberry shrubs common to my home in Wales. If the tender young buds had been nibbled, it meant that rabbits were in the patch. Rabbits kept the brier under control; otherwise the bush would spread like wildfire. A few hazelnuts under the tree could be the work of either the dormouse or the squirrel. Speaking of rabbits, I had my rabbit in the trap! I was not at all surprised when I found Poo Choo asleep in my bunk once again. But this time she was wearing one of my own sarongs. I was determined that she would definitely have to make the first move in this matter.

My cabin on the *Wilful Lady*

However, if she was waiting for me to make the first move, it could take quite some time, even though we happened to be sleeping together in the same bunk. I wanted to see if indeed she would, but I certainly had no intention of being a substitute for her fantasy.

Thursday, 3 April 1947

K'ung Fu-tzu is the true name of the Chinese philosopher Confucius, a thinker ahead of his time who exercised more influence on Chinese culture than any other thinker back then or even today. His *Analects* (collected sayings) do not in any way constitute a religion or carry a profound intellectual message but simply stress man's duty to man, within social units from the family to the state.

This morning my disjointed thoughts took me to that masterful classic from Leo Tolstoy, *War and Peace*; the saying "Everything comes to he who waits" is rather apt. The full quote is "Everything comes in time to him who knows how to wait … there is nothing stronger than these two: patience and time, they will do it all."

It was rather like one of those vivid wild dreams that young men are prone to, pleasurable yet deeply sensuous to the point of sudden awakening. Poo Choo was set astride the pinion tree! I blinked at her nakedness several times. This was the first time one of those fantasies had materialized, and I was at a loss. She chose the moment to descend at full thrust, pivoting herself to the hilt. Her samurai, Muka Saki, had taught her well. I was being seduced skilfully in the Japanese style, and she was doing all the hard work in the dominant position. Strangely, I was not angry with her. She had not in any sense belittled my own masculinity. We talked a little afterwards and both gradually drifted back into a deep sleep and satisfying slumber.

Dawn was breaking when I returned to the bridge and checked our position. We were off Peng Patah, making good headway against a slight groundswell. Our estimated time of arrival would be around midday at Bachok, from which point I would make a little foray to the village of Gunong. I looked at Roy's boat some 500 or 600 yards to my starboard, but there was no sign of him. Perhaps it was a little too early for the old plonker to be up and about. Don't get me wrong, Roy is not lazy, and when the chips are down or as they say, the shit hits the fan, he is a very good man to have around.

Poo Choo came up on deck at 0800 hours, together with her son. I put Shang Chi into the safety harness and watched him play around my feet.

"I thought you would leave in Bangkok," she said.

"Your friend would have left us?"

"You don't chase me around the boat like your friend did."

"That is all over now," I told her. "You have nothing more to worry about, and you are safe." I watched the smile of tenderness on her face as she gazed steadily at her son, Shang Chi. This was the inner side of her; the child meant everything. He was, after all, her Mura Saki, all that she had left to hang onto.

I have always held the view that life is a rather huge merry-go-round. It is like the ancient second-century BC Indian child's game called *mokshapat* or moksha *patamu*. In the West it is better known as snakes and ladders. You can climb quickly in the game, but you can also fall very far back down.

Round and round in a world spinning round,
Life is a ride on a merry-go-round.
Sometimes you are up, sometimes you are down;

334

You would like to get off,
But the world keeps spinning around.

Gunong village, Kelantan

It was 1130 hours when we arrived at Bachok, a little ahead of schedule. The night fishermen had long since driven up their boats, beached them, and retired to their respective homes where they would sleep during the heat of the day. We decided to anchor out rather than run into the beach at low tide, so we used dinghies for access to the shoreline. Transport to the village of Gunong was via mosquito bus, a rather infrequent service dependent on the availability of passengers, with no set timetable.

The village of Jelawat was much smaller than Bachok. *Jela* in Malay means "gadding about" of a woman. *Wat* is, of course, Siamese for a Buddhist temple. Kelantan was at one time a part of the Siamese Empire. *Gunong* means mountain in Malay, as opposed to the word *bukit*, which means hill. So there we had the village of Kampong Gunong, or Mountain Village, on this side of the mountain and the village of Bukit Marak on the other side.

My arrival in Kampong Gunong was a kind of unexciting coming after a rather exciting previous night, a kind of anticlimax, if you know what I mean!

Bachok, on the Kelantan Coast

The village was quite charming and picturesque, with a young cockerel herding a group of ambling ducks across the main road. People stood out talking here and there or ambled along in the unhurried fashion so very typical of the kampong Malay in these parts. People took life much slower here in contrast with the hard-working fishermen of Bachok. A Malay policeman walked the edge of the road, and a group of young Malay children immediately changed their chant from "*Orang puteh*", meaning white man, to "*Mata-mata, ayer dalam besi, api delam kacha.*" Malay young village girls all dream of marrying a policeman because of the police quarters they receive from the Malay government, where piped drinking water and electricity are standard. Who could blame these young girls for aspiring to something beyond that of their parents? We all have our dreams.

The village of Gunong was situated at the foot of the angry mountain, *Marak*—the Malay word meaning to flare up or flame. Wherever you found a Malay village, you would find the coconut palm. The Malays used coconut in their day-to-day cooking.

It is the casuarina tree (*Casuarina equisetifolia*) of the mountain forest that I was concerned with at that time, as I believed that was where the real money was going to be. It is also known as Australian pine, beach sheoak (she-oak), Australian beefwood, or ironwood. The Malay name for this tree was *pokok ru*.

Mind you, I also firmly believe that what we take in the forest must be sustainable. It is of little use to the environment or future generations to mass-scale cut down and deplete an entire mountain forest of all her tress. We need to replace what we chop down with fresh sapling trees, to safeguard the future of this region and the generations of people who will live here. Yes, I believe in sustaining our forests, and the earth, for that matter. Guess this makes me an environmentalist at heart.

Che Nemah

Che Nemah was seated cross-legged on the floor of the veranda, busily embroidering a cover for her *bantal*, a long Dutch bolster the Malays put between their legs when they sleep at night. A sarong containing a small baby hung from a steel spring at the end of a piece of rope, which was attached to one of the roof beams, making an effective cradle for the child.

"I have come about the land on the mountain," I said. "A friend of mine would like to apply for a timber concession to allow him to cut timber on your land. Perhaps I should wait and speak to your husband?"

"That won't be necessary, Tuan," she replied. "I am janda now. Anyway, the land belongs to me, as it was my own father's not so long ago," she further added with some conviction.

"Janda?"—that meant a widow or a divorced woman—"I'm sorry to hear that," I said.

"Don't be," she replied. "He was no good."

I quietly explained that she would be paid a lump sum of money in advance for the concession, plus a bounty on each and every log cut and taken from her land.

"This friend you speak of is a Tuan like yourself?" she asked.

"Yes," I replied.

"But will he will replant with many young trees?" she asked.

"I will put it to him," I said.

"If he will agree to replant for every large tree he cuts, then and only then he can have the timber concession," she stated in a matter-of-fact tone. I saw that this could prove an impasse, so I told her that I would take to my friend her proposition and that he would be in touch with her in person very soon.

"You will bring this other Tuan?" she asked.

"In all probability," I replied.

Che Nemah was rather self-assured for a Malay woman, very businesslike. Such a professional woman I had not expected! I paid her at this juncture 100 Straits dollars and secured an understanding for an exclusive six-month option on the timber concession. But then, in all business transactions, there will be the unexpected and some compromise. In my view it made good business sense for her not to devastate her land on the mountain but to preserve any forest future timber, or the environment, for that matter. Without living trees the mountains would break down, as would all the creatures who lived there when deprived of their natural habitat. This would also have an impact on the local population and their means of making a living there.

"*Tuan sudah lesut. Ka-mari lah sedikit semua aku urat. Sama-sama kita berchuchi reka, tangga dia pun ketak dan dia pandai menjamah.*"

"Sir, you have been scorched," Che Nemah had said. "Well, here is a little bit of my veins [implying a little bit of me]. We are of the same *berchuchi* [broken hearted] design, she touched the emotions on both of them, and he's good at hiding it.

The bus journey through the countryside on my return to Bachok was rather laborious, but I was glad when I found everything shipshape on my arrival back on board my boat. Another day and another adventure over. We put out to sea at 1800 hours, and I set a course for our next stop, Kuala Besut in Northern Trengganu, as I watched the sunset from my bridge of my boat.

Friday, 4 April 1947

I have never been a puritan who practises the urges of strict correctness. But I have always loved the basic simplicity of life, which I think is more my style. I do appreciate bona fide beauty, and between you and me, providing that every relationship is a well-defined, two-way relationship in every element, I will be sure to pick up the occasional flower along the way. Guess that's just the romantic in me. This has no connection with moral purity, for it is this which attracts the most criticism.

Yet the curious fact remains that most of this criticism is simple envy, born out of untruthful gossip by those who would judge us. For such people are fishwives. For those not in the know, a fishwife is a person who collects gossip and spreads it around to all and sundry, rumour-mongering, just because he or she can. Character assassination via the mischiefs from the tongue has caused so much unnecessary hurt. If only people would live and let live, we would have a better world.

I tell you naught for your comfort,
Yea, naught for your desire,
Save that the sky grows darker yet
And the sea rises higher.

—G. K. Chesterton
The Ballad of the White Horse (1911)

There was quite a sumatra blowing. It was a sudden attack of violent weather in the form of very high winds along with heavy rainfall, which lashed about angrily for a little over an hour. It was not one of those bad storms, but still it left a rather heavy sea swell running in its wake.

The sudden wrath of a sumatra can be rather terrifying at times. The high winds whirl and spiral around at gale force 12, willy-nilly, anticlockwise, a cylindrical body of swirling air akin to a small tornado at sea.

At 0400 hours the wind dropped from its high crescendo form down to a whisper, leaving a strange uncanny quiet about the sea. Zainal had started the bilge pumps when the storm initially hit us, and I made my checks of the gunnels, the upper edge of the side or bulwark of my vessel. Fortunately, we had not taken on much water. Bravura! It had been nature's brilliant, showy performance, and the *Wilful Lady* had brought us through with top marks; I felt rather proud of her and humble at the same time. The waves out there still remained large, although nothing my helmsman could not deal with effectively. It was now time for me to catch a little sleep. The young child, Shang Chi, was fast asleep in his hammock and oblivious to all and sundry, which was rather a relief. I had thought the sound of the sudden storm would have frightened him. Perhaps it was the reassurance of his mother together with the movement of his hammock.

It was not the Western style of motherhood that she focused on; it was the motherhood of patriarchal societies. These have a sensual absorption in babies and life. These situations are not always clear cut, so who am I to judge? Yes, Poo Choo had been rejected by her clan even though she'd refuted their charge that she had been a collaborator with the Japanese during the occupation. There was again the critical matter of her mother, that indefinable bond which could be wayward and elusive, or the reason why one child for no apparent reason would become the favourite. Poo Choo could have fled with her sister Kim Soo, leaving her mother to face the consequences with that group of soldiers. But she'd quickly found and brought Mura Saki, who'd saved the situation for the moment.

Mura Saki had taken them both under escort, which had placed the women beyond the reach of ordinary Japanese soldiers. He'd utilized the mother as a concubine for himself during the Japanese advance through Johore and, from all acknowledged accountable information, had not treated the women badly. It was only after the fall of Singapore, when the Japanese had been finally in full control and Mura Saki established in a large bungalow at Fallings Park, that he had turned his full attention to Poo Choo, though it was not until May 1945 that she gave birth to his child.

But by this time the writing on the wall had become rather obvious where the Japanese Imperial Army in the South East Asia region was concerned, being at the receiving end of major military defeats from the British. Rangoon had been retaken by the British and her Commonwealth forces, bringing Japanese morale to an all-time low. Mura Saki had been no fool; he'd been fully aware that the forthcoming battle for the British to recapture Malaya and Singapore would be a fight to the death on the part of the Japanese Imperial Army. Mura Saki, the Japanese samurai officer, had wanted his seed to survive somehow after the war and his new child, whom he named also Mura Saki (later renamed Shang Chi for obvious reasons) to be safe.

His child, being the only heir to his line, had to survive the war no matter what—perhaps that would be his only immortality. With the onset of the atomic age, the detonation of two atomic bombs on mainland Japan fetched in a new uncertainty for the planet between the new superpowers. The subsequent unconditional surrender of Imperial Japan changed drastically the situation for Mura Saki. He was later arrested, put on trial for war crimes, and subsequently hanged at Changi jail in Singapore. Perhaps the samurai had had a premonition of his impending death and used Poo Choo to ensure his immortality.

But what if the child had been a girl? According to Poo Choo, Mura Saki had been sure the baby was a boy from the very first moment he had talked to the unborn child, long before it was born. She believed the child understood his words, because she felt it jump and kick in her womb as he talked. Perhaps if the child had been born in 1943 or even 1944, the story that Poo Choo and her mother had been raped by Mura Saki might have had some credence with her people. But the child was born in 1945, and both Poo Choo and her mother had not been left to struggle under the yoke of Japanese oppression as had so many other people.

Saturday, 5 April 1947

Rarely have I seen anything quite so beautiful as the sunrise this morning. We made good headway and arrived at Kuala Besut at 0900 hours in the glittering sunshine. The Malay word *kuala* means estuary, the point where a main stream falls into the sea or a tributary into the main stream. The Malay word *besut* means a silken fabric (and the word proper is *besuta*). Life in this part of the world is a scenario of simplicity, a paradise lost! Perhaps Trengganu was once a part of Eden! I would not trade this morning's grace for all of the rice in China. Roy arrived some thirty minutes later and came alongside at my anchorage just as we were finishing breakfast.

Roy also had weathered the sudden storm without damage, but it had slowed him up a little. Kuala besut was in his show anyway; he had an appointment with some kingpin planter in the *kelapa bali*—oil palm—trade. There was also quite a lot of *copra* to be had in this area, dry *Cocos nucifera*—coconut, in other words. Me, I was going for a quiet spot of swimming with Poo Choo. Ali and most of the crew were ashore getting some quality time out, leaving Zainal once again to take the watch. But then again, he was my best man and the most reliable person on board as well as a damn good warrior in every respect.

The child, Shang Chi, was with his aunt, Kim Soo, on Roy's boat while Poo Choo and I were taking a dip in the warmth of the sea. We swam together, heading for the seclusion of a small cove sheltered from the quizzical eyes of the Malay village. She was a strong swimmer and rather agile underwater, moving easily and quickly through each dive until we finally made land and waded ashore together. She had a kind of mermaid quality about her I had not seen before, a kind of aquatic aristocratic beauty. She was at one with the sea and its immediate surroundings, rather gracefully slender and nymph-like of stature.

We spent an hour exploring the shoreline of the cove, turning over the occasional rock or stone. We finally put up the cocks accompanying a group of domestic chickens that were foraging along the upper line of the beach. They stretched themselves and flapped their wings rather noisily, but the hens did not fly. Perhaps they preferred to lay their eggs in the soft, warm sand of the upper beach and dream of the predatory fox.

Not wanting our nakedness scrutinised by the local peasantry, we took to the sea once again and commenced the long swim back towards the boat the way we had come, diving frequently in search of the venomous coral snake. The bite of this nocturnal hunter was supposed to be fatal within twenty minutes or so. They would lie up during the daytime in runs under stones or bark or in mossy clumps above the water. But they were sometimes active during the day, especially if there had been a heavy rainfall. Our protocol of diving and searching whilst swimming along these estuary shorelines was a safety measure we took, for it was always better to be safe than sorry. A plover was perched on the top mast when we climbed back on board the boat. Poo Choo said it was a good omen; something good was going to happen in the future.

A plover, a kind of sandpiper, is sometimes called a crocodile bird. This is because it supposedly enters a crocodile's mouth as it lies basking in the sun with its mouth open and picks pieces of meat from between the crocodile's teeth and leeches from its gums.

Poo Choo on the beach at Kuala Besut

Roy returned at 1200 hours, rather jubilant. He and I were to have dinner that evening with a planter friend and his lady wife at their bungalow amidst the oil palm trees on their estate. It would be a formal occasion, he declared. "White tropical colonial officers' evening dress suits for the outback of Trengganu?" I suddenly exploded with mischievous laughter. "What do they expect me to wear—sea boots and a bloody yachting club cap?" I said with a laugh.

"It will have to be an informal affair, with our apologies," Roy replied rather sheepishly.

A young Malay in a jeep with the canvas top raised against the heat of the midday sun arrived on the scene at 1230 hours, declaring that he had come to take us back with him, on the instructions of his tuan. Roy, garbed in his monkey suit, his jacket folded over his left arm, climbed into the rear seat while Rex, my dog, jumped in beside him. I took the front seat next to the driver, and we were off. While the jeep had all the normal paraphernalia conducive to the smooth conveyance of its occupants, it was soon apparent that quite by chance we had discovered the Malay equivalent of the original rough rider. It had just two speeds, it seemed—flat out and stop!

Bukit Kepala Bali Estate, the sign said some two miles down the road beyond Kuala Besut, announcing the domain of Bamford-Smyth with a hyphen. The estate itself consisted of 1,500 acres of productive oil palm, with the Bamford-Smyth residence smack in the middle, some seven or more miles from the small town of Kuala Besut. A dusty laterite track wound its way willy-nilly through hilly terrain, shaded on either side by hundreds of green, leafy palm trees. The heat of the morning sun had long since evaporated the heavy, cool predawn dew, so that the careering jeep hurtling along perpetuated a constant stream of whirling red dust in our wake. It was like driving though one of my life dreams to be an oil-palm plantation owner.

The red dust was borne like one great trailing pennant through the air between the corridors of lush green palm trees. Laterite is a superficial deposit caused during the weathering of rock in some wet tropical climates, a deposit rich in iron and aluminium oxides. "Menjangan," the Malay driver said suddenly; they [referring to the Muntjac deer] were very fond of the ripe fruit.

I saw a small group of five or six *Cervulus muntjac* cavorting along the track a short distance ahead of the jeep. Suddenly they changed direction and disappeared from my line of sight between the trees. "Barking deer!" I said. Roy just nodded his head in agreement.

The fruit of the oil palm grows close together in large clusters, rather like soft, sweet figs, turning orange and then a deep purple when ready for harvesting. I noticed several squirrels in the palm fronds, and further on into the estate we found a group of workers harvesting, while others were loading up the large clusters of fruit onto a lorry ready for shipment to the processing plant just outside Kuala Besut, where the palm oil would be extracted. The clusters of ripe fruit were never left on the ground overnight because of the abundance of wild game in the area. Palms and plants of the family *Arecaceae monocotyledonae* (mostly unbranched shrubs or trees with large persistent leaves in terminal tufts and sometimes rope-like stems with scattered leaves and stout spines) are the source of many economic products, for example dates, coconuts, raffia, and in this case, palm oil.

Suddenly the jeep turned off the main track and quietly ascended the slope of a winding tarmac road to the top of the hill. We had arrived. There in the centre of the large lawn stood the abode of the Bamford-Smyth clan. It was a large Malay style bungalow, aptly called *Sira Menanti*, which meant to sit awaiting! Rex, my dog, was the first out of the jeep, having found a female of his own particular breed in these remote distant parts. Indeed, boxers were quite rare in this part of the world.

Anthony Bamford-Smyth

Anthony Bamford-Smyth was tall in stature, 5 feet 10 inches and well built. He was a rather jovial man in his middle thirties, with a strong firm handshake. His only acknowledged eccentricity was the wearing of a trilby hat during his rounds of the estate, on which occasions he always carried a .45 ACP (auto colt pistol) Thompson sub-machine gun. This combination gave him somewhat the appearance of a Chicago hood in white shirt and khaki shorts. He claimed the tommy gun was quite effective in the continual control of Eurasian wild pigs throughout his estate.

The Eurasian wild pig inhabited both the primary and secondary forest throughout Malaya but also foraged in adjacent cleared or agricultural areas—such as oil palm estates. I smiled when he told me why he carried that sub-machine gun—that had to be a first! Sub-machine guns, more commonly known as SMGs, were of course primarily military weapons meant for close-quarters work. They were issued to British commandos as well as the Special Operations Executive during the Second World War.

Bamford-Smyth only employed Malays. He was quick to point out that Trengganu was part of Malaya and that his labour force was cost effective. No way would he have a Chinaman or Tamil near the place. Stella, his wife, had a rather boisterous voice, noisily cheerful without being rough, if you know what I mean. Believe me, the very sight of Roy in a formal evening dress in the middle of a hot tropical afternoon would make a bloody horse laugh. Mad dogs and Englishmen? Stella and Anthony had been married in India back in 1945. She was a brunette 5 feet 6 inches in height who spoke the Malay language fluently. Her father had been the British advisor to one of the sultans, and she had spent most of her childhood in the Malay states.

"I think perhaps I'm responsible," she said with a smile. "Of course, we don't dress formally for dinner out here."

"That was that old Java planter and his wife," Anthony said.

"Yes, I was going to mention them, darling," Stella interjected. "That was in Johore, pre-war," she went on. Maintaining British standards, I think they thought they were."

"The old white superior," Anthony said. "Quite supercilious when you come to think of it!"

"Are you superstitious?" Stella asked.

I thought the question over for a moment, swallowed the piece of beef I had been chewing, and said no!

"It looks like you are overrun with squirrels," Roy put in.

"*Ratufa*," Anthony said with a laugh. "No, it may appear so, but the damage they do here is minimal. There are five species of Asian palm squirrel, which are often called striped palm squirrels because they are striped much like chipmunks."

"That's a rather ludicrous statement!" Stella said.

Anthony frowned. "All right," he said.

Stella Smyth

"Palm squirrels are noted for having a dense, soft greyish brown fur but in parts almost black nearly all the year round. They show reddish colour on the head from December to May with three light stripes on the back; But on occasion, there is a further short stripe on each flank. Asian palm squirrels measure around seven inches in length, with a long head and body. Their bushy tail being the same length as their body. Striped palm squirrels feed by day, in the tress or on the ground. Their forage ranges from seeds, nuts, stems, bark, buds, leaves, and flowers, as well as insects and their grubs," Anthony said. "The different species of striped palm squirrels live in varied places amongst open palm forests and shrubs at low altitudes to dense jungle with very tall trees. Their habits are similar to those of tree squirrels of the northern hemisphere and, like some palm squirrels, they live near or around human habitation. One species, *Protoxerus stangeri*, is also known as the booming squirrel for the booming sounds it makes when alarmed," Stella said.

"Otherwise, its voice is like a bird twittering," Anthony further added with some conviction. There was a distinct glint of satisfaction in Stella's eyes when her husband finished speaking. Perhaps it was just my imagination, but I had the feeling they got on each other's nerves, maybe grown tired of the same old day-to-day routines in their lives. It could also be down to the continual remoteness of life on an estate isolated from civilization.

"Stella has a doctorate, a PhD," Anthony told us in a quiet, matter-of-fact manner.

"Anthropology," she said, before I could ask the obvious.

"An ology doctorate," I said. That was impressive for a woman out there! I wondered whether Anthony had been involved in some way with her thesis initially. Moment by moment we make the world. We create our own worlds step by step! Credible? Of course it's bloody credible; only a fool would think otherwise.

Stella was still talking, and I hadn't heard a word she said. It was as if I had stepped out of time.

"Have you any spare .45 ACP ammunition?" Roy asked. "Anthony requires it for his wild boar cull."

"Yes, I think so," I replied. "We can let him have a crate, but he will have to collect it himself."

"No problem," Anthony said.

"I don't believe you are not superstitious," Stella said.

"Stella believes all members of the seagoing community are superstitious," Anthony said. "She is currently compiling the facts and other information on various local common superstitions for a book she is writing."

"We all have our taboos, born of strong religious or social disapproval," I said.

"Certain rude words are taboo in general conversation," Roy piped in suddenly.

"Sex before marriage!" Anthony said.

"I suppose you are rather prejudiced in favour towards the Malay," I said, turning the conversation away from the obvious.

"Not entirely," he replied. "Certainly, their labour is much more expensive in comparison with the Chinese and Tamils. But then, it is more a question of loyalty. Most of the Tamils went over to the Japanese during the war. On the other hand, a large Tamil workforce requires several extra amenities, some of which are quite offensive where the local Malays are concerned."

"It's not so much their temples," Stella said, "it's *Kali*, the black earth mother."

Kali is hideous. She is depicted standing on the prostrate form of Shiva and grinning, with outstretched tongue. Her body is smeared with blood because she has waged a ferocious and successful war against the giants. Like Shiva, she has a flaming third eye on her forehead. Her body is naked save for a girdle of giants suspended from her waist; round her neck she wears a long necklace of giants' skulls. Like the Egyptian Isis, Kali can conceal herself in her long, abundant hair. She has four arms; in one she holds a weapon, in another the dripping head of a giant, and two empty hands she raises to bless her worshipers. Like the Egyptian Hathor, or Sekhet, the "Eye of Ra", she goes forth to slay the enemies of the gods, rejoicing in the slaughter.

Like Hathor, she too is asked to desist but heeds not. Then Shiva, her husband, approaches her and lies down among her victims. Kali dances over the battlefield and leaps on his body. When she observes what she has done, however, she ejects her tongue with shame.

As Sati, Shiva's wife is the true and virtuous Hindu woman. When Sati's husband is slighted by her father, the Deva-rishi, Daska, she casts herself on the funeral pyre, the sacrificial fire. Widows who died on the funeral pyres of their husbands were called Sati, because in performing this rite they imitated the faithful goddess. Sati was thus reborn as Uma, viewed as Light, the impersonation of divine wisdom, just as Amvika, the same goddess, was a sister of Rudra or his female counterpart.

Rudra took the place of Perusha, the first man. Par'vati was another form of the many-sided goddess. When Shiva taunted her for being black, she went away for a time and engaged in austerities, with the result that she assumed a golden complexion. A trinity of goddesses is formed by Saraswati, the white one; Lakshmi, the red one; and Par'vati, the black one. The three were originally one, a goddess who came into existence when Brahma, Vishnu, and Shiva spoke of the dreaded Asura, Andhaka (Darkness) and looked one at another. The goddess was coloured white, red, and black and divided herself according to Varaha Purana into three forms representing the past, present and future.

It is after Sati burns herself that the sorrowing Shiva is wounded by Kamadeva, the love god, whom he slays by causing a flame of fire to dart from his third eye. This is the son of Vishnu and Lakshmi. He is usually depicted as a comely youth, like the Egyptian Khonsu; he shoots flowery arrows from his bow. His wife, Rati, symbolizes spring, the cuckoo, the humming bee, and soft winds. As Manmatra he is the "mind-disturber"; as Mara, "the wounder'; as Madan, he who makes one "love intoxicated"; and as Pradyumna, he who is "all conqueror".

Ganeśa, the four-armed elephant god of wisdom, is the son of Shiva and Parvati. He is the general of Shiva's army, the patron of learning and giver of good fortune. Ganeśa is also called Ganapati and Vināyaka. At the beginnings of books he is invoked by poets, and his image is placed on the ground when a new house is built. Ganeśa is honoured before a journey is begun or any business undertaken. The elephant's head is an emblem of sagacity. A myth in one of the Puranas relates that the planet Saturn, being under a curse, decapitated Ganesa simply by looking at him. Vishnu mounted the back of the man-eagle Garuda and came to the child's aid. He cut off the head of Indra's elephant and placed it on Ganeśa's neck.

In conflict with the Devarishi, Ganeśa lost one of his tasks. Several myths have gathered around this popular elephant-headed one, who is also identified with the wise rat deity.

"I thought Kali was the goddess of the Thug," I said.

"The cult of the Thuggee was suppressed by the British in India between 1830 and 1840. But it is a very ancient system of worship, demanding blood sacrifice by the cult following, a group of professional robbers who murdered their victims by strangling them with garrottes," she replied. Then, "Are you both staying the night?" she asked us suddenly.

Roy looked across at me for some kind of reaction.

"I would like to," I said, "but one of us would have to spend the night on board. It is a question of security. Roy can stay if he likes."

"Good!" Anthony exclaimed. "What about a spot of wild pig shooting?" Anthony and Roy had a brandy and then took off together in the jeep.

"He's about to show off his marksmanship abilities with that damn Tommy-gun again," she said.

I'd declined his invitation on moral grounds. While I was quite prepared to kill for food when necessary, I could not kill even wild pigs indiscriminately just for the fun of it. Now, this may sound rather hypocritical, but I have a great respect for life, believing that all creatures have souls. I did respect Anthony's motives in culling out the wild pigs to protect his crop, but I could never understand why some people got a thrill out of killing some poor animal with high-powered rifles using high-resolution telescopic sights, just as a Sunday sport. When I must kill, I dispatch my quarry quickly and efficiently; I always take them outright with one shot.

If ever you wound an animal whilst hunting, you must hunt the animal down to kingdom come and finish the job. You should never walk away from a wounded animal, especially if the cause of their injury was your poor shooting skills. In plain speaking, hone your shooting skills and then develop well also your tracking skills before even considering going out on a hunt. If hunting is new to you, be prepared to see what you have done to the animal after you have shot it. The experience will not be pleasant and sometimes will be rather bloody and gruesome! Killing another armed human being remains a very nasty business that you never get used to.

"There is no hunting like the hunting of man, and those who have hunted armed men long enough and liked it, never care for anything else thereafter." So wrote Ernest Hemingway in "On the Blue Water", an article for *Esquire* in April 1936.

"You lead an interesting lifestyle," Stella remarked with a note of envy in her voice.

"Most of the stories are grossly exaggerated," I replied. "You know what the press are like. Notoriety sells newspapers. They like to make a mountain out of a molehill."

Stella laughed. "But there's no smoke without fire," she said.

I changed the subject. "I suppose you are planning your next long leave home."

"Anthony and I could do with a long break," she said, "but no, not just yet. He has too much work here on the estate, and I have my book to write. Of course, there are times when we seem to get on each other's nerves as the day-to-day routine rot sets in. But even the pain is better than being with anyone else. It's the isolation, living in the country in complete isolation."

We sat in the quiet shade of the traveller's palm there on the large lawn in the late afternoon, strangers in a strange land, with colour, not race, our only common bond.

"Perhaps it's just plain boredom?" I said cautiously, not wanting to sound presumptuous.

"It's surprising how soon you have accomplished everything worthwhile in a place like this," Stella replied. "Then you spend the rest of your time seeking some fresh field of challenge. I heard a rather strange story from my amah just before lunch," she told me. "It seems that some of the local village people saw a mermaid and merman off the beach this morning. Shortly after that, a young, bearded stranger appeared in the market, peddling some sort of concoction he declared contained the tears of a mermaid."

"*Minyak Tangis Duyong*," I said. "Potent love philtres. I know the young man in question; he is one of my crew.

"Can I take it that the mermaid is also a member of your crew?" Stella asked.

"Don't know anything about the mermaid, but the young man in question is probably one of mine. The concoction is just salt water and essence," I said. "Quite harmless. No one is hurt, except the gullible young buck is minus a few dollars. And it also gives their elders a laugh at their expense."

Wi-wi-wi-wi-wit! It was the female golden whistler answering the male's whip-calls. In this species of birds, both sexes sing during their courtship rituals. The golden whistler is found from Malaya down all the way to Australia and in the Fiji Islands. The male bird is yellow with a black band across the chest which continues up each side of the throat to the bill. The female, in contrast, is streaked with white on the abdomen. They are called "thunderbirds" because they are stimulated to sing by sudden loud noises. Most times these birds have a strangely wistful call, but other times they sound like a man calling his dog. Whistlers have alternative names such as robin, shrike-thrush, or tit-shrike. It was late afternoon and the insects were on the wing, a problem we did not have at sea. It was time for us to move indoors behind the permanently fitted mosquito screens.

Anthony and Roy returned from the hunt shortly afterwards, and it was soon time for me to thank my hosts for their kind hospitality and return to my boat, leaving Roy to spend the night there. There were times when I was forced to leave my boat in the hands of her crew, in particular my loyal and trustworthy helmsman Zainal, who always looked after her as if she were family. It was always a relief on my return, however, to discover that nothing untoward had occurred during my absence. I had a good crew, and these were peaceful waters. After I carried out a mandatory quick but routine check on my boat, it was time to get my head down for the night. I smiled, thinking, *Mermaid indeed!*

I would have a few choice words with Ali in the morning for spreading urban legends concerning my early morning swim with Poo Choo. It wasn't hard to imagine how Ali had seized the opportunity to help sell his wares, hitting upon the idea while watching Poo Choo and me skinny-dipping out on the estuary that morning. Before I forget, an *amah* or *ayah* is Asiatic, probably Portuguese in origin, for a girl or woman who is employed by a family to clean, look after children, and perform other domestic tasks. She is a house servant for all intents and purposes, who also usually lives with the family.

Saturday, 5 April 1947

I had often pictured myself as lord and master of my own oil palm estate one day. Strange though it may seem, this had been my dream for quite some time now—but we all aspire to greater things, don't we? I was not the only person living the dream in this part of the world. It is good and healthy for a man to have ambition. Poo Choo and I took our morning swim together around the boat, and this time I made sure there was no skinny-dipping. The bamboo telegraph is rather effective in these parts, and I wanted no more stories about mermaids on my account.

We saw what appeared to be a *Wobbegong* or carpet shark. Unlike most sharks, the wobbegong uses cunning instead of speed to obtain its food. Resting on the bottom, it looks like a rock overgrown with seaweed, a perfect camouflage to enable it to pounce on unsuspecting victims. Human beings are not its primary source of food. The wobbegong is quite unlike the usual shark in shape. It has a short, thick-set, flattened body, with a broad head and a blunt, rounded snout ending in a wide, straight mouth. Its teeth are slender and pointed, with those in the centre of the mouth being the largest.

Its eyes are small, with folds of skin below them, and the wide oblique slits of the spiracles are situated behind the eyes and lower down on the head. The last three or four external gill clefts on each side open above the bases of the pectoral fins, which are broad and rounded. The two dorsal fins are comparatively small. The anal fin reaches to or is actually joined at the base to the lower lobe of the tailfin, which is long and asymmetrical, with a notch in the end.

The one we saw was approximately six feet in length, but around

West Australia's coastline you can get wobbegongs reaching ten feet or more.

That was the very first wobbegong I had encountered in Malayan waters. Accordingly, we cut our morning swim short, for neither of us wanted to tangle with a shark before breakfast without the proper diving gear, even though these carpet sharks are bottom feeders. Wobbegongs have been known to attack swimmers who accidently stepped on them or even got too close. While the sudden shark encounter made me feel rather hungry, it left Poo Choo feeling both hungry and rebelliously randy all at the same time. Perhaps it had something to do with sudden danger and the need for reassurance. Stella had been right, I did live an interesting lifestyle, shark or no shark. I made sure that the crate of .45 ACP ammunition had been put ashore ready for Anthony when he arrived later.

I then got on with the routine chores necessary in preparation for sea later. I wanted to get underway once again, not that I was in any great hurry! But I had seen all of Kuala Besut that was of any possible interest and had an itch for the next port of call along the way.

I was not surprised when I saw the car arrive; I should have known. Her Ladyship would never have travelled in an open jeep. I observed through the telescope from my bridge, while Anthony attentively held the car door open, and I saw her alight. Gone was the tight-lipped, shrivelled-breast look I had seen the previous day. Anthony and his wife stood on the shore with Roy, waiting for the dinghy. Both of them were smiling, exchanging remarks concerning the need for rain again, and grumbling about the time it was taking the dinghy to get to them. Then the dinghy arrived. Roy was still wearing the shirt and shorts he had borrowed for the wild pig hunt the day before. He was the last one into the dinghy, and then they pushed off. Suddenly I realized that they were heading in the direct of my boat, not Roy's. A few minutes later they came alongside. Poo Cho, her sister, and the young boy were on deck, and they came to watch the new arrivals with great interest, the way Chinese people did, with delightful curiosity. I suppose it was something of a novelty for them.

I refuse to have many visitors on board my boat, for obvious reasons; the less people know of my boat the better. Zainal lent a hand with the boarding party and courteously took them on a short tour of inspection. Ali had started the engines, and I announced from the bridge that I would be taking her on a test run in preparation for the sea in ten minutes. Roy and Anthony said they had a little business they wished to finalize and quickly stepped across to Roy's boat, which was moored alongside mine. Stella, of course, elected to stay on board. She was just one strong-willed woman, used to having her own way most of the time.

Personally, I would not wish her on my worst enemy; two alphas in the same space do not make for a good mix! My crew cast off our moorings, and we got underway, taking her out in a rather wide circle, with her ladyship on the bridge.

"So, this is how you unwind!" Stella said. "I love your lifestyle—booze, music, sex!"

"I only drink in moderation and never before sundown," I told her. "And where women are concerned I am rather careful."

"Which one is the little mermaid?" she asked with a note of pretentious irony in her voice. "The one with the child would have the necessary experience," she went on sarcastically, answering her own question.

"They are both extremely good swimmers," I said.

"I bet they are," Stella retorted. "Why the preference for Chinese nooky, anyway?

"Availability," I said. "It's just a question of availability. They are never bored, because there is always something fresh on the horizon."

Stella got right to the point. "I will be in Kuala Lumpur around the middle of May next", she said, "and quite alone."

"Sixty miles from the nearest port, which is, of course, Kuala Selangor," I said. "*Kuala Lumpur*—mud estuary," I noted. "I don't know just where I will be this time next month," I told her.

"It's just a question of sorting out your priorities," she said. "You could be there in Kuala Lumpur if you wanted to meet with me. It's really up to you!" she insisted with indignation.

"My wants are few and soon satisfied," I said. "As I have already told you, I do not know exactly where I will be this time next month, as my job assignments are in flux, always changing with the winds. I never know where I will be going or what assignments I will be getting next."

Stella frowned angrily. "I am not going to give up that easily!" she snapped, rather like a spoiled child determined to get her own way.

I had no intention of becoming the other man in her life. Anthony and Roy were standing on the deck of Roy's boat when I brought my boat alongside. Zainal helped Stella across, and we said our cordial goodbyes. The crew cast off, and we were underway once more, heading for the open sea. I could feel the comfortable movement of the boat beneath me, and that in itself was reassurance indeed. At 1600 hours we were off Pulau Rhu, where a strong groundswell was running and we made good headway. The Malay word *Ru* is the name for the casuarina tree, which the island appeared to be full of. The windborne fragrance was quite pleasant. The large trees would be in full blossom now.

There were many of these small islands off the East Coast of Malaya, each with its own special fragrance when the wind was blowing in the appropriate direction. The groundswell slackened a little once we were beyond the island, due to the rip current caused by the ebb and flow of the tide around the island. That current always ran at full strength when the tide was on the turn. It was a question of knowing the waters together with the feel of the boat—in other words, what mariners call seamanship.

At 1800 hours I checked the engine revolutions on both of my boat's Packard engines with Ali, and by the smile on my engineer's face, I knew that she was running like a bird in full flight towards a new horizon. At 2000 hours we located the required offshore market buoy while making the necessary radar scan and adjusted our course accordingly. We then struck a strong cross-current, and I felt the boat shudder momentarily, like a dog shaking itself. This happened sometimes when we suddenly hit a strong surface cross-current at the wrong angle. This was nothing of great concern to an experienced navigator in these waters, although the unpleasant jar could be a little disconcerting to a novice.

I noted that the starlight was particularly bright and soft that night and the sea gentle with the sensuous thrill of excitement, like a woman young in the throes of her first love. I have always kept a little jotter for making notes, which I would later read and, if found wholly worthy, write up to add to my journals. I checked our course and made the necessary notation in my boat's log book. South-south-east of Kuala Stiu Bahru and off Pulau Chipu, one of those little islands. *Chepu-chepu* in Malay means the trunk of the mast.

This probably goes back to a bygone era when sailing ships put to anchored in the calm waters of the bay here for the vast resource of strong trees to fell as repair material for their broken masts after a heavy storm at sea. Kim Soo came up on the bridge, and I realized that until that moment I had forgotten she was still aboard. She looked much younger standing there in the bright moonlight, saying nothing. She was probably waiting for me to speak first.

"I should have put you on board Roy's boat," I said rather apologetically.

She smiled and replied, "No, he told me to stay on board with you. Hope you don't mind," she went on. "You cannot imagine how worried I was at the time; guess I didn't know how you react after what happened. It is because of that *hang-mor-kee-ah*," she said in a matter-of-fact tone.

"Poo Choo?" I asked.

"Sleeping," she replied hesitantly, and then she added, "In your own cabin."

"Did Roy treat you with care?" I asked.

"He's a very hard man," she said, "Quite rough at times."

"Poo Choo is very hard up at the moment," I told her.

"Hard up?" Kim Soo said, repeating the word quizzically.

"To be hard up is an English idiom meaning lack of money," I said. "Have you any idea what I am trying to explain?"

"English idiot," she replied.

"No, of course not," I said and laughed. "An *idiot* is a foolish person. An *idiom* is just a phrase which means something rather different."

"Roy is an English idiot," she replied. "Not sensible at all."

Roy has never been sensible over a woman, ever, I thought for a moment. Roy was not a devious person by any means, though on this occasion I had the feeling he was planning something a little dishonest. Perhaps it was just to impress the Bamford-Smyths. I was quite prepared to keep an open mind and adhere to the routine we had set. For the present that was more than adequate for the purpose.

Zainal arrived on the bridge at that moment, and I spent the next twenty-five minutes familiarizing him with the routine he would be required to follow for the next four hours of the watch. Curiosity is addictive, and I soon discovered that Kim Soo had lost none of her resilience, with quite a difference that was rather remarkable.

I would have to do something about my impoverished Chinese ladies. It would be my intention to finance them with their own business but to remain their silent partner in the business venture. Fate had a strange way of making things happen even under strange conditions. But exactly how I would accomplish that was an entirely different matter; at that moment in time I was uncertain how they would feel about going into business with me after all that had taken place. Throwing good money into a bad investment, especially if it were still tainted with ill feelings towards me, would not be to anyone's benefit.

I had to be certain of their commitment to the venture, the risks involved, and their loyalty towards me as a business partner. Despite all my shortcomings, I had saved their lives from the Tiong street gangs who would have most certainly wanted revenge and payback; they would have made an example of these poor women. I remained a little apprehensive about the very dangerous business of running guns into Burma, a volatile hotbed of mini wars and cut-throats. This was one of those times when the need to make money had to balance out with the risk to the lives of all my men.

Sunday, 6 April 1947

I was going to change the world and make it a better place! Perhaps I was naïve, but the world outside my boat was more often than not indifferent, cold, and rather hostile towards women. It was a masculine, masochistic rat race of abuse, sometimes unkind and even cruel. We might find ourselves placed in situations where we were forced to learn the hard way—disparaging talk, Roy would have said! But then, he took everything for granted. We were now halfway on our quiet journey back to Singapore, and it was time for me to take stock and make my decision.

All actions or inactions have consequences, and Roy, despite his demeanour when it came to chasing after pussy, had been my friend and business partner. There was an old saying that went something like this: "A bone on has no conscience", but I would never take another man's women unless he no longer wanted to be with her. After all, there were rules in every game, and the universe did have a plan somewhere in all the emotional euphoria. For a few moments, the *Wilful Lady* creaked and groaned her protest against the sudden change in the swell, like the sound of a badly oiled door. Then she settled down to her change of routine like the good sturdy ark that she was.

I never in the smallest degree felt that I had disobeyed some moral or social rule. I'd believed that she was bartering a commodity. She was *chieh*, and I'd paid in cash for the privilege. It had been a business deal, giving me immediate access for the next five years. Kim Soo was good even now, but never like those first few days. Poo Choo, on the other hand, had not changed!

I had to come up with some sort of living for them both once we returned to Singapore. My plan was to set them up in the shellfish business but remain as a silent partner. You could never have enough consensual sex on tap or secondary sources of income. Some people might have a morality fixation with that, but I did not.

I have a kick bag which I hang from the frame above the bridge to practise kicks, punches, elbow strikes, and so on. I keep in training by doing high-kicking stunts. You cannot practise enough where martial arts are concerned—though a good steady session of wick-dipping is rather a good heart stimulant which always encourages and increases more activity. Those sisters! Well, I had to take care of the two of them. The alternative would be to take them along with me on my mercenary travels all across the South Pacific Ocean, but that was out of the question. I enjoyed my journeying. It was rather helpful where avoiding the selfish greed and ambiguity of the rat race was concerned.

At 0600 hours we were off Batu Rakit, heading in towards Kuala Trengganu, which was now some four hours away. I left Poo Choo asleep in my cabin while I checked the course on the bridge. I had made my mind up about the two sisters, and it was nothing I couldn't cope with when the time came. Perhaps it was the rogue in me to enjoy women! I had shared my bed with both women, and now I intended to have them both again, but this time together! There was no immediate hurry. First I would have to see what developed at Kuala Trengganu with my next business venture, which would pay the bills and my crew's wages and keep me moving forward.

It's not impossible, just impracticable. Common sense makes it rather obvious that seduction is best undertaken in a one-to-one situation! Ali, who has three wives, regulates their conjugal relationships on a weekly basis, spending one week, in strict rotation, with each of his wives. This is a good arrangement, according to Ali. He says the wife with just one child is the most passionate of the three; the other two wives are what he termed puritanical. There is, of course, a very special chemistry which makes up the universe and every living thing. It is more apparent in women, in this case, but who am I to judge?

As far as women go, they are more concerned with the perpetuation of the human species, as this is what their biological function is designed for. The whole attraction chemistry is part of their biological allure, and that is worth remembering. A case in point was that of Che Nemah of Gunong, mentioned earlier, who'd decided to consummate a business arrangement with a roll in the hay. The incident was reminiscent of a story Ken Christian was fond of relating over a pint of beer. He'd had a young Malay female servant who was rather good at her job and went about her work with the energy of three people. Then, after a while, for no apparent reason, she became flighty in behaviour. One morning while Ken was having his breakfast, she carelessly broke some crockery, and in a fit of tears, fled into his bedroom.

Bent on consoling her, Ken took her into his arms. She flashed a smile at him, and the inevitable happened, after which she was her old self again. No more broken crockery. According to Ken, she would flash a smile at him and head for the bed. The glory of the nude female form is unaffected by the hue of skin, for it resides in perfection of the line alone, the purest form of beauty, over which the eye, undistracted by shades, tints, or intensities of colour, travels with lingering delight for every curve and contour.

The Malay word *chium* is rather interesting: to smell, to kiss in the Malay way of kissing; *menchium* means to snuff; *penchium* is the sense of smell. Chium is a kind of face rubbing. Malays don't kiss the way we do! The Malay, and indeed the Chinese, apply the mouth and nose to the cheek and inhale: chium. It is interesting to note in passing that the Romans distinguished various kinds of kisses, such as the kiss on the cheek, which was a mark of friendship, and the kiss on the lips, which was a sign of affection. The kiss proper, which consists of applying the lips to some part of the face or body, appears to have been a European innovation.

Applying the French kiss to a Malay woman requires quite a lot of ability and tact if you are to avoid offending her. But once you can apply the kiss properly, she will quickly come to her full volume of activity, rather like a volcano, and you will be able to reach full penetration before she realizes it.

At 0900 hours, I scanned the beach rather carefully, and I got quite a surprise when I saw what appeared to be a Bamford-Smyth car parked near one of the buildings onshore. This car was approximately 160 miles from where it was supposed to be! I considered that Roy was somehow involved in this.

What the hell had he been up to now? Roy had given me no

heads-up or indication of his intentions, but of course there was nothing unusual in that. Roy was as Roy did. We both were actively independent but never predictable. *Bukit Besar*—great hill—appeared large and volcanic from our anchorage point. Yes, it was large, but it was no volcano. There were several legends concerning this mountain, or rather hill, some of which were probably true. Idris and I headed out in our dinghy towards the small but rather picturesque town of Kuala Trengganu, with Ali taking the tiller and singing quietly to himself for most of the journey.

The tide was at its lowest ebb, and there were plenty of jellyfish floating near the surface inshore. This meant there were no sea urchins around. I hated the floppy creatures, jellyfish, I mean! But even jellyfish have their place in the scheme of marine life. We are wise to live our lives in accordance with nature.

To me, life is an acknowledgement of the great adventure, strange at times and exciting. But also, in my case, it could be very dangerous. Perhaps with all great adventures there is a certain degree of risk. For risk-taking is the very spice of life with high adventure, and getting there for me is just half the enjoyment, akin to some sort of adrenalin high. Together with the need for a fast-forward in your life, it is an unbeatable combination.

We came to the small dock, and I quickly disembarked from my longboat, sprinting up the wooden steps onto the quay above. The driver was fast asleep on the back seat of the car, which was parked near one of the many sheds used for storing cargo in transit. There was no sign of the Bamford-Smyths, so I left their Malay driver to his slumber. Perhaps it was the imp of perversity within, but I felt an overwhelming relief at not having to offer dubious explanations to another irritated husband at that early hour of the morning.

Anthony must be on board with Roy; they were quite capable of managing their own affairs. Having spent the next hour placating odious officials of the Etonian playing fields old school tie brigade or rather, the rank has its privileges crowd of old fuddy-duddy civil servants. These old-school British Empire farts were like spoilt class monitors whose parents could not be arsed to raise them properly but instead abandoned them as children to grow up in English boarding schools. Those guys, it seemed, didn't want me in their backyard at the moment, and I wondered what these morons had to hide. Call me biased, but I never had much time for pink-gin civil servants or those who grew up with silver spoons in their mouths.

Yet I have always enjoyed turning over the occasional stone just to see what comes crawling out from underneath. The woman had a face like Ingmar Bergman and looked bloody ridiculous standing on top of her desk in the outer office, speechless, mouth open, and legs crossed. The next few minutes proved somewhat challenging. A stealth intruder from the Malayan bush had somehow managed to find its way into the offices, very much to the dismay and shock of the occupants.

"*Ular katang tebu!*" Idris shouted and jumped to one side to distract the snake, giving me the opportunity to grab the reptile at the end of its tail and crack it like a whip several times on the floor.

On the third whip of the snake on the office floor I was sure it was dead, as its head was splayed open. I then severed the snake's head completely with my jungle machete to be sure of the kill and carefully placed it on a table in the room for all to see. Ular katang tebu, or *Bungarus candidus*, is a venomous snake from the family *Elapidae*. More commonly known as the Malayan krait or blue krait, it is a natural stealth intruder that frequents human habitation. The banded krait, like most snakes, travels at speed by keeping those parts of the body not in immediate contact with the ground at an angle of .25 degrees, thus providing the reptile with fast and continual motion. The pink-gin civil servant was full of praise, and we left the office, taking the dead krait with us. Idris, of course, wanted the skin, most likely to make a magic charm with.

Roy arrived on the scene at 1300 hours and tied up alongside my boat at our anchorage half a mile offshore. The Bamford-Smyths were very much in evidence on the bridge of his boat, and Roy himself looked happy as a pig in shit. I could not help feeling that some dodgy dealings were going on between Roy and the Bamfords, unbeknownst to me. He must have misread her intentions. Perhaps

I had misjudged her myself. However, I was sure of one thing; she had an ulterior motive of some kind or another. I thought at the time of the character Bunbury, that mythical friend whose misfortunes provided the hero with pretexts for absence in Oscar Wilde's play "The Importance of Being Earnest".

The meeting was impromptu and to the point, brief and detailed. Anthony produced an old Japanese naval chart plotting the last known position of the wreck some five miles offshore. This wreck was supposed to have been one of three secret Japanese cargo submarines en route back to the Japanese homelands. She had gone down with all hands in March 1944, allegedly carrying Nazi gold bullion, amongst other valuable vital supplies for the war effort against the Allies. This had been no ordinary submarine but rather a long-range cargo-carrying submarine with a much larger displacement than the ordinary attack subs. Poring over weather and tidal charts, we plotted and worked out the necessary rough equations, for even at the bottom of the sea, wrecks had been known to move with the tidal drifts. I told Idris to start the compressor and charge the bottle bank with compressed air, ready for the dive.

Because of the large number of jellyfish I had seen close to the surface of the inshore waters, I decided that full wetsuits would be the order of the day. The sea urchin, that small ball-shaped animal with a hard shell and many sharp points feeds on jellyfish; its lack of presence here in these waters explained the profusion of these invertebrates. What we are at risk from is the profusion of floating blue balloons with nasty, venomous stinging tentacles. Better known as the Portuguese man-of-war, which is a siphonophore, or colony of organisms working together rather than a jellyfish in the true sense of the word.

These creatures possess four separate polyps; the uppermost polyp has a gas-filled bladder, also known as a pneumatophore. It is this that makes it resemble an old-world wooden warship at full sail. Its venomous long tentacles deliver a rather painful sting, possibly fatal to divers under certain conditions. As with all beautiful things on the ocean, the rule is see but do not touch. I didn't want any injuries to any of my dive crew; bacterial or viral infections would go septic rather quickly in this heat. It took us another hour or so before we had moved out into position to begin our dive search patterns. After thoroughly cross-checking all the dive bottles, we kitted out in scuba gear and were ready to make the first dive though the coral reefs.

On the reef three miles off Kuala Terengganu

Roy went in first, followed soon after by Idris and me, together with Poo Choo, my latest addition to the dive team. It was her very first experience of a wetsuit, although she was already a natural in the water and a rather good skin diver as well as an excellent, strong swimmer.

During the Second World War, Japan had possessed among the most diverse submarine fleet of any nation, in part because of her aspirations to rule the entire South Pacific, which was a great distance away from home territory. What is not generally well known is that her great submarine fleet included manned (suicide) torpedoes, midget submarines, medium-range submarines, long-range fleet ocean-going submarines, and submarines capable of high submerged speeds as well as ability to carry multiple bombers. Designed and manufactured by the Mitsubishi Corporation around 1943, the Japanese Type C-3 cargo submarine was state-of-the-art naval design back in the day.

367

These top-secret Japanese submarines were rumoured to possess an early type of invisibility technology applied to their hulls, which absorbed sonar search signals from Allied enemy destroyers. They had a surface speed of eighteen knots or seven knots submerged. Japanese torpedoes of that period were far more reliable that those of the Americans, with a much-extended range.

The submarine wreck we were hunting was a Japanese Type C-3, with a displacement of about 3,644 tons submerged. It had had an approximate range of 21,000 nautical miles and a crew of about 100. With a total length of some 365 feet, you would think that this vessel would be an easy find, even in the vastness of the open seas, if you had a general idea where to look for her. Imagine if you will a small pebble tossed aside on a vast sandy beach, and this will give you an idea of how difficult it is to find a lost submarine in a previously uncharted underwater landscape.

On our initial dive down, Poo Choo and I sighted what appeared to be a rather large school of barracudas in the distance, moving like a solid body of elongated silvery predatory fish towards our dive position. This large body of predators, some around five feet in length, was quite a sight to see, although the experience could be perplexing.

For the inexperienced scuba diver, urban legends abound regarding the aggressiveness of these sea creatures which are sometimes feared much more than sharks—who, incidentally, feed on barracudas.

There are rules in the sea that every diver must adhere to, and staying calm instead of panicking must be the order of the day.

Barracudas, like cats, are curious and love to investigate what is moving about in their environment; this does not necessarily mean they will attack you on sight! Resist the urge to bolt quickly or make any sudden movements towards them, which may be misconstrued as a threat to the barracuda school. Above all, stay calm. But more importantly, stay cool. Barracudas will nearly always pass you by, as scuba divers are not their natural prey.

When the barracuda school finally passed us by, we commenced our dive search pattern in twos along the seabed, hoping for clues as to whether there was indeed a submarine wreck on the sea floor in this region. Despite all our dive efforts on this occasion, we came up empty. All we had was the old Japanese naval chart citing the location that one of her cargo submarines had come to rest in these waters. We searched diligently until our compressed air and dive time were up. We would see what the new day brought tomorrow.

Tuesday, 1 January 1952

I am in the second decade of my life in a rather fascinating part of the world, among the delicate desire and the destructive. The poor are not conscious of their poverty or the rich conscious of their prosperity. Not a pin to choose between them, for their own poetry does go beyond, into the subject and object—a priori into the existence of transcendental man. I am here seen and not seen, heard and not heard. There is a time and season for all things. Believing this one truth, I write this, my journal, for my children and my children's children. I do not seek for them to justify me, for I alone am responsible for my own actions. I wish rather that my people may know and perhaps understand their own grandparents, parents, great-uncles, and aunts but remember other relatives, plus their friends, in their quest for their own identity.

A British Intelligence officer walked through the defensive perimeter set up by the Royal Marine Commandos to parley for the surrender of a thirty-strong group of Indonesian enemy paratroopers. These had been observed being inserted via parachute on the mainland and hunted down over many weeks, until they were fully surrounded by British and Malayan forces.

British Royal Marine Commandos were specifically dispatched to be the first point of contact, but with local Malay troops in reserve had tightly cordoned off the coastline area, surrounding completely the enemy infiltrators, whilst Royal Navy warships covered any seaward escape attempt by those not-so-lucky failed stealth intruders. Carrying a white flag of truce, the Intelligence officer in plain clothes approached the enemy's position to parley for their surrender, communicating with an enemy officer in local Malay/Indonesian language, which was universally understood in the region. "These are our terms for your surrender," the negotiator suggested calmly, "but you will be respected and treated well as prisoners of war."

The Indonesian commander rebuked him boastfully. "What is to stop me shooting you dead right here where you stand?" he demanded.

The negotiator paused and considered carefully before responding. "Where is your president, Sukarno? Will he die with you also?"

After a long pause, the enemy para commander shook his head.

The British Intelligence negotiator then responded, "Yes, you can shoot me dead; that is your choice. But if you decide on this course of action, we will all die together and cover this field with our blood, which serves no purpose. You are surrounded by a larger force of elite marine commandos, with no possible escape route out of this. What I am offering you is an alternative of life with your honour intact and no further bloodshed. There is no loss of face when you cannot possibly win."

Knowing the game was up, the enemy Indonesian commander ordered his flight of men to stand down and to surrender to the British commandos. These same prisoners were then handed over to local military forces of Malaya, our allies who took them into secure custody as prisoners of war. One of the Royal Marine Commando non-commissioned officers remarked, "Who the hell is that guy savvy with the lingo of the Indonesians?" The Royal Marines commanding officer replied, "The locals here call him the Dutchman. Forget you ever saw him or that this incident ever happened." It was a case of "need to know" only.

There was yet another little-known, very bloody war back then, known as the Indonesian Confrontation (1962–1966). But that is another story. The title of this book comes from my time working with British Special Intelligence.

Challenge: By the tail
Response: Dragonfly

This book is dedicated to my very good friend and confidante, Fame Alvares. For nothing is ever as it seems. Remember: a lifetime of mediocrity or one day the hero. That is entirely up to you. If I can do all of this from nothing, anyone else with the same mind, determination, and courage can. But you should always have at least two escape strategies in place.

My Journal 1947, Volumes 1 and 2
The journal of an itinerant soldier of fortune in the fourth decade of the twentieth century.

Round and round in a world spinning round,
Life is a ride on a merry-go-round.
Day follows night, night follows day;
You may like it or not, but God made it that way.
We live in deeds, not words,
In thoughts, not breath,
With feelings, not figures on a dial;
We should count time by heart-throbs.
He most lives who thinks most,
Feels the noblest, acts the best.
When imperfection ceases, heaven begins.

MALAYSIAN security forces are tonight closing in on a group of about 30 crack Indonesian commandos who parachuted into the Labis area of Johore at 2.40 a.m. today in an operation officially described as "an invasion."

One Indonesian has been killed. Several others have been captured—and two Malaysians found acting suspiciously in the airdrop area were also detained by kampong vigilantes.

The Cabinet was told of the air invasion soon after its weekly meeting began this morning and the Prime Minister, Tengku Abdul Rahman, announced later that counter-measures would be taken "after discussions with our allies."

The Deputy Prime Minister and Minister of Defence, Tun Abdul Razak, said: "This is a flagrant act of aggression by Indonesia. They have not only violated our airspace but also our territorial sovereignty."

Note to U.N.

He said Malaysia would be sending a Note on the airdrop to the United Nations Security Council.

He added that the Finance Minister, Mr. Tan Siew Sin, in the face of this new threat, would ask for additional military aid in the talks which he will have tomorrow with the Finance Ministers of Britain, Australia and New Zealand.

Jakarta flight

He said the Malaysian Government had already ascertained that the commandos took off from Jakarta in a Hercules C130 transport aircraft soon after nine o'clock last night.

The plane stopped to refuel at Medan in Northern Sumatra at 1 a.m., took off again soon after and was over the Labis area a few minutes after 2 a.m.

The plane flew low and dropped flares from 1,000 to 1,500 ft. before disgorging its first paratroopers.

Kampong vigilantes not far from Labis town saw the flares and the parachutes and raised the alarm.

They captured two Malaysians found acting suspiciously in the area

★ SEE BACK PAGE, COLUMN ONE

Lightning Source UK Ltd.
Milton Keynes UK
UKHW010309180719
346343UK00001B/39/P